FORMERLY BRI'l

A Profile of the New ...ation of Belize

books by the author . . .

THE ORIGIN AND HISTORY OF THE FAMILY SETZEKORN
LOOKING FORWARD TO A CAREER IN ARCHITECTURE
HERALDRY: The Ancient Art of Designing Coats of Arms
FORMERLY BRITISH HONDURAS: A Profile of the New
    Nation of Belize

FORMERLY BRITISH HONDURAS:

A PROFILE OF THE NEW NATION OF

BELIZE

William David Setzekorn

Ohio University Press
Chicago   Athens, Ohio   London

Previously published by Dumbarton Press, 1975

Revised edition published in 1981 by
Ohio University Press
Athens, Ohio

Library of Congress Catalog Card Number: 81-80917
ISBN 0-8214-0568-3

To Illene who shared all

CONTENTS

Preface

A number of years ago I attempted to find something in my local library concerning British Honduras and discovered a lamentable gap in the "917" shelves. Little of a general nature has been written on this subject since Archibald Gibbs' dissertation in 1883. To my knowledge, no up-to-date survey is available for the student, general reader, or for the tourist and investor for whom this country has recently begun to hold great interest.

What is available are a few commendable books and monographs about specific features of the country; many written for the political scientist and most with a definite British slant. Most of these are listed in the Annotated Bibliography at the end of this volume. Some offer invaluable, and often penetrating, views into certain narrow aspects of Belizean life or history.

Yet, the general reader may find these studies difficult to appreciate without a proper background in local history or knowledge of the human factors which have molded life in Belize. The purpose of this book is to provide that background.

This book aspires to provide an overview of the country as it is today; its geographical, cultural, social, and economic features against a comprehensive historical background to demonstrate how these features have developed from the Settlement's founding in 1638 to the present. It is written primarily for the non-Belizean reader, but hopefully will serve as a handy reference book for Belizeans as well. I believe this "mini-encyclopedia" on the subject of Belize will prove a helpful tool for anyone interested in the country: scholars, journalists, businessmen, tourists, history buffs, or general readers.

To my friends in Belize who have offered encouragement and advice, I owe a special debt, as well as the many librarians, clerks, and archivists, who have helped in my research. While much of this book is based on personal impressions formed in the course of residence and travel in the area, I have been influenced by the scholarly works of the authors listed in the bibliography, and in some cases have borrowed extensively. To them I am also grateful.

I owe a very special thanks to Illene for her help in too many ways to mention, and to my children for their patience and interest.

Fremont, California
January, 1975

FORMERLY BRITISH HONDURAS:

A Profile of the New Nation of Belize

ruin

Statute miles

Consejo

Corozal Town

Progresso

SWAMP

COROZAL

Orange Walk Town

Tower Hill

Trinidad

Ambergris Cay

NORTHERN HIGHWAY

San Pedro

Shipyard

San Felipe

Revenge Lagoon

Blue Creek Village

Aguas Turbias

Indian Church

ORANGE WALK

Crooked Tree

Altun Ha

New River Lagoon

Salt Creek

Hill Bank

Bermudian Landing

Mussel Creek

Big Falls (ranch)

BELIZE INTERNATIONAL AIRPORT

+831

Belize

BELIZE

Northern Lagoon

BELIZE CITY

WESTERN HIGHWAY

Roaring Creek

BELMOPAN

Sibun

Turneffe Islands

Lighthouse Reef

BARRIER REEF

Central Farm

San Ignacio

Xunantunich

Benque Viejo del Carmen

Southern Lagoon

Gales Point

Mullins River

Caribbean Sea

+3,348

Augustine

+1,200

Middlesex

Pomona

Stann Creek Town

CAYO

Millionario

Caracol

STANN CREEK

Hopkins

Glovers Reef

Cockscomb Range

Victoria Peak 3,680

MAYA MOUNTAINS

2,100

Maya Beach

Selne Bight Village

TOLEDO

Placentia

Bugle Cays

Medina Bank

Deep

Monkey River Town

Lubaantun

San Miguel

San Pedro

San Antonio

BARRIER REEF

Punta Gorda

Gulf of Honduras

Belize

Dolores

Sarstoon

Barranco

GUATEMALA

MEXICO

GUATEMALA

Introduction

"British Honduras is not on the way from anywhere to anywhere else, has no strategic value, is all but uninhabited; *"IF THE WORLD HAD ANY ENDS, BRITISH HONDURAS WOULD SURELY BE ONE OF THEM."* So wrote British author Aldous Huxley in his *Beyond the Mexique Bay*, written after a visit here in 1934.

British Honduras, or BELIZE, (pronounced BA–LEEZ) as this self-governing colony is already called in anticipation of the day it will attain full independence, remains somewhat remote. This 8,867 square mile New Hampshire-sized Central American colony, one of the last remnants of British Empire in the Caribbean, is located on the east coast of Central America facing the Spanish Main. Bounded on the north by Mexico's Yucatan Peninsular State of Quintana Roo and on the south and west by Guatemala, Belize boasts a population of a little more than 120,000 people—comparable to Cambridge, Massachusetts (or even Sioux City, Iowa), which gives it the lowest population density of any Central American country—about 12.4 persons per square mile. One-third of this population is clustered in Belize City, her largest city and seaport. Its greatest length is 174 miles, and greatest width is 68 miles.

Belize is not the smallest nation in the Americas; San Salvador is slightly smaller in area, though that country has a population nearly ten times that of Belize. The importance of the role that the "microstate" of Belize may have in future western hemisphere affairs should not be judged by its present lack of population and its current low standard of living, but by its rapid rate of progress over the past decade since achieving nearly total independence from Great Britain. This is best evidenced by its new capital built at Belmopan, the latest of a series of planned administrative centers around the world, and by the improvement of the state of the nation's health, education, and general welfare since that time.

Immigration to Belize has been severely limited by government control pending a clearcut policy being framed by the government, which realizes that its undeveloped land is a national resource worthy of careful study and regulation. The local government has resisted British efforts in the past to induce immigration from over-populated Caribbean states and other former colonies, preferring instead a slow, well-planned influx of multi-racial peoples from many different backgrounds and with diversified talents who would more easily fit into the national plan for the future of their country.

Rich in history, a port-of-call for white sail fleets of the Caribbean two centuries ago, her shoreline protected by a barrier reef that once gave refuge to buccaneers and pirates, for centuries seldom visited except by wandering foreign craft, mahogany freighters, and a small fleet of local boats carrying fruit to New Orleans and Tampa, Belize for many years was the most inaccessible place in Central America. Until only recently few tourists had visited this country, and still no railroad or acceptable highway connects her capital with any other Central American capital.

Founded by accident in 1638 by a group of ship-wrecked British seamen, the settlement known as Belize, "Belice," or the Honduran Bay Settlement—a British enclave surrounded by hostile Spanish neighbors near the mouth of the Belize River—struggled for two hundred years before gaining the recognition and protection it sought as a British Colony. Hurricanes, endemic to the area, have taken their toll; Spanish wars, Indian massacres, malaria epidemics, and other disasters have tried the fortitude of the Colony's courageous people. That the Belize Settlement has continued to survive for 335 years is a tribute to the determination of a handful of mixed-blooded English-speaking settlers. The major asset of the country today is not its delightful climate nor its fascinating geography, which one anticipates, but these innately innocent and sincere people—for the most part, descendants of the early British settlers and their African slaves imported to help in the harvesting of dye-wood and mahogany from the jungle. An amalgamation process has gone on quietly for centuries resulting in the modern, racially-blended Belizean. Belize has a functional literacy rate of over 90 percent and an insignificant crime rate.

Belize is different . . . exciting . . . scenic . . . memorable. It stands apart as an independent-minded progressive nation that blends in perfect harmony both the cultures, traditions, and beauties of the West Indies and that of Central America. Belizeans reflect the hospitality and diversity of their clime. They are a gracious and gentle folk whose ancestors, through struggle and adversity, have endowed them with an abiding love of freedom and a deep sense of respect for education, law and order.

ECONOMY

A poor country by any standard, Belize's gross national product is but U.S. $46 million, or less than $400.00 per capita per year—at that, higher than most of its Central American neighbors. Of greatest concern is its huge trade deficit which has to be propped up by foreign aid (primarily from the United Kingdom), tourism, and foreign investment. Chief among her imports are foodstuffs and manufactured items.

With over 1.6 million acres available for cultivation, Belize is still not self-sustaining in agriculture and is making little headway in overcoming the popular aversion in the country toward farming and farm labor.

After centuries of a one-crop economy, the national leaders are attempting to switch the economic emphasis from the dwindling timber industry to agriculture and light manufacturing. In this country that has exported wood to the world since the seventeenth century, wooden clothes-pins are imported from Czechoslovakia and wooden matches from Belgium.

The cost of importing foodstuffs from Britain and the U.S. keep the cost of living extremely high and the price of everyday commodities out of reach of the average Belizean.

The unit of currency in Belize is the Belize dollar. The rate of exchange varies with the fluctuation of the pound sterling, but ranges from U.S. $1.00 = $1.53 Bze. (June 1972) to an all time low of $1.82 Bze. in January, 1974.

Belize began issuing its own money for the first time on January 20, 1974 and is gradually replacing all the old British Honduras imprints still in circulation. Coins and bills are issued in denominations comparable to U.S. coinage, except that the twenty dollar bill is the highest valued note in use. The new Belize coins, in cupro-nickel, nickel-brass, and bronze, all bear portraits of distinctive birds of Belize—the toucan, parrot, curassow etc.—on the obverse with the national coat of arms on the reverse. They are the first coins minted for use in Belize that do not bear the portrait of the reigning British sovereign. This follows a trend begun in mid–1973, when all the nation's postage stamps began carrying the name Belize overstamped on the British Honduras imprint.

Prices in local stores are sometimes quoted in U.S. dollars and sometimes in Belize dollars, requiring one to constantly inquire, "in Belize or U.S. money?"

Belize has monetary reserves on deposit with the Commonwealth to back up its currency. These reserves earn only about three percent interest. It has been proposed that these funds be withdrawn and transferred to the United States where they could be re-invested at a more favorable rate of interest. Belize has lost, however, whatever chance she may have had of returning to the U.S. dollar parity she enjoyed prior to 1949 when her currency became linked, instead, to the pound sterling.

Principal banks in the country are Barclay's Bank of London, the Royal Bank of Canada, and the Bank of Nova Scotia. There is also a Government Savings Bank.

Table 1

NATIONAL BUDGET
(In Belize Dollars)

	1971	1972	1973	1974
Revenue (recurrent)	17,504,871	18,272,712	21,000,000	23,500,000
Expenditure (local sources)	16,107,850	1,495,880	2,600,000	- 0 -
United Kingdom Development Aids, other grants and loans (capital expenditures)	11,228,509	13,512,853	10,800,000	14,800,000
TOTAL EXPENDITURE	44,841,230	33,281,445	30,800,000	38,300,000

THE NATION'S HEALTH

The standard of living, as indicated by per capita national income figures, places Belize somewhere in the middle of the world range. While better off than the vast majority of underdeveloped countries, enjoying higher income than almost any of the new Asian or African countries, Belize lags a long way behind the countries of Europe and North America. Poverty is certainly widespread and most Belizeans live at a level that would probably be considered as unacceptably low in Europe or North America.

Such information that is available on nutrition suggests that many families are still undernourished with a caloric intake barely above that normally considered necessary for a healthy existence. Throughout the country, diets tend to contain an unduly high proportion of starches; local sources of high-protein foods are inadequate. This situation has improved considerably, however, from what it was prior to 1964.

One consequence of an improving nutrition is a resulting improvement in health standards. The most dramatic improvements are shown in the fall of mortality rates. In 1967 life expectancy at birth was 45 for males and 49 for females. Childhood mortality rate for children one to four years was 14 per 1000. This is roughly on the level with most of Europe. This improvement has been largely the result of the elimination of yellow fever, malaria, and small pox which were formerly frequent causes of death. This, however, is but one aspect of improved health standards. There is still much scope for the reduction of preventable though non-fatal disease, and the consequent lessening of personal suffering, through improved sanitation and medical services which are overstrained.

Belize has one physician per 3158 residents, one nurse per 620, and one hospital bed per 203 persons. There are only about ten dentists in the country. Though not ideal, Belize cannot be considered in any sense an unhealthy country nor can its medical facilities be regarded as intolerably inadequate. Its hospitals and clinics are well distributed between the larger towns and villages and there are no serious endemic diseases, with the possible exception of gastroenteritis, a national scourge which has persisted long after the common yellow fever and malaria have been wiped out. This can only be eliminated with the improvement of living conditions.

The great majority of the houses in Belize are without proper cooking or toilet facilities. Domestic electricity, running water, sewer mains, and street lighting are uncommon. Drinking water is obtained from "catchment," i.e., rainwater drained from the galvanized metal roofs and stored in less-than-sanitary cisterns. Durable household goods are minimal and a high proportion of the houses contain but one room, overcrowded with relatives, children and pets. It is in the area of housing where deviations from levels acceptable in more advanced countries are most obvious, and where improvement is most needed.

For those that can afford them, there are three very well staffed hospitals in Belize City, and several private physicians.

The new National Public Health Department sponsors Pre-natal and Child Welfare Clinics for children up to age five; some school health services are carried out by Public Health Nurses assisted by the British Red Cross.

There are ten urban health centers and fourteen rural health centers located throughout the country with organized programs for Infant Welfare, Pre-Natal Instruction and Clinics, T.B. Control, Immunization Services, Midwife Instruction, Communicable Disease Control, Out-Patient Service, and assistance to the chronically ill.

Other Government Public Health Department activities include Environmental Control Service (sewage and water supply), Malaria Eradication Service, V.D. Control, Rabies Control, Port Health Service, and the regulation of Food Supplies and Establishments. There are currently two professional Medical Health Officers on the staff.

NATIONAL GOAL: INDEPENDENCE

Although the world knows little of Belize, Belizeans have achieved a new awareness of the world and an acute sense of their own national identity in this generation. This has been brought about primarily by one man: George Cadle Price, their 56-year-old Premier. Price, a studious mild-mannered auctioneer's son from Belize City, was educated at Belize's St. John's College, run by American Jesuits, and at a Mississippi seminary before forsaking the priesthood for politics.

A complex wedding of Christian Democratic maxims of the church and Mayan mysticism, his political philosophy has had a universal appeal to the various ethnic groups in this country of polyglot racial blends which Price likes to describe as the "Belizean personality." A true "Belizean personality" himself, his ancestors include Spaniards, Mayas, Africans, and Welshmen.

Upon becoming the country's first Premier in 1964, Price launched into the business of nation-building with fervor. He gave his people a new flag, a name, an anthem, and a national prayer. He has even written a pageant to be performed on Independence Day. Although succeeding in arousing the easygoing Belizeans to the cause, he has been unable to deliver on his promise of independence.

The one seemingly insurmountable obstacle is their unsolved "Guatemala question." This Spanish-speaking Indian neighbor-republic claims to have inherited Spain's sovereignty of Belize and now, armed with American-supplied rifles and airplanes, lies ready to make good her 135-year-old claim as soon as the last Grenadier Guard returns to Yorkshire. Former Governor Sir John Paul has stated: *"So long as British troops are required to insure peace, Great Britain cannot leave British Honduras."* Thus, what may prove to be the longest period of labor in the birth of a nation, keeps Belize an emerging nation in suspended emergence.

Despite the ferment of recent years, Belizeans accept their plight with a piquant mixture of philosophy and naivete. As one young Belizean told the author with a shrug, *"It's no big deal, man. When it comes, it comes."* Of less concern in this land where a soothing calm pervades and warm tropical days flow by unmetered, time seems endless and undemanding.

For administrative purposes the country is divided into six districts: Belize, Corozal, Orange Walk, Cayo, Stann Creek, and Toledo; all except Belize are administered by district commissioners. District Town Boards have authority over most municipal affairs. In August, 1970 the seat of government moved from Belize City to Belmopan, a new Capital City built fifty miles inland, near the junction of the Western Highway and the Hummingbird Highway which leads to Stann Creek.

The British Government, represented by a Governor, retains responsibility for foreign affairs, defense, internal security, and civil service employment. There is an independent judiciary whose members are appointed by the Crown. The highest court in Belize is the Supreme Court headed by a Chief Justice. The United Kingdom gave up control of the national treasury in 1966.

The women's liberation movement in the United States in the 1970's was felt at least as far away as British Honduras. In 1972, for the first time in the nation's history, women were allowed to sit as jurors in a court of law. In a complex ordinance originally signed by His Excellency, Governor Paul in 1970, but not put into effect until March, 1972, qualifications for two types of jurors, regardless of sex, were set down at that time in a circular issued by the Registry. Common jurors and special jurors were defined: a special juror being one who, in addition to qualification as a common juror, also owns real estate drawing an annual income of at least B.H. $360., owns real estate of value not less than $5000, and is in receipt of an annual income of not less than $1800.

The Government of Belize, now headed by its first elected Premier, is, and has been for more than 150 years, characterized by political stability. Growing out of its long Commonwealth association, Belizeans have an ingrained respect for the constitution and the law—part of their British inheritance.

THE CARIBBEAN SETTING

Not quite so remote today as in Huxley's time, Belize City is now easily reached by daily jet flights from Miami and four times weekly from New Orleans. Approaching Belize, seen through the Mexican Gulf's whipped cream cloudscape, as the waters of the Gulf blend into that of the Caribbean Sea, one is struck with the beauty of the shifting patterns of indigo, bottle-green, turquoise, jade and violet as the warm West Indian sun reflects off the many-hued coral formations lying under the clear crystalline waters below. The coastline of Belize, scalloped with thousands of coves and bays, inlets and anchorages, skirted by hundreds of Polynesian-like, palm-covered islands called Cays (pronounced Keys) is the first dramatic landfall.

Second only in size to Australia's world-famous Barrier Reef, Belize's 190-mile-long chain of semi-submerged coral heads is a spectacular sight from the air. A white line of surf pushed up from the depths of the deep blue Caribbean is nearly unbroken for the 190 miles length. The surf crashes on the reef and damps into the brilliant aquamarine lagoon-like strip of quiet water that separates the Barrier Reef from the mangrove and jungle-covered coastline. In the distance, seen beyond the low coastline, lies the Maya Mountains appearing in a misty green haze under immense tropical clouds. As the airliner descends, one can see hundreds of tiny cays dotting the surface of the sea which is often blackened by large schools of fish feeding in the shallow waters surrounding them.

The waters along the Barrier Reef are everywhere dotted with starch-white sails of coastal schooners carrying their occupants out for a day of spear fishing. These native divers will return in the late afternoon from working, without benefit of air tanks, in forty- to sixty-foot clear blue water along the Reef, laden with many varieties of fish, 14-pound lobsters and local stone crab (truly a gourmet's delight) to sell in the native market in Belize City.

All of the nation's population centers are on the Caribbean Coast and it is the most West-Indian-oriented of the countries of Central America. It shares a similar climate, culture and colonial history with the former British islands, yet Belize is uniquely anomalous (as we shall see).

In keeping with the climate, life is unhurried in Belize, flowing with a vague rhythm of pattern. The author once tried to buy a local newspaper the day following a five-day holiday at Eastertime and was told, *"The paper's staff is recovering from their long holiday but will publish for sure tomorrow."*

GEORGE PRICE

The People and Their Culture

THE PEOPLE

The population of the country of Belize is slightly more than 120,000. More than one-half of these people live in six urban areas and nearly one-third live in metropolitan Belize City, the former capital and chief seaport. The population is growing at an annual rate of about three percent. Most Belizeans today are of multi-racial descent.

The history of British Honduran population growth has been one of forced immigration. Shipwrecked British seamen, deported Sepoy soldiers from India, Spanish-Indian refugees fleeing from the War of the Races in Yucatan, deported Black Caribs from across the Caribbean, Africans liberated from slave ships, persecuted Mennonites from Mexico, and even Maya Indians re-entering from neighboring territories after British settlement have provided the diverse ingredients which make up today's Belizean. That groups of people of such ethnic variety could be brought together with such vigorous civic unity as exists today is a tribute to their national leadership as much as the common cause that unites them: a desire for independence from Great Britain.

Table 2
POPULATION BREAKDOWN BY ETHNIC ORIGINS
(Based on April 1970 National Census)

American Indians (Mayas) 13%
Africans (pure African, Creoles and Caribs*) 57%
Mestizos (mixed European and Maya Indian)........... 22%
East Indian....................................... 1%
European 4%
Others (Lebanese, "Syrian" and Chinese).............. 3%

*The Black Carib population is estimated at 7%.

Table 3
POPULATION BREAKDOWN BY DISTRICTS
(Based on 1970 Census, provisional figures)

District	Male	Female	Total Persons
BELIZE DISTRICT and CAYS (excluding Belize City)	5,514	4,844	10,358
COROZAL	8,081	7,322	15,403
ORANGE WALK	8,744	7,894	16,638
STANN CREEK	6,343	6,669	13,012
TOLEDO	4,386	4,568	8,954
CAYO	8,422	7,601	16,023
BELIZE CITY	18,602	20,655	39,257
TOTALS	60,092	59,553	119,645

Maya Indians

The Maya Indians, the only peoples indigenous to this country, once heavily populated the entire area which is now Belize but mysteriously emigrated to Yucatan in the tenth century A.D. Today their numbers make up only approximately thirteen percent of the country's population, only ten percent of what it once was. Most of the present-day Belizean Mayas re-entered the country during the period of British occupation. The government granted them land in the Toledo District of the south but did not restrict them to that district. Villages were built in the north as well as the southern highlands. Belizean Mayas fall into three distinct groups and moved from three separate areas into Belize. Besides the group moving to the Toledo District, Mayas also settled in Orange Walk and Corozal Districts, and Mopan Mayas live in Succoths near Benque Viejo.

Belizean Mayas are largely situated in the more remote regions of the country and remain less assimilated than the other peoples of Belize. Following the timeless patterns of their ancestors, they are sustained on small plots of maize and black beans and raise a small amount of tobacco, pigs and cattle. Their century-old way of life is based on the shifting cultivation of one- to ten-acre plots of land.

Still an extremely rural people, by 1946 only one out of every eight lived in towns, and of that two out of three Mayas who were gainfully employed were working on their own land or as unpaid helpers and they had a lower proportion of wage earners than any other group in the country. Living in this way, they remained out of reach of schools. In 1911 ninety-seven percent were illiterate. Through intense government effort amazing progress was made so that by 1946 they had a literacy rate of fifty-seven percent, and since then this rate has been vastly increased.

The Mayas in Belize consist of three groups, each located far from the other, each speaking a different dialect of the Maya language: one Yacateco, a second Mopanero, and the third Kekchi. Today's Maya, if not a farmer as most are, prefers to work in the chicle forests where Mayas constitute the majority of all workers employed in that industry.

The Kekchi, as the Maya tribe in the Toledo District is called, have kept their old ways and old beliefs even more intact than the other two less-remote groups. There are about 4000 of these Mayas living in the villages of San Miguel, San Antonio, and Crique Sarko near Punta Gorda. The village women no longer weave their own cloth. Vendors hike from another Kekchi village, Coban, in Guatemala, to sell these items to their fellow Mayas in Belize. The journey, on foot, is said to take them three months.

The villages are governed by an *Alcalde* (headman), who is elected each year and paid a salary of $4.00 a month by the Belizean government. He has the power to levy fines for misconduct and is assisted by a second Alcalde and about five policemen.

Creoles and Africans

By the time the Bay Settlement formally became a British Colony in 1862, the population had become remarkably mixed. In addition to the British settlers who began settlement of the area as early as 1638, and the remaining Maya Indian tribes, Negro slaves had been introduced to work in the thriving timber industry. Being in a small isolated frontierland, living with daily threats from hostile neighbors and impending natural disasters, the Baymen had little time for racial prejudice. There was no "plantation" economy to perpetuate the slavery institution as in the islands of the West Indies so these Negro immigrants, while technically slaves until emancipation in 1838, found a place alongside the European woodcutters as companions and willing allies against the challenges of their inhospitable land and soon outnumbered their "owners" three to one.

Not all of the Black men arrived in Belize as slaves, however. On March 12, 1817 when the all-Black 5th West India Regiment was disbanded, five hundred of these men were given land grants and temporary rations and transported to Belize where most became free woodcutters. Their families joined them the following year.

In 1836 a slave vessel captured near Havana was routed by the Colonial Commission to Belize and its passengers, 193 male and 59 female Africans, were allowed to settle. On November 15, 1836 another ship on its way to a projected settlement planned by a private London company on the River Polochic, ran low on provisions and put into port in Belize where its unfortunate cargo of ninety African men, women and children were allowed to land. Employment was soon found for them. In December of the same year a Portuguese slave schooner was also captured, and 158 of its captive passengers became inhabitants of Belize.

There are no records of armed clashes occurring between African slaves and their masters as in other Caribbean settlements and, in fact, old records from the colony, still extant, contain accounts of many emancipations granted for civic service or on payment of a trifling sum. It was not difficult for them to earn this fee, as slaves were allowed to work for wages in private enterprises after their normal duties were completed. There are also accounts showing that the bequeathing of valuable property to a slave by his master upon his emancipation was a common practice.

Intermarriage has been common and socially acceptable in Belize since early colonial times and it is the English-speaking people of mixed European and African ancestry, the descendants of British woodcutters and their slaves, that predominate in the country today. These Afro-Belizeans, or "Creoles," vary in appearance from ebony black to near Caucasoid and make up over one-half of the total national population. The Creoles prefer to live in urban centers, especially Belize City. They dominate the ranks of the nation's civil service and occupy key positions in government, education, business, and commerce. While most of the Creoles were at one time employed in the seasonal timber industry, they now are found earning a living as farmers, fishermen, industrial workers, and especially in the growing construction industry where they have been quick to learn trades.

Mestizos

By far the largest single influx of people came as a result of the bloody War of the Races which broke out in Yucatan in 1848, when the Indians rose against their Spanish (Mexican) landlords and all other Europeans or people of mixed European ancestry. Thousands of mixed-blooded "Mestizos" (Maya Indians with some Spanish blood) fled into the protection of the Bay Settlement. By June 1859 it was recorded that between twelve to fifteen thousand Spanish-speaking Indians were then living in Punta Consejos and Corozal Town, within sight of their ruined native land across the River Hondo.

The War of the Races lasted until 1874. Of the thousands of Mestizo refugees who sought the shelter of British protection in Belize, over eight thousand remained permanently, settling mostly along the River Hondo, Belize's northern border shared with Mexico. Some worked as logcutters but most settled down in small clearings, cultivated maize and fattened pigs. They soon built a church in Corozal. Perhaps their most important contribution to their adopted country was the sugar cane that they brought with them, which is the origin of Belize's now-flourishing sugar export industry. The Mestizo people today are found largely in the Corozal and Orange Walk Districts and make up some twenty-two percent of the nation's population. Their influence can best be seen in the fact that Spanish is now the mother tongue of approximately forty percent of Belizeans (although English is spoken by virtually the entire population) and as a second language by another twenty percent.

The Black Caribs

Since the year 1797 there has been living on the southern coastal region of Belize an unusual group of people known as the "Black Caribs" who make up about seven percent of the present population. They are descendants of West Africans and Red Caribs, a fierce cannibalistic group of Amerindians who occupied parts of the northern coast of South America and the

Lesser Antilles at the time of Columbus. This warlike tribe had seized the Lesser Antilles and were progressively working their way north, overrunning the more pacific Arawaken tribes along the way. Their raids, made over long distances in dugout canoes, usually resulted in the women being taken as captive mates and the Arawak men killed and eaten in elaborate victory celebrations. Their northern thrust was effectively checked by the arrival of the *conquistadores* whose armor, horses, and gunpowder proved superior to Carib arrows and blow-guns. These island Caribs were greatly reduced in number and scattered during the Spanish Conquest.

The ethnic origin of the Black Carib can be traced through their strange eventful history to the year 1675 when a sailing ship carrying West African slaves ran aground in a storm off the tiny island of Becquia, near St. Vincent in the Windward Island chain on the eastern rim of the Caribbean. The surviving shipwrecked Africans found this island inhabited by Island Caribs. Intermarriage between the Africans and the Red Caribs gave birth to the present-day Black Caribs.

After many years on Becquia, the Black Caribs spread to the larger island of St. Vincent, already inhabited by runaway slaves from Barbados. In 1795, under a leader named Chattoyer, the Black Caribs participated in an unsuccessful rebellion against British authority and were promptly deported to the Bay Islands of Roatan and Bonacca where many reside today. Some of them eventually migrated to the mainland, settling first in Trujillo, Honduras.

Settlers in Belize first had contact with these black Indians with strange customs and language in 1802 when they began making frequent trips from Spanish Honduras to Belize City and back, smuggling British goods into Honduras. Some remained longer to work in the seasonal mahogany harvest. In 1832 large numbers of Caribs made their way north along the coast and settled permanently in Punta Gorda and later in Stann Creek Town, Hopkins, Seine Bight, and Barranco after they had cooperated in an ill-fated attempt by Royalists to overthrow the new republican government in Honduras.

Black Caribs have always presented a puzzle for anthropologists who are hard put to consider them Afro-American or a variant Amerindian, but all agree that their total culture resembles no New World African culture but is uniquely their own. Regardless of where the Black Caribs live today, they form a separate ethnic group which may be considered a caste. They tend to be endogamous, hardly ever intermarrying with even the rural Creoles in Stann Creek, with whom they mix freely in daily life, but prefer to return to their own group for the more intimate functions of life including recreation, marriage, birth and death.

The Black Caribs are a superstitious people. Many steadfastly cling to old folkways which include a belief in the supernatural. Their culture today is a catch-all blend of Indian, Creole, and African influences and when they do practice a religion, it is invariably Roman Catholic. The Caribs have traditionally made their living by fishing but in recent years more and more are forsaking the sea to become farmers, an occupation they once believed fit only for women. Great strides have been made in the social integration of the Carib into the Belizean community, but the urban Creole still hesitates to accept this strange Negro who speaks an Indian language-form and retains Indian cultural traits.

The Caribs themselves maintain a certain amount of hostility toward the Creole, whom they regard as the perpetrator of the "spoiling" of their racial character. The remark of a young Carib schoolteacher, *"I could go and kill every Negro in Africa for having spoiled our race,"* quoted by Douglas Taylor in an exhaustive Carib study, speaks volumes for the sense of shame and frustration that consumes many Black Caribs.

In a country with a history of easy racial relations, where mixed blood is more common than the exception, and with the present rise of nationalistic feelings of unity, perhaps little importance should be placed on isolated incidents of disharmony and this quotation therefore deserves less emphasis today than it did when it was first published in 1951. With the improvement of communication and education the old differences are becoming less. Many young Caribs are leaving home to seek jobs and higher education outside of the Stann Creek and Punta Gorda areas and many have found their place in the mainstream of Belizean society.

East Indians

In 1857 a revolt took place in India against British rule. In New Delhi the British-trained-and-equipped Indian soldiers, known as Sepoys, mutinied and killed many British inhabitants of that city. Joined by insurrectionists in Lucknow and Cawnpore, they proceeded to massacre over a thousand British men, women, and children before the bloody Sepoy Rebellion was finally put down by British and a few remaining loyal Sepoy troops.

Escaping the horrible reprisals suffered by many of the defeated Sepoys, 1000 of the convicted rebels were deported by the British government to British Honduras. These East Indians were first sent to the Corozal District to work in the sugar plantations. Today their descendants can be found throughout the country, still rather poor and subservient to their neighbors in Belize City, and others still working in the sugar industry, both in the North and in the Punta Gorda area, making up about one percent of the population in 1970.

"Syrian" and Lebanese

There are a number of Lebanese mercantile families living in the country. They are among Belize's most successful businessmen. "Syrian" is a generic term used throughout the Caribbean for the group of immigrant traders who originated in any of several French-speaking areas of North Africa and Southwest Asia. There has been little intermarriage between these groups and others. Together with the Chinese, these people constitute about three percent of Belize's population.

Chinese

By the year 1865 the economic situation in Belize had reached a crisis stage with the depletion of its vast mahogany reserves imminent, and a severe drop in the world market for this wood due, in part, to the introduction of iron and steel for ship construction. It had been obvious for over a decade that the Colony needed to foster an agricultural industry on which to shift its economic base. Toward this end, several immigration schemes were proposed to induce agricultural workers to the Colony. In 1864 an Immigration fund was established by a government loan contracted by the Colony. Through this fund, a few large landowners in Belize arranged for the importation of Chinese farm workers. The first group arrived in Belize on June 1, 1865.

The Chinese were at first welcomed and greeted with much natural curiousity, as few of the colonists had ever seen an Oriental person, but the experiment did not work out. The Chinese, first sent to northern areas of the New River and Corozal Town, met with resentment by the Spanish-speaking Mestizos of that region. In an official complaint to the Legislative Assembly the Mestizo settlers suggested: *"It might reasonably have been supposed that where population and labor were so necessary for the development of the resources of the country, and when Chinamen and East Indians were being sent for to distant parts of the world at an expense of more than $100. per head, a quiet, industrious, and inoffensive people at the very doors of the Colony (Yucatan), would have been encouraged in every way to enter and remain, especially when the cost would have been trifling . . ."*

In August 1866, the Chinese were withdrawn from the Corozal District and transferred to the Toledo District in the south and no new Chinese groups were introduced. On October 23, 1868, the Immigration Agent reported to the Assembly on the present numbers, state, and condition of the Chinese immigrants in the Colony, stating: *"Great diminuation, however, has taken place from death and flight. Of the 474 who landed in 1865, only 211 remain."*

A scattering of people of Chinese ancestry can still be found in Belize. Today most live in Belize City and Punta Gorda where some are merchants and store proprietors, but on the whole they have not prospered.

North American and Europeans

Of the remaining eight percent of the Belizean population, half are of unmixed white European stock, mostly American, Canadian, and British. Several hundred southern Americans settled in the Toledo District after the Civil War to escape the unsettled conditions in the South. The Belizeans welcomed the ex-confederates and offered them landgrants in the Toledo District where they established large sugar plantations a few miles from Punta Gorda. Many former army officers, doctors, and ministers were among these settlers who emigrated from nearly every southern state, attracted by advertisements and posters displayed by Young, Toledo and Company, a private immigration company in New Orleans.

Although many became discouraged and returned to the United States, for those settlers courageous and enterprising enough to survive price drops in sugar and the cholera epidemic of 1868, British Honduras offered ample reward. Those who remained introduced bananas to the southern part of the Colony. Through their contacts in the United States, communications were established and economic and social ties are maintained to this day between Belize and the southern states of the U.S. as a result. Many of these settlers' children were sent back to the United States for education but, unfortunately for British Honduras, more and more of them remained in the U.S. after college where economic opportunities were greater.

In August, 1879, 450 distressed Italian farm laborers left Guatemala and located new farms on public land provided by the government near Manatee.

The most recent group to immigrate to Belize has been the Mennonites. Mostly Canadians of German extraction, these people left the Canadian prairies when that government levied heavy taxes on them for refusing to send their children to public schools. These devoutly religious people who speak a form of "Old German," preferred to educate their own children. In 1920, President Obregon of Mexico invited them to come to Mexico, and between 1920 and 1930 several thousand Mennonites did immigrate to the States of Chihuahua and Durango in Mexico where they remained for thirty years. During that time the Mennonites multiplied and land became scarce for their cooperative farming activities. Arrangements were made in 1959 for 3000 of them to relocate to Belize. The Mennonites bought 100,000 acres of forested land along the River Hondo and constructed a road to Orange Walk. There are now two other Mennonite communities, one at Spanish Lookout and one at Shipyard.

The Mennonites set up self-sustaining communities and do not participate in public affairs or local politics. Not well received at first, they soon proved themselves an asset to the country by intelligent and diligent farming which, for example, reduced the price of eggs on the local market from $1.10 B.H. to $.75 B.H. a dozen.

In Belize City they maintain a market building which serves as an outlet for their farm products and a community center for their members' use while in the city. They also sell much of their garden produce door to door or along the road from their horse-drawn wagons. The Mennonites do not believe in using motor vehicles and all their farm work is done with horse-drawn equipment.

Although the Mennonites have not become assimilated into Belizean life, they have been good neighbors and made a contribution to their new homeland. Belizeans felt a loss when, in June, 1973, Mennonite families from Blue Creek and Shipyard began an organized withdrawal to a new settlement in Bolivia. Initially, about five hundred left, via SAHSA Airlines, and some fifteen hundred are expected to leave before their exodus is completed. Following their Amish teachings, the Mennonites are not permitted to use farm machinery and the Belizean jungle proved too much of a challenge for their hand labor methods. The area selected in Bolivia is thought to be better suited for their type of farming, and at least equally important, Bolivia imposes no market price controls on them. Caucasians, especially newcomers to Belize, are still often referred to colloquially as "Backras." This term, a carry-over from slavery days, is the equivalent of "tenderfoot" and refers to the white man's tendency to underestimate the intensity of the West Indian sun which often results in a painful sunburn, or a "raw back." Though most have forgotten its origin, the term is still used much in the same way mainland Americans are called "Haoles" by native Hawaiians; serving more as a means of identification than a derogatory term.

SOCIAL ATTITUDES AND LANGUAGE

From the time the first African slaves arrived in Belize they represented a wide cross-section of Africa, both geographically and culturally. They were former aristocrats, tradesmen, hostages taken in inter-tribal wars, dupes betrayed or sold unknowingly into servitude, delinquent debtors, or unfortunate captives taken in raids on their villages by the slave-traders. It was difficult to ascertain an individual's African origin in America as they were identified with their port of shipment which may have been immediately adjacent to their home or, more likely, several hundred miles inland. The slavers roamed the African coastline for a thousand miles from Senegambia and the Gold Coast where the trade began, to Nigeria and Angola whose ports were most often visited by the slavers at the time of emancipation.

While the slaves had a common African heritage, they represented over twenty different tribes: Bibi, Fulani, Mandingo, Tambi, Sokko, Kalibari, Mangree, Watje, Fida, Arrada, Ibo, Akim, Mondongo, Kanga, Papaa, the war-like Elminas, and the peoples of the vast Congo and Loango areas. Each tribesman spoke a different language-form but most came from similar agricultural, nomadic and pastoral backgrounds.

As Belizean society began to take form, each new arrival of

slaves from Africa were forced to become "Creolized," or to adjust to the new environment. The true Creoles, the lighter-skinned of mixed white parentage, who were second or third generation Belizeans were most effective in forcing this transition and provided a model to be emulated. Tribal language was scorned and today's "Creole" language evolved, a sort of pidgin-English still used throughout the colony by many of the natives in speaking among themselves, though nearly all now also speak a fine, almost-nineteenth-century, very proper English in addition.

Social strata developed, based not as much on wealth and position as on the effectiveness this assimilation had on an individual which was best told by his language. Skin color, although not to the extent of the sugar plantation-based British Islands, held another key to a person's social standing even in Belize. The most marked racial bias in the colony's history has been between brown-skinned Creoles and their black-skinned African brothers.

Free Creoles soon rose to positions of importance, owned slaves themselves, and aspired toward considerable social and civic prestige. There developed a friction which exists on a small scale even today between the upper-class Creole and their darker brothers. Black servants sometimes resent working for Browns who often show them a condescending manner. The Blacks have been heard to say of the Creole: *"They seem to think they are doing us a favor by wearing our color."*

In the lower classes of society, below the Creole elite who considered themselves white, stratification was intricate. In Africa, the Blacks knew only three classes: aristocrats, serfs, and slaves. In Belize, the nuances became more complicated. At the top of their social scale were the soldiers and "fort Negroes," the smart-uniformed Jamaican regiment guards and the local militiamen who were considered sufficiently trustworthy to bear arms and trusted with the defense of the colony.

After the fort Negroes came the skilled craftsmen—cabinet-makers, masons, barbers, tailors, and boat-builders. After them the wood-cutters, which group accounted for by far the largest proportion of nineteenth century Belizean society. These were freemen who labored in the timber industry under contracts with their employers.

After the wood-cutters came the house servants, and there was even division there. The children's nurse was at the top of this order followed by the cook, the ladies' maid, etc., etc. At the bottom of the social ladder was the agricultural worker—the field laborer, whose lot was the hardest and whose skin was usually the blackest.

The heritage left by the early slavery days of Belize is still in the attitude of its people, especially in the contempt present-day natives have for physical labor which they feel to be demeaning. A cook will not scrub floors for fear of losing her "status." The author once asked a Creole taxi-driver to carry his luggage to the waiting taxi, and was told, "That is porter's work." The driver only reluctantly picked up a bag after his fare had already carried two of the largest himself and it was obvious that no porter was available. This attitude accounts for the problems that Belize has had in converting their unemployed wood-cutters to agricultural workers. While the labor of the wood-cutter is just as hard and back-breaking as that of the field worker, the former is a "contractor," contracting his labor, while the latter works for wages. The small nuance may seem unimportant to others, but to Belizeans it is very important indeed. It is this emphasis that society puts upon maintaining personal prestige that makes the native eschew manual labor, not their laziness. Belizeans are not lazy, as anyone who has watched a gang of mahogany loggers can testify.

Another interesting characteristic of the natives of Belize is their innate courtesy. The politeness shown employers and visitors, often a surprise to the first-time tourist to this country, may to some extent have filtered down from early days when punishment was swift and severe for wrong-doing, and a former fear of causing their superior's displeasure may explain this present tradition of avoiding any responsibility that may result in failure. Belizeans never say "no"; always "maybe," or "possibly," which one must learn usually means "no." Instructions are always carried out literally with no improvision to meet changed conditions. Instructions given to a local newspaper concerning a change of address was directed to a particular individual whom the author knew to be a reliable and conscientious employee but who, by the time the letter was received by the paper, no longer was employed there. Asking why the request had not been honored, the paper replied, in all sincerity, that the party to whom it was directed, not being there, had been unable to comply. No thought had been given to someone else handling the simple matter.

A local businessman in Belize with an agency for the rental of Land Rovers has a stack of reservation requests on his desk inches thick. When asked why he didn't answer them, he replied, "I don't have enough cars to fill all their orders, and I wouldn't want to disappoint anyone."

Yet another incident which illustrates this desire to please occurred when the author returned from a fishing trip with his first kingfish. Not having a scale on which to weigh the fish and anxious to learn its approximate weight, he recruited the help of four commercial fishermen standing at the rail of the dock. The first held the fish up, and after much deliberation, said it weighed 14 pounds, probably very close to its true weight. In mock indignation I replied, "Fourteen pounds! Why man that fish must weigh forty." Solemnly each of the next three men held the fish at arm's length, and each in turn thoughtfully determined that the fish weighed forty pounds. Almost all new residents to Belize have had similar experiences in encountering this old and distinctive culture, which locals make no attempt to explain. The newcomer's confusion upon experiencing this unusual psychology only serves to amuse the residents.

The English language as spoken in Belize today is a rich patois of English, Creole, local words, and foreign expressions delicately blended and delivered with light, sing-song, Calypso-like intonations, difficult to understand but delightful to hear. Scots and Irishmen have left their mark in the lilting speech and some students of languages have likened it to King James' English, the language of the British buccaneer—founders of the country. Many antiquated phrases do find common usage in Belize: dresses are still "frocks" and automobiles are "coaches," but then Americans are constantly amused at out-moded idioms in use in London today. Belizeans use the term "tea" colloquially to refer to any meal.

The Belizean's speech is well-seasoned with Creole proverbs that go as far back as the slaves themselves, but still contain considerable humor, much practical wisdom, and sum up whole philosophies.

"Creoles can say in a few words what takes the English three hours to say," is a popular sentiment expressed in Belize. Some of the quaint solecisms expressed in idiomatic Creole are:

"Fence has got ears and tokada (blind) got eyes," "Punkin never bear watermelon," "Fool dey talk, but dey no fool – dey lisson," "When fish come from rivah bottom and say alligatah got bellyache, you believe 'em," "Coward man keep sound bone," and, *"Same place Pelican wanto go, sea breeze blow 'em."*

This last bit of philosophy expresses best the attitude of the overwhelming majority of the citizens of Belize today. Resolutely calm, they wait with infinite patience, confident that the sea breeze of political change will blow them where they want to go.

SUPERSTITITIONS AND FOLKLORE

According to a law introduced throughout the Caribbean as early as 1971, the African practice of Obeah, brought by the slaves to the West Indies, has been punishable by death. In Belize, Obeah has never had a strong hold, though it is known and those persons reputed to be practicing it are feared. Inquiry into this Black Magic by an outsider is met with cold disapproval, but with some persistance it is possible to learn something of its practice which apparently today is diverse and limited only by the imagination of its practitioner.

Today in Belize, Obeah is of vital concern only to one people—the Black Caribs of the far southern regions of the country where it is blamed for many deaths, allegedly brought about by Obeah-men hired by an enemy of the deceased to work their magic spells. This is usually accomplished by the use of a black doll constructed from a black stocking stuffed with feathers from a dark fowl, held together with black thread and black pins. (Possibly related to the sticking-a-pin-in-a-doll voodoo ritual of which we've all heard.) The doll is then buried under the victim's doorstep.

In addition to causing death, Obeah is thought to have the power to affect the outcome of a love affair, the well-being of one's crops, or the success of a business venture. Black Caribs paint an indigo cross (with household bluing) on the forehead of an infant to ward off the evil spirits of the Obeah. This exact practice is, curiously enough, common in Puerto Rico where Obeah is unknown, but there it is done to ward off the "evil eye," an evil spirit who preys on children.

Most educated Belizeans scoff at belief in Obeah, and even ones who do believe admit that "there aren't as many evil spirits about as there once were," as one told me. But nevertheless modern Belizeans still hold a fear for a certain species of black butterfly, prevalent in the country, said to bring an early death or at least bad luck to its beholder. A carved trinket suspended from a bracelet worn by a teenager in Belize City, a small black clenched fist with the thumb inserted between the index and middle fingers, which I took for a modern Black Power symbol, turned out to be an Obeah charm dating back to the African "bush" days, and even commonly found in Egyptian tombs. Shoes are frequently crossed before going to bed to prevent the "evil ones" from occupying them during the night and to insure the wearer from harm on the morrow.

Maya superstitions, even more mystical and fatalistic, are countless and have been absorbed into Belizean culture. Many of them are survivals from their ancient religion, mixed with European folklore and African beliefs. There are many omens believed to foretell death. If one dreams he is floating on air or that he is having a tooth pulled, a close member of the family will die, as does a dream of a black bull attempting to enter one's home or of breaking a water jug. To dream of red tomatoes means a baby will die.

Sickness is believed to be caused by dwarfs and that by placing gourds of food in the doorway for them, one can prevent an epidemic. If one gives away embers of burning wood, his turkeys will die. Eggs laid on Friday will not hatch. Fridays are considered, along with Tuesdays, as unlucky days while Saturdays and Mondays are lucky. Many Mayas won't buy a lottery ticket except on Saturday or get married on any day but Monday.

Typical Mayan folk stories are mystical, like the tale of the young Indian who observed a bright blue snake crawling upon one of the pyramids. A few minutes later, after walking on, he turned to see a young woman in a bright blue garment standing at the top of the pyramid with her ankles bound and arms outstretched. Then she disappeared. This story, or similar versions of it, has been popular with the Mayas as long as they can remember, as have various stories of ceramic statues taken from one of their mounds and transported many miles away, stealing back to their jungle resting place.

There are many weather omens. Thin cornhusks indicate a mild winter, thick ones a cold winter. If the swallows fly low it will rain; if high, it will be clear. Evil winds often take the form of animals, and individuals struck by them will die.

Most Maya superstitions have unpleasant connotations. Many more things are thought to bring bad luck than good. This fatal strain is perhaps a heritage of their past, where sacrifice was common and more of their gods were hostile than friendly.

Most folk tales are identified with one ethnic group or another but some are typically Belizean. One such story which is given wide-spread credence in Belize concerns a phantom pirate ship, called "Jack O' Lantern" or "Flying Dutchman," claimed to be sighted from time to time off Colson's Point near Mullins River in the Stann Creek area. This derelict sailing ship, traveling at night with its rigging illuminated by flickering lanterns hung from its yardarms, is blamed for luring many unfortunate seamen onto the coral reef off that point.

Two similar spirits, locally created, are the "Greasy Man" and the "Ashi de Pompi" who live in abandoned houses, the latter in the ashes of burned houses, and come out at night to frighten people. On one occasion half the residents of Belize turned out to chase a Greasy Man back to his haunt.

Any collection of Belizean Mythology must include an accounting of the dwarfs, called by their Spanish name *Duende*, who play such an important part in the lives of the local children. Every school boy knows what to do if he enounters one of these elfin creatures in the jungle. He gives him the *Duende* salute, that is a four-fingered salute being very careful to conceal his thumb in his palm, only exposing the backside of his hand to the *Duende*. This is because the *Duendes* only have four fingers on each hand and can become very jealous of anyone with an ordinary five-fingered hand. *Duendes* can be very mean and terrible but they also are capable of doing all manner of miraculous things. They speak all languages and can grant wishes. One especially popular belief is that if one becomes captured by one of these goblins two things happen: you lose your mind and you achieve instant mastery of the musical instrument of your choice. Natives living in Gales Point swear that a man living there was carried away as a child by the *Duendes* and when he returned he was a little strange in the head, but he sure could play the guitar!

Most educated people living in Belize City look upon the "little people" as characters of a fairy tale, but many men who live and work in the jungle not only believe in them but have evidence of their existence. A British naturalist working in the jungles of British Honduras in the 1930's made a study of these reports and interviewed dozens of forestry workers who had encountered *Duendes*. Among those to whom he talked were forestry officers who had received their education in the United States and Europe.

One junior forestry officer told of seeing two of them on several occasions watching him from the edge of the forest reserve near the Maya Mountains, not far from El Peten where he was marking young mahogany trees. This whole area is a tangle of sharp ridges, tall peaks, deep gorges and ravines choked with tropical rain forest. It has not been explored nor mapped, and what it may contain no one really knows.

The pair of *Duendes* this man reported seeing were from three and a half to four feet tall, well proportioned, but with heavy shoulders and rather long arms. They had flat, yellowish faces, and their bodies were covered with a thick, short brown hair not unlike a short-haired dog's coat. They left deep footprints with pointed heels. When observed, the *Duendes* usually appeared suddenly from the edge of the forest, observed men silently, and then disappeared just as quickly into the jungle. Forest workers have little fear of them as they have never been known to make a threatening move toward them, but have sometimes been reported to carry off dogs.

Further evidence that these little people did exist, at least at one time, can be seen in Maya bas reliefs which depict pairs of tiny folk with no clothes except for a large Mexican Hat or banana-frond held over their heads. These were at first dismissed as merely the Mayas attempt at depicting low social status, but since then murals have been found showing *Duendes* and peasants—the lowest social strata known to the Mayas— with *Duendes* appearing much smaller.

From time to time evidence of human habitation is found in unexplored, inaccessible regions of the Belize jungles, as Shell Oil Company aerial photographs have revealed, yet no one has been known to have come out of these utterly isolated spots and we have no idea as to what manner of men might inhabit them. Perhaps they are Mayas who fled there at the time of the conquest or earlier, pre-Maya survivors of a race we do not know, or maybe even little *Duendes* with four fingers on each hand. Who can say?

Far more dreaded than the *Duendes* in Belizean mythology is the Sisimito or Sisemite, a great hairy creature larger than man and stronger than a wild animal said to inhabit the Montane jungles of Guatemala and range as far as the western range of Belize's Maya Mountains. Though not seen as often, nor by witnesses as reliable, the Sisimito has the fearsome reputation of tearing men to pieces and carrying off their women as mates.

One of the first stories published concerning this creature was in a 1959 issue of *Museum Journal*, of the University of Pennsylvania, and tells how a Sisimito carried off the wife of a young Indian farmer who was later imprisoned for her murder since the people didn't believe his story. A group of hunters in the area where she had disappeared one day captured what appeared to be a wild woman drinking at a brook. She struggled to get away, and all the more when a Sisimito appeared on a hillside, waving his arms and answering her cries.

"On his back was a child, or a monkey child," the hunters were quoted as reporting, "which he took in his hands and held aloft as if to show it to the woman, who renewed her struggle to be free. The Sisimito came down the hillside almost to the brook where we stood, dropped the child and tore off great branches from big trees which he threw at us."

The wild woman was taken before the imprisoned husband, but he simply said, when asked if he recognized her; "My wife was young and beautiful; this woman is old and ugly." She never spoke a word, refused to eat, and died in a few days. This story, attributed to different people, times and localities, has been told throughout Central America and even in South America where Baron Alexander von Humboldt encountered it more than 180 years ago.

Local legend has it that these Sisimitos are impossible to trail as they have the miraculous ability to reverse their feet and run heel foremost. "If a Sisimito sees you," a wide-eyed ten-year-old has told me, "you jump behind a bush. If the Sisimito comes to look for you he will walk around the bush, see his own backward tracks leading the other way, think they are yours, and will follow them. That's when you get away."

There are two things the Sisimito desire desperately to learn: the arts of speech and firemaking. They reportedly build up little piles of twigs and sit in front of them for hours but do not know how to light them. When they find the remains of a hunter's fire in the forest they sit by the embers until they grow cold—and then eat them! Sisimitos kidnap children in the hope of learning to talk. Men who are unfortunate enough to look into a Sisimito's eyes are said to die within a month, but a woman who sees one has her life prolonged.

The legend is old—and new. As recently as the 1940's in the Guatemalan town of Coban, the police investigated the complaint of a man who charged that his son-in-law allowed a Sisimito to abduct his daughter. Witnesses said they saw her carried off while the husband sat shivering with fright. In view of the Sisimito's bad reputation, no arrest was made.

RELIGION

Belize's early inhabitants were nearly all Protestants. The Church of England (Anglican) was officially established in Belize City in the month of February, 1777, and as soon as the city was finally surveyed and regularly laid out, in 1812, St. John's Cathedral, the first Anglican church in Central America, was built at government expense. This church, presided over by the stern Bishop of British Honduras, served as a pompous setting for various ceremonies of state and was attended regularly by only the government officials, the small European community and the Creole elite. Christianity was still the religion of the "white man" in Belize until late in the 1820's.

Working against slavery in the West Indies within the government in England, a group of humanitarians had been able to force a policy of amelioration to be adopted by the Colonial Office which included such reforms in slave codes as restriction of physical punishment, prohibition of separate sale of parent and children and encouragement of Christian marriage among slaves. The Colonial Office requested that Governors of colonies with Assemblies urge the passage of similar legislation. Even when such laws were passed, the extent of their effect was slight, as it was from the white or Creole slave-owning classes that the law enforcement agencies and judicial authorities were drawn.

Although the campaign for amelioration suffered from

constitutional and practical limitations, the missionary wing of the movement had for some years been engaged in the West Indies on what they considered to be the most important means of slave improvement—Christian religious instruction. The hesitancy of the Church of England to carry out this work against the wishes of the slave owners, who feared the effect of the education of their slaves in Christian doctrine would in some way endanger the delicate balance of their society and might lead to revolt, gave rise to an anti-establishment evangelical movement within the Church of England. It also led to the establishment of vigorous nonconformist churches, like the Baptist and the Methodist, who operated outside the Church of England. By 1815 an increasing number of these missionaries began arriving throughout the West Indies to administer to the Africans and convert them to Christianity. The first such mission was established in Belize with the building of a Baptist Church in 1822 and followed three years later by a Wesleyan Methodist Church.

That these first missionaries, contempuously called "Methodizzies," had good effect on the Blacks of Belize cannot now be denied. For many, their first instruction in the English language was at the mission schools set up in Belize, and the missionaries helped the Blacks with the difficult transition from slavery through "apprenticeship" to full-free status achieved in 1838.

While the Anglican Church still has adherents in Belize, many are nominal and the most dynamic element of Protestantism in Belize today is represented by these fundamental evangelical sects, the largest being Methodist, who draw their parsons, as well as their followers, from the lower ranks of society. Religion in its most fundamental form plays an important part in the life of these people. The churches provide opportunities for satisfying status aspirations not available in the wider society as a whole, and their services provide important opportunities for emotional release.

While it cannot be said with impunity that the fundamentalist Protestant sects in Belize have been an obstacle to national integration, it can be charged that they have reinforced certain racial or class divisions which already existed. There is ample evidence of class hatred shown the East Indian Moslem minority by Blacks, recently converted to evangelical Christianity. Conversely, Blacks from these denominations find it difficult at times to gain appointments and advancement because of the stigma inherent in this association. As a case in point, the leader of the minority political party found it advantageous to convert to the Catholic religion and this fact was duly noted by his opposition in the political campaign, reminding the voters that their opponent was a Catholic *convert*.

Another problem encountered by the evangelistic churches in Belize results from their method of setting up mission churches in outlying districts under half-educated Black preachers and thereby often losing their members to native evangelical sects whose traditions owe as much to African witchcraft as to Christian principles.

Catholicism, which today encompasses sixty percent of the population, was at the outset slow in taking hold in Belize. Until the mid-nineteenth century the only Catholic communities of any size were at Mullins River, a village a few miles south of Belize City, where a few hundred refugees from Spanish Honduras had settled, and in the Black Carib villages in the south. These villages were visited irregularly by English-speaking Irish priests who traveled along the coast from Corozal to the Guatemalan border performing a few marriages and baptizing hundreds of infants. Most of their early followers spoke Spanish or Carib dialects and were accustomed only to Spanish Padres, but the periodic sight of the foreign priest's vestments was reassuring to these isolated Catholics.

The War of the Races in Yucatan after 1848 brought thousands of Catholic Mestizos into the confines of the Settlement. In 1851 two Jesuit priests arrived in Belize to administer to this growing congregation which at one time approximated twelve thousand. They built the first Catholic Church in the Colony at Corozal Town, and another in Orange Walk soon after.

In January, 1883, six Sisters of Mercy arrived in Belize and established a convent and St. Catherine's Academy for girls. St. John's College, a Jesuit-operated secondary school was founded four years later. Both these institutions were destroyed in the 1931 hurricane but have since been rebuilt. The St. Vincent de Paul Society is active today in charitable work among the poor. Membership in the Roman Catholic Church had increased continuously and has now far surpassed all others in size. There are Roman Catholic Churches in every district.

Although not particularly religious, the Mayas add their members to the Catholic rolls in Belize. Roman Catholicism introduced to them by the Spanish has replaced their own forgotten religion. At the present it is interesting to note that worship among the Mayas is carried on almost exclusively by the women, though in ancient times religion was largely an affair of the men. Practically all children are baptized but few receive additional instruction in the tenets of the Church due to the scarcity of priests in the smaller villages; hence the majority know little or nothing of the real meaning and significance of Christianity.

In 1891 Seventh Day Adventist missionaries came to Belize. A thirty-five ton ship was built in the colony for them and, six years later with other missionaries, they launched the ship, called *The Herald*, and plied the Caribbean bringing dental, medical and spiritual help to inhabitants of the Belize Coast, the Cays, and other West Indian Islands. They built their first church in Belize in 1932. In April, 1972 ground was broken for a new hospital and clinic on the outskirts of Santa Elena in the Cayo District by the Seventh Day Adventist Mission in Belize. This facility will initially provide for twenty-five patients plus out-patient service for many more. It was planned as a sanitorium where mental therapy as well as medical treatment will be provided.

Besides a Scottish Presbyterian congregation formed in 1850, the only other Protestant churches in the country (other than those already mentioned) are the Salvation Army, who came in 1915 and operate a day school, Baptists, Nazarene, and the recently-arrived Mennonites. The total estimated membership in all the Protestant church groups is 28,000, mostly Methodist and Anglican. That of the Roman Catholic faith is 65,000. There is a small group of Muslim, Hindu and Jewish faith but their total numbers scarcely over one percent of the population. The Persian Ba'hais sect is also represented by a small group. Freedom of worship is guaranteed by the constitution.

EDUCATION

Religion and education have always been synonymous in British Honduras and are still closely related. Had it not been for the churches, education would surely have remained neglected for a much longer period than it was. Today, due to the efforts of her various church organizations maintaining nearly two hundred schools with the help of government aid, Belize can boast an astounding literacy rate approaching 95 percent, the highest in the Americas. As Premier Price proudly puts it, "the highest literacy rate of any country from the north pole to the Strait of Magellan." Though this is literacy in its loosest sense, the test being the ability to write one's name and the date, it is nevertheless an enviable record.

Until as late as the 1930's the local government had little concern or interest in the education of its people. The Legislative Council, controlled by the lumber industry, spent little money on schools, feeling that the woodcutter had no need for education and their own children were privately educated.

Basic in Belize's social problems, of which the plight of her educational system was but one, was the relative absence of a middle class professional group to elevate the moral and intellectual culture of the society. What passed for the middle class were local bankers and lumber export consigness whose very life was dedicated to private gain from the labor of the uneducated forest workers. Both the owners of forest concessions and the woodcutters alike spent six months a year in the jungle and had no real interest in setting up schools and colleges. Education of the poor was entirely in the hands of the Belizean churches.

In 1839, when John L. Stephens passed through Belize City, he reported visiting two Negro schools in operation under the auspices of the Anglican Church. They were housed in two small buildings behind the Government House on Regent Street. The students ranged in age from three to fifteen years. The boys' department had over two hundred pupils with only one schoolmaster. The girls' department, nearly as crowded, had but one mistress though both teachers were reported to be well-educated and experienced.

The schools, being so impossibly understaffed to handle the task, a pupil-teacher system had to be introduced to meet this deficiency of qualified instructors. With no special institution for the training of teachers, student teachers were selected from scholars whose only requisite was that they had passed primary grade five and were fourteen years of age or older, to teach in the elementary schools.

Secondary school education began in the 1880's with the founding of a Wesleyan High School in 1882, followed by the Roman Catholic St. Catherine's Academy and St. John's College in 1883 and 1887. St. Hildy's was founded in 1897 and St. Michael's in 1921.

One very important legacy of British rule is the high value placed on education today in Belize. In 1932, the year after a devastating hurricane, the British Government took over complete control of the colony's treasury, exacted from a reluctant Assembly as the price demanded for reconstruction loans. The British allocated $9 out of every $100 in tax revenue (not a large amount compared with other countries) for education and set up a program for improving the education system. The first Superintendent of Schools was appointed, scholarships were provided so that poor children might go on to secondary schools, and compulsory education was made law. Today, school attendance is compulsory for everyone between 6 and 14 years of age.

The Belize Technical College was opened in 1952, a

Government Training College in 1954, and a junior high school in 1968. Education has a high priority with the present government. Since the very beginning of the independence movement, Premier Price has stressed the importance of literacy and the common language. English is the medium of instruction in all the schools and an organized effort to encourage school children to teach their parents English, if necessary, has had a surprisingly effective result. English is now spoken, at least as a second language, in virtually every home in the country. With the aid of some forty-eight Peace Corps and forty-one Papal volunteers Belize, in 1970 when the last available figures were published, had 182 primary schools with 30,591 pupils enrolled, 20 secondary schools with 3,597 in attendance, 3 technical colleges with 267 students and 130 students attending universities outside the country, 71 of these at the University of the West Indies in Jamaica.

Most Belizean schools are still sponsored by various religious denominations, but all are now government-subsidized and under the control of the National Board of Education which is responsible for the standardization of instruction.

In 1962, following the advice of the UNESCO Educational Planning Mission, a National Council for Education was established and a Minister of Education was vested with the power to make subsidiary legislation. The National Council of Education, consisting of the Chief Education Officer and 16 members appointed by the Minister of Education, acts as a consulting body and advises the Minister on questions of educational policy. Membership is drawn from the National Assembly, Chamber of Commerce, Minister of Agriculture, the Catholic Education Association, The Union of Teachers, the Roman Catholic, Anglican, and Methodist churches, churches of other denominations, and trade unions. Besides those so nominated, three members must be practicing teachers from an Anglican, a Roman Catholic, and a Methodist secondary school, and one each to represent adult and further education. Appointments are for two years and renewable.

Four Standing Committees are appointed by the Council to

represent Primary, Secondary, and Further Education, Technical and Agricultural Education, and Teacher Training.

Of Belize's 182 primary schools, 166 are aided, two are government schools, 12 are private, and two are "special" schools maintained by the government: one for the mentally handicapped and one for the physically handicapped.

Secondary education is provided by 20 schools, two of which are government and the others are under denominational management.

Belize Technical College holds both day and evening classes. It offers part-time day training in various trades and evening classes in English, Commercial Science, and Home Economics. This vocational training center was opened in Belize City in November, 1965.

An experimental junior secondary school was opened in January, 1969. It is a government institution which provides a three-year course for children 12 through 15. Those students who show promise after completing this course of instruction are given two years' tuition to be used in further study at either Belize Technical College or at an academic secondary school.

A special secondary school specializing in agriculture is conducted by the Roman Catholic Mission in Stann Creek and presently has an enrollment of 110. Three denominational secondary schools provide an additional two years to prepare students for G.E.C. Advanced Level examinations.

The Belize Teachers College offers a two-year course of instruction together with an additional year of internship in a school under the supervision of the college staff. Tuition is free, though successful candidates are required to serve a minimum of five years as a teacher in one of the nation's schools after graduation.

THE ARTS IN BELIZE

The creative life of Belize is roughly divided between that of metropolitan Belize City and the traditional folkways of the African immigrants, Maya Indians, and Mestizo settlers of the outlying districts. The former has responded to the changing fashions of the times and is largely influenced by the tastes and dictates of the United States and Great Britain. Folk art has become partly divorced from African and native origins and has begun to develop as a more indigenous and true Belizean expression.

The arts in Belize suffer from the conflictive influence of two diametrically opposite forces. An innate feeling of cultural inferiority threads through the mentality of the Creole city elite who shun their own folk art and imitate the brash material manifestations of other, more advanced, foreign cultures. With the rise of nationalism, the government has initiated efforts to preserve and promote appreciation of certain forms of folk expression and to build identifiable Belizean art forms. This has been only mildly successful.

The arts have as yet relatively few local patrons and have to rely for most of their support on wider markets—particularly from United States tourists, whose tastes apparently tend toward either the wildly exotic or highly conventional, with a little Belizean color added.

Shortly after the Second World War there was an organized effort by the government to encourage "cottage industries," with the hope that local artists and artisans could be encouraged to produce items of folk art for the tourist souvenir market. Instead of creating articles expressive of their unique and distinctive culture, all that were, or are so produced today, are poor imitations of Mayan or Guatemalan Indian items, varnished sea-shells, poorly carved turtle shells and other novelties with little value and less imagination. The one brilliant exception is a young American-educated sculptor who works in the fine native woods and creates commercial, though beautiful and imaginative, carved wood items for the tourist trade. His stylized sailing ships and native bird pieces, inspired by the local scene and sensitively executed, offer hope for this industry's future. In view of the relatively lucrative possibilities and the general limitations of the market, it is perhaps remarkable that even limited progress has been made toward creating specifically

Belizean art forms as an expression of a Belizean cultural identity.

There are no fine art schools in the country outside of the elementary art taught in the grade and secondary schools. Many young Belizeans are returning from overseas universities inspired to foster and preserve their country's culture, and art forms in particular.

Belize has, over the years, produced a few fine artists. Manuel Carrero's paintings have been used on a British Honduras postage stamp and one was, in less troubled times, presented by the government to the President of Guatemala. Another artist, a young boy from Corozal Town, has painted very forceful paintings and murals depicting Maya Indian life, but the mainstream Creole society has not yet produced an outstanding artist.

The theater, long neglected in Belize, now has a center for the performing arts which provides for an annual Festival of the Arts.

One would suppose logically that Belizean architecture would pattern after the provincial English, as does the official language. Such, however, is not the case. The possible exception is perhaps the residences; white painted clapboard West Indian bungalows which contrast with the typical adobe dwellings of their Spanish-speaking neighbors.

Architecture is, as yet, controlled by outsiders. There is but one professional architect practicing in the entire country, an Englishman in Belize City, and the nation's only public buildings of any consequence built in recent years are the new capital buildings at Belmopan, and they were designed by a British firm. Fortunately they were designed thoughtfully, with the local people and conditions in mind, and have been highly successful in establishing a precedent for future government buildings. The government favors functional, well-designed, modern structures which reflect their own culture and attitudes of no-nonsense practicality while preserving the feeling of permanance and stability epitomized by the only native building forms of the region—Maya Indian ceremonial structures. A United States Peace Corps volunteer serves as architectural consultant to the government.

The profound influence of the United States on Belizean culture is best expressed in their preference for American popular music. Old native music forms, so popular as late as the 1940's, have all but disappeared in Belize. Rock music is now heard at all their dances and in the night clubs in Belize City. Latin American music predominates in popularity in some sectors, but only rarely is the traditional Belizean music, the "break-down," heard except at private gatherings.

Break-downs are original Calypso-like compositions played by local musicians and often improvised on the spot. After World War II they were nearly always accompanied by a steel band. Break-downs relate a story, usually based on some local incident or relating to some local person. They poke fun at some prominent personality—often British—and are full of saucy puns. Break-down singers are judged by their wit and ability to ridicule people humorously. The more prominent the ridiculed person is, the more the song is enjoyed.

For many years musicians like William Trapp and Roderick Brown introduced new break-downs at the Christmas festivals in Belize City which were hummed by the man on the street the rest of the year. All break-downs are original, sometimes biting, and many are slightly vulgar. The best have survived and some like *"Captain Foote's Money Gone,"* about Captain Frank Foote, a Nova Scotian coconut trader who established the first, though unsuccessful, lobster canning plant in the 1920's, and Roderick Brown's *"Tea Kettle is a Lovely Place"* have become nearly forgotten classics of the break-down era. The music of the logging camps, once provided by steel bands and break-down singers, is now the "Three Dog Night" received on Japanese transistor radios via Radio Belize. Even the few local entertainers are careful imitators of popular United States stars.

Poets have been encouraged with national poetry competitions and the like, but few creative works have yet emerged that are both good and Belizean. Although a great deal of literature has come out of the independence movement, patriotic writings and protest literature aimed at the state of the colony, most of what is good is only slightly Belizean and what is thoroughly Belizean is inferior. Belize still awaits writers, poets and artists of genius to aid in her quest for identity.

HOLIDAYS AND SOCIAL LIFE

Public Holidays — 1975	
January 1	New Year's Day
March 9	Baron Bliss Day
April 20 thru April 22	Easter
April 21	Queen's Birthday
May 1	Labor Day
May 24	Commonwealth Day
September 10	National Day (St. George's Cay Day)
November 14	Prince Charles' Birthday
December 25 and 26	Christmas

Although Belize City was never the wide-open wicked city that Port Royal, Tortuga, or some of the other Caribbean ports were in the early days, it was nevertheless a frontier town with its share of hard-drinking, hard-brawling roustabouts and mahogany loggers. Many of them were recently retired pirates and privateers forced out of the piracy business by the new attitude of the West Indies and the end of Britain's toleration policy toward them. Having prodigally spent several fortunes acquired over the years in lucrative freebooting, most of the seamen found themselves wanting in subsistence, without the wherewithal to return home. They were forced to turn to the Settlements of Campeche and Belize, where they arrived with axes, saws, and a "pavilion" to sleep in, to try their hand at the grueling business of logwood harvesting.

These land-locked seafarers did not forget their taste for strong drink and merry-making, although only the most industrious sort remained when they learned what a dull and toilsome life these Settlements held for them. The irregular arrival from Jamaica of a trading ship with a cargo of rum to trade for local logwood was announced by a cannon fired from the ship's anchorage at St. George's Cay and answered by cannon fire from Fort George which signaled a three- or four-day holiday marked by riotous drinking, carousing, and indiscriminate cannon firing. The loggers would spend thirty or forty pounds each at a sitting aboard the trade ship for rum, served as a formidable punch. The ship's crew were entertained at the loggers' camps where they were treated to "pig, port and peese" or "beef and doughboys," the favorite dumpling dish, which gave them the nickname of "doughboys"—still applied to Belizean woodcutters. It would take at least a week for the logging camps to return to normal after each visit by a rum ship, with stragglers returning weak and ill from the unrestrained drinking bout, unable to lift an ax or drive a wedge.

Possibilities of great wealth existed for the hard-working logger who kept off the drink, though of the many sober men who came into the Bay Settlement to cut wood most succumbed by degrees to the old standards of short intense work, most of the revenue from which was lost to the rum traders.

The singularly most important social event of the year in the early Settlement was the festival during the Christmas season when ships from all over the Honduran Bay and Jamaica put in to the port of Belize to join the loggers in a mad week-long Mardi Gras-like celebration. During this season merchants set up booths and temporary grog shops, sometimes numbering one for every ten inhabitants, to satisfy the apparently unquenchable thirst of the Christmas revelers. Even more awe-inspiring than the amount of liquor consumed was the quality—it was potent stuff. One contemporary reported, "One might wonder at the sickness of our people, until they learn of the strength of our drinks; then they wonder more that we all are not dead."

The loggers and the sailors were joined for the holiday by

women eager to separate them from their money. A common nocturnal sight in any of the grog shops or punch parlors was a logger, with a girl draped on each arm, recklessly spending several month's earnings; toward morning with his head full of drink and pockets empty, he generally found himself devoid of feminine companionship as well. These ladies of easy virtue, besides the ever-present camp followers, found their way each year to the Belize Christmas revelry from as far away as Spanish Honduras, Mexico, or San Salvador (buying their passage with favors bestowed on willing captains of ships Belize-bound for the holiday season) and returning with untold wealth.

With the increased influence of British administrators, the Belizean Christmas festival began to take on aspects of a more civic nature and came under a greater amount of regulation. Christmas was the driest and coolest time of the year, before the worst rush of the logging season began, when the least attention was needed for agriculture. Thus it was the ideal time for celebrating the close of year's work and the start of another. The undisciplined, senseless, drunken brawl of the loggers' yearly celebration became restrained by the special tradition of all British colonies in making the Christmas season a period of martial law and the time of the mustering of rag-tag and bob-tailed Citizens' Militia, in which all free men of reasonable physical fitness were required, by law, to enroll. Due to this mustering of the militia, all business was at a standstill and this time became not only one for serious military duties but for balls, *al fresco* pleasures, and all manner of amusements. The Military provided parades, firings of the cannons, and various maneuvers for the entertainment of local spectators.

As an anonymous poet in 1846 put it:

> "When Christmas came in former days
> The time for Martial schoolery
> Three guns from Fort George battery were
> The signal for tomfoolery.

*　*　*　*　*

Then all our townfolk turned as red
As lobsters in hot water;
And, had there been an enemy
There might have been much slaughter!

* * * * *

But after vapouring a week
The scarlet fever vanished
And till next Christmas Martial thoughts
Were from each bosom banished."

The colorful uniforms of West Indian regiments, the some-times humorous accoutrements of the militia, and the white of naval uniforms added to the carnival-like costumes of African and Mosquito Indian revelers gave the usual dull, squalid sur-roundings of Belize City a holiday air of great color and excite-ment.

This tradition lasted well into the nineteenth century but with the repeal of the Militia Law in 1846, devout Wesleyen missionaries, with the aid of straight-laced British Governors, brought it all to a close. As the evangelical churches, preaching Christianity and abstinence, slowly but surely gained control of the colony's social life, the last spark of uninhibited merry-making and civic gaiety became snuffed out.

To what extremes and to what extent this missionary con-trol went can be seen in a report as late as 1945 written by a North American visitor to Belize City: "I was surprised to find that in Belize City all social gatherings are church-centered. The only theater groups here are connected with the church. A strict law calls for a license for all entertainment and the only groups which are given a license are the churches. Public dances are forbidden. Private dances can be given by invitation only and even then all those attending are required to sign a list provided by the host or hostess and this presented to the police who actually supervise the entrances to assure that only those on the list are admitted. Night clubs and other common types of enter-tainment are not even allowed in the city."

Thus was the dismal state of Belizean social life until very recently. It is little wonder that one of the concerns of Belizeans at this time was the trend of their young people in leaving the country to seek employment in Mexico, Guatemala, or the United States.

Still not known for its nightlife, Belize City is recovering from this overreaction and long-lasting suppression of amusement. Today's social life revolves around the two major hotels, the scene of most of its parties, and several night clubs and private clubs.

Boxing, polo games, football matches, and horse racing are now sponsored by private social clubs, outgrowths of the severe public amusement restriction laws.

Since the independence movement, St. George Cay Day, September 10th, has gradually changed from a day of recognition of a British victory over a superior Spanish force to a national holiday commemorating its local heroes, who gave the nation a claim to their land by right of conquest, as well as their long-standing right of settlement. It is celebrated with patriotic speeches, parades and a pageant.

Carnival, particularly common in Roman Catholic regions throughout the Caribbean, is kept alive in Belize by two very different peoples: the Mestizos of the Corozal District and the Black Caribs.

Carnival is the term applied to the entire holiday season from Christmas to Ash Wednesday, the first day of Lent, and especially the days immediately preceding it, and is characterized by a contagious gaiety, brilliant verbal sallies, and comic buffoonery.

Among the Caribs the season is ushered in on December 24 by the *warin*, a group of men dressed in costumes made of dried plantain leaves with papier-mache or insect-screen masks. They go from house to house, dancing to a drum accompaniment, and are rewarded with a cup of rum, wine, or a bit of food at each. The origin of the dance of the *warin* is not known to the Caribs, and has no special significance to them today, but the costumes are identical to traditional masques used in Trinidad at Carnival.

On Christmas Day and again on January 1, another Black Carib dance group appears on the streets of Punta Gorda and Stann Creek dressed in short full skirts, blouses with yokes and long full sleeves, flesh-colored stockings, masks, and elaborate head-dresses decorated with feathers and ribbons. Ribbons are also tied to the dress to stream out in swirling motions during the dance which they perform. Their dance is called by the Caribs *wanaragua*, meaning "mask," but known throughout the West Indies by the name of the character it portrays, "John Canoe," a Jamaican folk hero. The dance is characterized by a rapid crossing of the legs, terminated with a sudden stoppage.

Another unusual sight appearing on the streets from time to time during Carnival is a pair of performers known to the Black Caribs as *pia manadi*. These two are always seen together, dressed as a man and a woman, with padding appropriately placed to emphasize their sexual characteristics. They are ribald comics with an amusing repartee, always somewhat lewd, and animated with obscene gestures. They accost passersby on the street with verbal abuse meant to embarrass and amuse them.

Carnival in Corozal is more church-oriented but is also devoted to revelry and riotous amusement with masked street dances and parades leading up its climax at Shrove-tide, the day before Lent.

Funerals in Belize are solemn, widely attended social affairs. Notices of a death are posted in prominent public places and relatives and acquaintances immediately begin to gather at the home of the deceased. Wailing begins and continues throughout the first night wake. Those attending keep the vigil by praying, singing, dancing, or by playing games such as bingo or checkers. Folk-tales are told by men who specialize in this art and who perform only at wakes. Refreshments are served several times during the night, the food, rum, and coffee having been brought in by the guests.

One of the most popular dances performed at wakes is the Punta, or "point." In this dance, a couple occupies the center of a ring formed of hand-clapping and chanting onlookers. Accompanied by a drum, the man and woman alternately pursue each other around the circle, at times attempting to get as near as possible to the other without touching. In the dance, the feet move rapidly in a kind of sideways shuffle, the hips shimmy, and the arms are held alternately over the head, akimbo, or extended backwards. Occasionally a partner will drop out, leaving the other alone on the floor until some other person from the spectators enters the circle. Often too, one person, usually a woman, will dance alone without making an attempt to draw another partner out on the floor. The words to the songs which accompany the Punta are often derisive and critical, never naming the subject, but making his or her identity entirely clear.

The deceased is usually buried the next day. A long line of mourners follow the horse-drawn cart to the church, dressed in their finest black or white clothing. As they pass the business section, store keepers close their windows and doors in respect, and reopen them as soon as the procession passes. The first night's wake is repeated again nine days later in exactly the same manner as the first.

Customs surrounding death have been greatly affected by Christianity but still retain a flavor of non-Christian sources. For example, masses for the dead are as important to the Black Carib as they are to other Catholic people, but they are given at irregular intervals in response to dreams in which they are requested by the dead ancestor.

The Boledo

The current national pastime in Belize is the national lottery, called the Boledo, and is as much a part of the local scene as the Tierce in France or the soccer pools in Great Britain.

Nightly, the streets of Belize City fill with gay, noisy crowds waiting for two numbered balls to be selected at the public drawing. The odds for payment are 73 to 1, but the odds against are 99 to 1, giving the government a comfortable edge.

THE CITIES

Belize City Population 43,000, Altitude 1.6 feet. The nine-mile drive into Belize City from the country's little, one-runway, International Airport is often the visitor's introduction to the natural beauty and warm sub-tropical climate enjoyed by Belize. A dense living wall of climbing, entwining mangroves closely line the warm, narrow asphalt road, broken only by occasional small clearings hacked out of the jungle where black native children, dogs, and chickens play among the slender poles that support little wood frame houses built six feet in the air—a precaution against yearly inundation. Tourists, being as welcome as they are rare in Belize, are always greeted by the children and often by the adults as they pass by.

One's first impression on entering Belize City might be of its similarity to the capital of one of the new African republics, as the preponderence of its citizens seen on the streets are of African or Creole descent. One might be surprised to find the homes here, too, are built several feet above the ground; of wood and sheet metal, they were hastily constructed following the devastation of Hurricane Hattie which roared into the city in 1961 with 160-mile-per-hour winds, dragging a fourteen-foot tidal wave behind her and razing over seventy percent of the city. "We never need a slum clearance program here," a taxi-driver once told me, "our hurricanes take care of that." The city has never fully recovered from this storm that hit October 31, 1961, which took the lives of 275 Belizeans and left over ten times that many homeless. When the water finally receded to reveal the twisted and torn debris that had once been buildings, boats and automobiles, the damage was assessed at $50 million B.H. Insurance claims alone amounted to $28 million.

Belize City, the former capital, major seaport and administrative, cultural, and geographic center, sprawls across both banks of Haulover Creek, as the natives call the last four miles and the delta mouth of the murky Belize River; so called from its being the place where cattle, taken to market in Belize, were made to cross. Various explanations have been given for the name of this city, lying only eighteen inches above sea level. One, and the most probable explanation, is that it is derived from the Maya Indian word for this river, *be likin*, meaning literally, "road to the East." Until the tenth century A.D., this river was a very heavily-traveled trade artery of the ancient Mayas. Other residents steadfastly hold to the belief that the name comes from the Spanish mispronunciation of the name of its original founder, pirate Peter Wallace.

Regardless of its name, the happenstance location of this city in this improbable locality on the coast, in the middle of a mangrove swamp a few inches above sea-level, has proven unfortunate. In its earlier days, Belize City was not a very healthy place to live, requiring its citizens to retire to St. George's or one of the other nearby cays during part of the year to avoid "the fever" prevalent in the city. Its high water table has made the installation of underground water supply nearly impossible and, except for hospitals and the hotel buildings frequented by tourists, the other quarters of the city still obtain their water by "catchment," i.e. by draining rainwater off galvanized iron roofs into cisterns where it is stored for household use. For the same reason, there is no underground sewerage system. The houses have septic tanks into which chemicals are added and then, since the water table is too high for leeching laterals, the effluent is drained into open trenches running along the street curbs which find their way eventually into the ocean. As Jack Olson wrote concerning this subject in a 1972 *Sports Afield* article on Belize, "The British sent magistrates and soldiers and engineers, who laid out the city's odorous system of sewage disposal. No matter what unkind remarks are made about the British in Belize City these days, it cannot be denied that they brought the city law and ordure."

Indispensable to the unique sewerage system of the city are the swarms of salt-water catfish (called "Shittifish" by the Creoles) and the Gar which inhabit the mouth of the Belize

River in such numbers that one wonders that they don't impede the travel of the "pit-pans" and other small boats on the river. So spectacular is the panorama of these huge catfish, gregariously feeding on the effluent of the city, that one nightclub, the Bombay Club located on the bank of the River in Belize City, has installed underwater lights which, when requested, are turned on to illuminate the river revealing tens of thousands of these scavengers at work.

The salt-water catfish are protected by the government because of their usefulness, and fishing in the river within the city limits brings a stiff fine. A number of years ago a local entrepreneur seined the river. His catch, in one night, was enough to supply his canning plant with several weeks work. His catfish were marketed as "whitefish" and brought him huge profits, which he found unable to spend from his cell in the Belize National Prison after his operation was discovered.

Strolling through Belize City's narrow streets one finds a certain charm. The city's two main thoroughfares, Regent and Albert Streets, are still referred to locally by their more convenient original names—Front Street and Back Street. Pink, orange, and purple bougainvillea and red poinciana trees fill in the spaces between flimsy, unpainted, wood and corrugated sheet-metal houses. Despite evident poverty, the streets ring with laughter of happy children. One encounters few beggars or impudent street vendors, common in the Latin countries, and can find much to please the soul; the sun-bleached white sails of schooners tied up at the water's edge along Haulover Creek, the wrought-iron and red Georgian brick facade of the old Court House still flying the Union Jack (Britain still has responsibility for the judiciary), and exotic cooking smells mingling with the perfume of a frangipani tree when its pink-flowered limbs stir in a soft gust of heavy tropical air. One can wander into the great open market near the city's famous old "Swing Bridge," which connects the two sections of the city, to find ragged black natives bartering loudly over bananas, papayas, bags of charcoal, strings of brightly colored fish, curious huge brown roots, and a live iguana or two.

The shops in Belize City are small and thinly-stocked, with the notable exception of one large department store (Brodie's) that dominates the city's drygoods business. Belize has several churches, among them St. John's Cathedral, the oldest Anglican Cathedral in Central America (built in 1812) and the scene in former years of the crowning of several "Kings" of the Mosquito Coast Indians amid great pageantry and splendor. Other ancient buildings include the Government House (1814) and the old slave quarters located on Regent Street.

The town possesses some twenty elementary schools, eight secondary schools, a teacher's training college, a vocational center, a technical college, five libraries, and three centers for adult education. A center for the performing arts, founded in 1953, provides for an annual Festival of the Arts.

For the tourist trade Belize has two full-service hotels, the Fort George and the Bellevue, both located on the waterfront furnishing their own charter boat service for fishing or exploring, first-hand, the Cays seen from the hotel balconies. The British-built Fort George Hotel is run with the seemingly incongruous pomp and circumstance of a good British resort, but moderated with the warmth and friendliness of its local staff. The largest in Belize, it has but thirty-five spacious rooms, each with private terrace for sitting and contemplating the unique beauty of the multi-hued Caribbean below. It is built near the spot where the pirate Peter Wallace first built a base camp in 1603, from whence he sailed out to plunder the Spanish plate fleets sailing from Panama, laden with gold and silver bars, ducats, and doubloons for the Old World. The rooms at the Fort George are air-conditioned but most guests prefer the natural ventilation of the balmy trade-winds which blow off the Caribbean throughout most of the year. The rooms have a fully louvered exterior wall facing the sea which provides a delightful means of tempering the humidity.

The entire area of the city surrounding the Ft. George Hotel is called Ft. George and includes a small park on the waterfront. Belizeans like to point out that the hotel stands on British soil, which in fact it does. Once a tiny coral island off a promontory point near the mouth of Haulover Creek, hundreds of British ships arriving in Belize to pick up cargoes of logwood and mahogany have, for centuries, unloaded their ballast at this island. Through the years it has been filled in, and is now part of the mainland and a "bit of the auld sod," so to speak. It was called "Fort" George because on it were positioned 11 antiquated cannons salvaged from the Yeldham, an armed British merchant ship which foundered on the reef off Ambergris Cay in 1800. For many years these guns fired regularly at sunrise, noon and sundown. Two of them can still be seen in Fort George Park today.

A program for improvement of the water supply is prominent in the current development plans. Six large steel rainwater collection tanks, with a total capacity of 2.25 million gallons, were erected in 1936 and this supply has since been supplemented from three wells located about 11 miles northwest of the city. Water from these sources is pumped to the town's reservoirs from which it is then supplied, at low pressure, through a primitive street distribution system to the few homes and commercial establishments having this service. A Water and Sewerage Order passed in 1970 established a Water and Sewer Authority consisting of a Minister and seven Water Commissioners to study the problems and attempt to improve on the present situation.

Amenities in Belize City include electric, telephone, and telecommunication systems, three modern well-staffed hospitals, a national radio station (Radio Belize), and public recreation facilities. There are, except for the hotel facilities, only a few good restaurants and night clubs in this city never known for its night life. It has a municipal airfield and a horse-race track used for one or two days in connection with the Baron Bliss holiday in March.

Belmopan, the Nation's Capital   With the exception of a brief period in the eighteenth century when the business of Government of British Honduras was conducted on St. George's Cay, the capital of this country had traditionally been Belize City.

Disadvantages to this location as the national capital are many, not the least of which is its vulnerability to hurricanes. Belize City has an acute housing shortage and has neither a modern water supply nor sanitary waste disposal system. The population, overwhelmingly Afro-Belizean, for years monopolized the nation's civil service and elected constituency in the Assembly, which tended to alienate the minorities living outside the city. Digging out from under the wreckage caused by Hurricane Hattie in 1961, the thought of a new capital city, located away from the coast, began to germinate in the minds of the country's leaders.

In 1965 ground was broken for a new capital at a jungle-covered site situated 50 miles inland to the west, near the intersection of the Western Highway and the Hummingbird Highway leading to Stann Creek. This new city was built on land purchased by the local government from their Baron Bliss legacy (see chapter 7) and constructed with money from British grants and loans. Total cost of the project has been nearly B.H. $25 million. The name "Belmopan" was officially adopted by the House of Representatives for the capital after a Maya tribe that had successfully resisted subjugation by the Spanish conquerors, the Mopan, and "Bel" for Belize.

The population of Belmopan on its first day of operation, August 3, 1970, was 1000 people; mostly government employees. It was projected to increase to 5000 by the end of 1970 when all government offices were transferred. The predicted growth has not yet materialized due to a great reluctance of the people to move away from the seaside location of Belize City. The present population is only 2700, but planners envision a city of 30,000 within twenty years.

The first phase of construction, now complete, comprises a National Assembly building, two three-story Government Office buildings, a Police Headquarters building, and a Public Works Department building. Included in this phase are residences for 700 civil service employees' families.

The modern, bone-white, concrete masonry buildings of Belmopan, designed by the London architectural firm of Norman and Dawbarn, successfully interpret, in today's idiom, the same reverent feeling one experiences upon viewing a Maya temple for the first time. The country's new blue and white flag proudly flies atop the National Assembly building which is itself raised on a high platform of monumental steps and provides a focal point for the long green court formed by the Government Office buildings on either side. Belize is proud of this nucleus of accommodation for the administration of the country worthy of her future.

In addition to the government buildings there is a permanent native market, equipped with refrigeration, to deal with local produce; a government hospital; an elementary school; and fully-serviced commercial and industrial sites to encourage local industry. A civic center and library are planned for the near future.

What Belmopan does not have are the supermarkets, drug stores, cinemas, dry-goods stores, dress shops and recreation facilities which must be provided by the private sector. Merchants say they must wait until the population is sufficient to warrant the establishment of these facilities, while prospective residents refuse to relocate to Belmopan until these amenities are provided. Meanwhile, hundreds of civil service workers commute by bus daily to Belize City over the corduroyed and pot-holed roadbed of the uncompleted Western Highway, still under construction and showing signs of being so for many more years, judging from its rate of completion. There are no hotels or motels in the town and only one restaurant, a temporary accommodation in a converted three-room duplex. But for all its problems, Belmopan is already losing its raw edges. Palms and flowering decorative trees now line the streets and well-watered lawns soften its profile. Belizeans throughout the country look upon Belmopan as a symbol of their independence and a prophesy of their country's future.

Stann Creek Town   (Stann Creek District), Pop. 6876, Altitude 6 feet. In 1629 a party of Englishmen with Puritan backgrounds established a colony on one of the Honduran Bay

Islands which they named Providence (now called Old Providence). This small colony, located within easy reach of the Spanish forces on the Isthmus of Panama, lasted only 12 years before being wiped out by a Spanish fleet. Just prior to its being destroyed, several Puritan settlers relocated to the mainland to trade with the Mosquito Coast Indians for silk-grass, a thick-leaved bromeliad used for making rope. One of these, Captain Elfrith, sold potatoes, pumpkins and other crops brought from Providence from two trading stands (called *Stanns*) which he built at Lower and at Upper Stann Creek. A few of his fellow colonists located on a nearby Cay where they raised tobacco which gave the name to the Tobacco Cays. Puritans also established a fairly large settlement of six hundred at Placentia.

The town that developed around Elfrith's trading stands, called Stann Creek Town, is Belize's second largest city. It has a population of nearly 7,000 and is a very busy town, sustained by the thousands of acres of citrus cultivation in the nearby fertile valley to the west. The majority of Stann Creek's residents today are Black Caribs, descendants of those who settled in this area in 1823. Each year the arrival of these Caribs is commemorated on November 19 with house-to-house dancing, public ceremonies, and reenactment of the first landing.

Stann Creek Town has a piped water supply, a government rest station, two banks, two secondary schools, a Town Hall, five elementary schools, two churches, a public library, civic center, a hospital and a cinema. It is a major market center and port city.

An interesting legacy left by the Puritan founders of this town is the name of Bluefield which has survived since the 1600's, when it was originally given to a road in the Town to honor a Dutch buccaneer whom the Puritans found inhabiting Providence Island when they landed there. Captain William Blauveldt (Anglosized Bluefield) had been a great help to the settlers in getting established and in fortifying their island. The main street in Stann Creek is called St. Vincent Street, in honor of the island where the Black Caribs originated.

The town provides a convenient embarcation point for

excursions to the many off-shore islands or to Belize City which is only 36 miles by sea but 105 miles by automobile via the inland Hummingbird Highway route.

Almost completely destroyed in 1961 by Hurricane Hattie, this town has since been restored and expanded. Little evidence of the storm's destruction can be seen today.

The city's new piped water distribution system was installed in 1966 at a cost of $250,000.

Punta Gorda (Toledo District)   Although this town bears a Spanish name, it is inhabited by 2600 English-speaking people of Black Carib, East Indian, and African (Creole) stock. Punta Gorda originated as a small fishing village and was one of the sites selected for settlement by the Black Caribs when they fled Honduras in 1823.

The Town is situated on a shelf ten feet above sea level, on the margin of the Caribbean, and is flanked on the West and North-west by hills and by a large promontory at the southern end of the Town. Small boat traffic is frequent between Punta Gorda and the nearby ports of Barrios in Guatemala and Cortez in Spanish Honduras. Communication with Belize City is by coastal boats, small aircraft served by a nearby airstrip, and by the yet-unpaved Southern Highway, a hundred-and-fifty-mile trip. A paved road runs inland for twenty-one miles to San Antonio Village, from where roads connect a dozen Maya villages.

A few miles from Punta Gorda one can still find traces of the former Toledo Settlement started there by Civil War refugees from the United States and not far away is the important former Maya Center of Lubaantun.

One is captivated by the lush tropical beauty of this little community and for anyone who visits its mile-long waterfront on a clear night, with a soft warm breeze coming in from the sea, it is sheer magic to watch the sky glow over Livingston across the Bay of Amatique, in Guatemala to the south. But clear nights (except in spring) do not come often to the southernmost town in Belize which is drenched with over 170 inches of rain yearly.

Once a very isolated and little-known village, Punta Gorda now boasts of a fine secondary school, three elementary schools, a cinema, a hospital, and a public library. It is a quiet place that still lives on fishing, some logging, and bountiful crops of rice, corn and red kidney beans.

Domestic water stored in vats have been supplemented by four reinforced concrete rainwater collection tanks with a total capacity of 360,000 gallons. Drinking water is augmented by well water and supplied by a distribution system completed in 1963.

San Ignacio (Cayo District)   San Ignacio, the administrative center for the Cayo District, sits on the bank of the Macal River, a branch of the Belize, 72 miles from Belize City and 22 miles from Belmopan. It is surrounded by hills—an inland town of entrancing beauty.

Although the beginning of San Ignacio goes back a hundred years, it preserves to this day a robust, pioneer atmosphere. The early settlers were mainly Mestizo and Maya immigrants from nearby Guatemala and a few Lebanese businessmen who carried on a trade with the Indians. The town has now annexed the neighboring village of Santa Elena, linked by the Hawkesworth Suspension Bridge (named for former Governor, Sir E. G. Hawkesworth, who served from 1947 to 1949).

The Western Highway leading from Belize City through San Ignacio to the Guatemalan border at Benque Viejo del Carmen nine miles southwest, runs through high canopied forest and passes through villages with such striking names as Tea Kettle, Fire Ball, and More Tomorrow, where Spanish-speaking natives peddle snake skins and live iguanas which are said to taste very much like chicken.

Not far from San Ignacio lies the former Maya Center of Cahal Pech ("Place of the Ticks"). The scenery of the country-side around San Ignacio is dominated by rolling pasture land with herds of Brahma-related cattle recently introduced from Guatemala. The Macal River at San Ignacio is clear and quite suitable for bathing and boating. The town at one time prospered as a terminal in the chicle and timber trade and had an intimate connection with the saga of the old "Caya Boat" run, which preceded the opening of the Western Highway to Belize City.

San Ignacio today has a population of about 2750 and has a secondary school, three elementary schools, three churches, a government hospital, a cinema, several small hotels and nightclubs and a modern piped water supply. Radiating from its Central Park are a Police Station, Public Library and District Government Office buildings.

San Ignacio obtains drinking water from the nearby Macal River which is pumped into two reservoirs with a total capacity of 200,000 gallons. A modern distribution system, with house connections, came into operation in 1961.

Benque Viejo del Carmen (Cayo District), Population 2,500   Benque Viejo is the country's most westerly town, located 81 miles from Belize City and a few hundred yards from Guatemala's El Peten frontier. Set on the eastern bank of the swirling Mopan branch of the Belize River, this town of 2500 is one of the country's best examples of town planning. Its orderly streets and well-defined public spaces are the result of sound municipal design rarely seen in Belize. Benque Viejo has two large elementary schools, both a government and a church-affiliated health clinic, a public library, and a modern water system.

The early history of this predominantly Spanish-speaking town is lent a touch of drama and excitement by hectic episodes of banditry, border raids, and ribald living of the hardy "chicleros" who once lived here.

Today Benque Viejo del Carmen is a charming Mestizo town. The marimbas, fiestas, and colorful social customs centered around such events as Christmas, baptisms, and marriages; its highly seasoned "Spanish" food; and nightly serenades, still heard in the streets, are reminders of Benque's Mestizo heritage.

A few miles from Benque Viejo is the famous Maya Ruins of

Xunantunich ("Maiden of the Rock"). Of particular interest in this easternmost outpost of the group of ceremonial centers which flourished in the Peten district of Guatemala from the fourth to the ninth century A.D., is a finely-carved astronomical frieze from the roof facade of the main temple. The ruins are reached by ferry which crosses the Mopan River at a point about ten minutes' walk from Benque Viejo.

Corozal Town (Corozal District), Population 4200   Located on the fringe of the picture-book Corozal Bay, this town is set off by a multitude of coconut palms and scarlet flowering flamboyant trees. It is 96 miles north of Belize CIty and just nine miles from the Rio Hondo, the river dividing Belize and Mexico. Corozal Town was substantially destroyed by Hurricane Janet in 1955 and is now a well-planned restored community with wide thoroughfares and many parks.

A private estate until 1849, Corozal Town was settled generally by Mestizo refugees fleeing the War of the Races in Yucatan. An old fort in the center of the town recalls the days of frequent Indian attacks from across the border during this war. The town's 4200 citizens are mostly Spanish-speaking with English a second language.

Ringing the Central Park (Plaza) are a modern Catholic Church, Public Library, Town Hall, a Protestant church, and various Government buildings. Corozal has two secondary schools, five elementary schools, two banks, a Government Hospital, a health clinic, several small hotels and nightclubs, a cinema and provides modern power and water services.

The town is surrounded by many smaller villages, whose economies are sustained by the large sugar industry of this district with a processing plant nearby. Corozal's major products, besides sugar, are rum, corn, citrus and coconuts.

The 1955 hurricane caused a major set-back to the town's economy and required government aid in the form of loans to replace the many homes and commercial buildings destroyed in the storm. The town's first piped water supply was installed at this time, using a well some miles distant from town for its source. The natives, used to using rainwater, found the well water so hard that most still prefer "catchment" to provide their drinking water, although they have a modern distribution system with house connections.

Surfing and fishing for small fish in the bay are ideal, but larger tarpon and barracuda are found in the lagoons across the bay.

One of the most important post-classic Maya ruins, Santa Rita, is located just east of Corozal Town. A temple uncovered in 1896 contained murals in the Mixtec style and ancient hiero-glyphic dates. These murals have been the subject of much speculation in recent years as some interpret their symbols as evidence of North African origin of the Maya people. "Cerro Maya," another interesting archaeological site, is found at the head of the bay across from Corozal Town.

Corozal is famous for its many festive holidays, chief among them being Carnival, Columbus Day Celebration, and many "fiestas" shared with the neighboring villages.

Orange Walk Town   (Orange Walk District), Population 3000, Altitude 60 feet.   Orange Walk Town, on the left bank of the New River, is located 66 miles north of Belize City and thirty miles south of Corozal Town. From here roads lead off in four directions, linking the more than twenty villages of the Orange Walk District.

Orange Walk Town is one of the oldest settlements in Belize, having been one of the original timber-producing encampments. After 1849 it was largely settled, as Corozal Town was, by Mexican refugees and the Mestizo make-up of its population today reflects that. Her peasants for many years thrived on crops of chicle and maize, but the establishment of a modern sugar factory and extended sugar cane production through the district have had an impact on the area.

Today the town is a contrast of modern and traditional as, besides the new mechanized industrial complex of the sugar factory, it has a very ancient Catholic Church and the ruins of two forts: Ft. Cairns and Ft. Mundy, which were used during the turbulent years of the War of the Races.

Public amenities include a tree-lined park, Town Hall, two banks, a secondary school, two elementary schools, a cinema and a Public Library.

Geography

CLIMATE

Belize is fortunate in its climate. It is subtropical with a well-defined dry season. For most of the year, soft trade winds blowing off the Caribbean keep the temperatures in Belize City from October to May an even seventy degrees, day and night, and temper the humidity (average 83%). Even in the summer months, July through September, the temperature never exceeds 96 degrees. The mean temperature in July is 83°. In the interior, daytime summer shade temperatures often exceed 100° but the nights are cool, and from October through December north winds bring cool drier air. A rare cold spell might bring a 50° temperature reading, but it would be very short-lived.

Two meteorological phenomena occur yearly to mar the otherwise idealistic weather of this part of Central America. One is a series of frontal storms, called "northers," which sweep down over the Gulf of Mexico from the interior of North America during the winter months (December–February). These storms appear suddenly, bearing down the coast of Belize in a nearly continuous squall line, bringing dangerous surface winds which often dismast or capsize unwary coastal schooners caught away from immediate shelter. Several days of gusty, rainy weather accompanied by *chubascos,* or thunderstorms, persist in the wake of these winter storms.

At the other weather extreme is the unique phenomenon known locally as the "mauger" season; a period of extremely dry, calm weather occurring usually in the month of August. This "season" is characterized by oppressive heat, still air, and life made miserable, night and day, by noxious insects. Life in general stagnates until it passes, which may take a week or more.

The hurricane season is in early Fall, but hurricanes have been known to occur as early as June. Belize City has been devastated by hurricanes in 1787, 1931 and 1961. Corozal Town suffered a similar fate in 1942 and 1955.

While recordings of hurricanes are unreliable, one authority estimates that hurricanes have struck the coast of British Honduras no less than twenty-one times since the year 1787. Severe physical damage is usually restricted to a narrow area. However, high winds, heavy seas and torrential rainfall often extend far beyond the track of the storm center.

Rainfall increases sharply from the north to the southern extremes of the country, with dusty droughts occasionally occurring in the Corozal region which has a mean annual rainfall of 52 inches, contrasting to Barranco on the southern frontier with 180 inches. Belize City receives 65 inches, but year to year variations are everywhere large. The dry season lasts from February to April and the wet season from June to October. An abundant rainfall, coupled with high temperatures, accounts for the fact that all but ten percent of the country is covered with lush, verdant, tropical forest.

Since the damage caused by Hurricane Hattie in 1961, the Government has constructed a number of large and small hurricane shelters at various points throughout the country. Each coastal village and town has at least one reinforced concrete building designed as a public shelter in case of a storm. Tropical storm warnings are received by Radio Belize from a network of sources—Belize Meteorological office, the U.S. Weather Bureau

Forecasting Station in Miami, the San Juan Puerto Rico Weather Bureau, and the Jamaica Meteorological Service, who broadcast periodically until the storm threat is over.

PHYSICAL GEOGRAPHY

The northern half of the country, containing the Districts of Corozal, Belize, and Orange Walk, is low and undulating, gradually rising from the coast to the Guatemalan border in the west, but rarely exceeding 200 feet in elevation. The area is drained by the New River and the Hondo River which flow into Chetumal Bay in the north, and by the Belize River, flowing easterly, which is navigable for at least 120 miles. Although broken by many dangerous rapids at its western extremity, it still serves for native transportation from the interior to produce markets in Belize City.

This low-lying land is composed of parallel, subdued ridges and depressions, the ridges being noticeable only by reason of the differences of soil and vegetation. The jungle-covered ridges and intervening gullies run north and south, parallel to the seacoast and are, in fact, backbones of former coral reefs. If the present seacoast is considered to lie along one of these reefs, the next reef seaward and approximately ten to fifteen miles offshore is a string of small islands (called Cays) some of which possess palm-covered opulence while others are partially or occasionally submerged and mangrove-covered. These islands string out along the entire Belizean coastline. The next ridge just a few miles seaward of this chain of Cays is the famous Barrier Reef whose coral formations appear above the surface of the waters only tentively from time to time and serve to protect the entire 175-mile coastline of Belize from the rough sea.

Belize City, barely eighteen inches above sea-level, is backed by extensive mangrove swamps extending many miles inland in some areas, and lie like a moss-green algae between the sea and land, wedding the salt water to the verdant tropical forests.

The southern half of the country is a plateau, dissected by the relatively low-rising Maya Mountain Range running north and south, and fringed by a narrow coconut palm-covered coastal plain averaging about fifteen miles wide and some ten feet in elevation. The southern plateau widens and declines toward the west, ending in the north by a broken escarpment falling rapidly to the Sibun River Valley. The Cockscomb Range, an isolated group of peaks, rises close to the irregular seaward edge of the plateau at its northern extreme. This long row of uneven, abrupt humps look for all the world like a lower mandible of a gigantic crocodile laid along the otherwise flat skyline. The highest of these quartzite and granite peaks, Victoria Peak, is 3680 feet in elevation and the highest measured point in Belize. The Maya Mountains are jungle-covered limestone hills, for the most part still unexplored, pierced by caves and ribboned by streams feeding the many short jungle rivers which cut through the coastal plain to the sea. The fabulous Mountain Pine Ridge Area of the Cayo District is on the higher elevation of the rolling southern plateau, ranging in altitude from 1500 to 2700 feet. Partially open land, it is crossed by rushing mountain streams with white water rapids and spectacular falls.

VEGETATION

Seasonal broadleaf forest covers at least ninety percent of the country. On the limestone soils of the north, the forest is deciduous; the sapodilla (Achras sapota), which when tapped like a rubber tree gives a white resinous latex called chicle, the basis for chewing gum, and the 150-foot towering mahogany (Swietenia macrophylla) are dominant. Mahogany wood, a principal export of Belize, is of the finest quality known. Axe handles, door posts, and golf club shafts are among the special uses of sapodilla wood. Chicle bleeding is carried out in the wet months, July through February, when the rains induce a good flow of gum from the trees.

On the lime-poor soils of the plateau country, mahogany is rare and Santa Maria (Calophyllum brasiliense) is the most important timber tree. Santa Maria wood is extremely hard and is the source for lumber for local home building, as this wood is relatively safe from termite attack, a constant hazard in Belize. It was once used for ship masts. Another tree of commercial value is the pink-flowered mayflower tree whose decorative graining is preferred locally for wall paneling to the more universally popular mahogany. The short jungle rivers are largely bordered by dense, swampy jungle growth and tall-fronded banana trees.

The Mountain Pine Ridge area of the Cayo District, at its higher elevations, has coniferous forests, carrying oak and carib-bean pine (Pinus caribaea). Its mountain-fed streams dramatically cascade over rocky falls. They have recently been stocked with trout by the Forest Department which maintains a forest station (St. Augustine) there and a landing strip for light aircraft. The Belizean pine found in this region has the character of the pitch pine and reaches heights of over 100 feet. Cedar (Cedrela Mexicana) and rosewood are also prevalent. The fine-grained, hard, durable, red-hued rosewood is used for fine cabinet work. The local rosewood trees are relatively large but the percentage of marketable wood from them is small. Cedars are used for making native dug-out canoes, called "pit-pans." The insect-proof, nicely grained cedar wood is used for cigar boxes and drawer and wardrobe linings.

A word of caution: the term "ridge," as in "Mountain Pine Ridge," is a local expression used in the sense of a patch of vegetation of like kind, and does not necessarily imply an abrupt change in topography. Thus the "High Ridge," "Broken Ridge," and "Cohune Ridge" one sees on a map are common vernacular expressions to describe plant cover in Belize.

Grass savannahs with scattered oaks, pines, and palmetto palms (Paurotis Wrightii) are characteristic of the southern coast and north-central regions. Mangroves fringe the northern coast and river inlets and cover many of the cays.

Other commercial timber trees found in Belize are the nargusta tree; the chechem or "black poisonwood" as it is locally called (although innocuous); ironwood, with a notably fine grain; local "redwood," which has good rot-resistant properties;

and balsa wood, here called "polak," occurs in the far south but
not in large abundance. The cabbage-bark and Billie Webb trees
were once used for truck beds and wheel spokes and the banak
tree's wood is still exported for core material for mahogany
veneer in furniture. Logwood trees, to which Belize once owed
its very existence, are still found in the swampy northern area,
although now of little commercial interest. Yemerie, used for
building siding and interior paneling, is a good substitute for
pine and does not burn easily.

A common tree of potential commercial importance,
although hardly exploited, is the royal palm of cohune
(Orbignya cohune). From its hard stony nuts a valuable oil is
extracted and, when burned, leaves a charcoal of great purity.
This substance was once used by the Britih army for gas mask
filters. The cohune starts as a one-leafed affair, then grows a
fleur-de-lis of beautiful great fronds that sprout from just above
the ground. At this stage, it has the appearance and dimensions
of a mature oil palm but it has hardly begun to grow. The
hard-wooded cohunes don't flower or fructify until their heads
reach the sunlight; that is, grow up to the height of the forest
canopy. The trunks become smooth and ringless, looking more
like hardwood trees. One can only recognize the cohune as a
palm tree by looking up at its wing-leafed head, a titanic
distance up in the sky.

The ceiba (Yaxche) tree, the national tree of Guatemala, is
found in Belize. This slender-trunked, uniquely-shaped tree was
once considered sacred by the Mayas who believed that this tree
grew in Paradise and, in its heavenly shade, deserving tribesmen
would someday rest, forever free from labor. It is still supersti-
tiously protected in Belize as well as in Guatemala.

Flaming red blossoms of the slender flamboyant trees (Delo-
nix regia); thickly flowered hibiscus of every color; oleanders;
pink, orange and purple bougainvillea; red blooming royal
poincianas; and the frangipani (Plumaria), whose pink-flowered
limbs emit a pungent perfume, all give a fragrant and colorful
accent to Belize's tree-lined roads and vine-choked jungles.
Great purple bunches of orchids grow around the wide-spread

roots of "bullet" trees, and lofty "cotton" trees stand singly, their crowns spreading like open parachutes, adding to the character of Belize's "back country." There are some 240 species of wild orchids alone, growing in Belize!

WILDLIFE

If British Honduran politics is a laboratory for the political scientist, as newsmen are prone to term it, then Belize's jungles are certainly a laboratory for the naturalist. This country is the home of some of the most fascinating creatures in the world, including an opossum only three and a half inches long, turtles that climb trees, ants that practice agriculture, and the "two-snakes-in-one" which is exactly that. But before venturing into the awesome depths of the tropical jungle with a Belizean guide, to avoid confusion one must first take a course in local terminology. In Belize jaguars are called "tigers," jaguarandis are "tiger cats," howler monkeys are "baboons," deer are "antelope" and moths are called "bats." True bats are "rat-bats" and thought by the natives to be of the same genus as the moth.

One need not leave the confines of Belize City to find exotic specimens. Here mangrove swamps teem with wildlife; lizards, frogs and endless varieties of crabs. Once each year, about mid-September, the entire crab population migrates to the sea to deposit their eggs. The most common Belizean crab, the Blue Mangrove Crab (*Cardisoma guanhumi*), comes in an array of colors from sky-blue through grey-blue, yellowish-blue to, in rare instances, bright straw-yellow. The most unusual feature of this crab is that one claw, his right, is much larger than the other and gives the appearance, as he lumbers along, of carrying one hand in a huge muff. They are the prized ingredient for the local culinary delicacy, crab gumbo. Crabs of another species (Uca minax) live in small water-filled holes. I found them even within the city limits of Belize. They have a trait in common with the Blue Mangrove variety. Small, with brown backs and red undersides, they too have one outsized claw. Their claw is red with a white tip and looks for the world like a tiny hand sticking out of a red muff. As a friend in Belize commented, *"It must be spectacular to see those two types of crabs shake hands!"*

Both the Northern and Western Highways, upon leaving Belize City, run parallel with the coastline for a number of miles. These mangrove-lined roads must be crossed twice each year by countless thousands of crabs trekking to and from the sea on their yearly business. The road is often so thick with crabs that traffic is halted for hours, and the road and ditches along the shoulder are black and blue with them.

Sharing the mangrove swamps with the frogs and crabs is the Yucatecan Crocodile (Crocodylus moreletii), locally called "alligator," naturally. They grow very large; a ten- or twelve-foot one is not a very large specimen, I am told. Some natives make a livelihood selling "alligator" skins.

One rarely sees the base of a mangrove tree, as they grow with roots submerged in the stagnant water of the swamps. Peering into these still, fresh-water pools at the base of the mangroves, one can see thousands of tiny fish called "Billums." Billums are present in nearly all still pools in Belize and come in a great variety of shapes and colors; some with ruby eyes, some with brilliant peacock-blue tails, others with mauve-colored bands or shining skins not unlike mother-of-pearl. They lose their color soon after being taken out of the water.

Everywhere one travels in Belize, hair-raising stores are told of a snake that jumps out of trees, is extremely poisonous and aggressive, and will chase and strike repeatedly. This short fat snake is the Tomigoff (Bothrops mummifer) or "Tommy Goff" as the natives say, and deserves every bit of his bad reputation. While it doesn't leap as far as it is locally credited, "Tommy Goff," because of its great muscular girth, strong band-like ventral scales, and relatively short body (18 to 24 inches), can spring from a limp state to absolutely rigid in an instant. This action propels it in, what appears to be, leaps. When it travels, it does not "snake" along as others do. It also has the bad habit of lying in the head-high lower branches of trees and, when disturbed, has been known to project itself right out of the tree. It appears to be utterly fearless and attacks on the slightest provocation. Although usually olive-green in color, it may be grey or brownish with a pattern of lateral darker, black-edged triangles along the back. Its long fangs, with highly toxic venom, are responsible for more deaths than any other American snake.

A near relative of the jumping variety of "Tommy Goff" is the longer "Yellow-Jawed Tommy Goff" which in Belize also goes by the romantic name of "Fer-de-lance." Named by French pirates, the true Fer-de-lance is found only on the island of Martinique but the Belizean variety *(Bothrops atrox)* is equally deadly. Colored much the same as the jumping Tommy Goff, this snake sometimes reaches eight feet in length. It has a habit of vibrating its tail to produce a sound in the bush similar to a rattlesnake, although it has no rattles.

Belize also has the common boa constrictor (Constrictor constrictor), here called "wowla," which grow to incredible lengths; but the wildest, most unusual snake in the country must be the "two-Snakes-in-one." This rare creature is not a hybrid but a separate species known as *Sibynophis annulata* and has the combined features of two entirely different common snakes; the coral snake and the *Coniophanes fissidens.* The astronishing beast has a black head and for the first several inches of its neck is vividly banded with the red, cream, and black markings of a coral snake. The body then abruptly changes, is larger in girth, rougher, and olive-brown, with vague dark longitudinal lines. On the underside it, too, changes from the smooth pink belly of a coral snake to the yellowish-cream of the brown snake. It is speculated that this snake commonly lies with its head sticking out of a hole to fool its enemies, who mistake it for the poisonous Coral. The "two-snakes-in-one" is not poisonous, but little is known of its habits.

Not to be omitted from any list of Belizean reptilian oddities are some of its many varieties of lizards and iguanas. There are green iguanas (Ctenosaurus similis) on tree limbs;

ground lizards (Ameiva undulata), some with bright blue and others with salmon-pink undersides; little maklalas, and countless wild-eyed basilisks (Basilicus vittatus). These are very beautiful lizards of the iguana family, called "cock maklalas" by the locals, the same name given to a plant in the Virgin Islands and elsewhere. The males bear tall, fin-like combs, or crests, on the back of their heads and change color continuously, developing intense greenish-yellow lines along their upper flanks. They have very long hind legs and tremendous tails. They climb low trees with some difficulty, but usually prefer to remain on the ground where they rely on their prodigious speed to escape their enemies. When sufficiently frightened, "cock maklalas" raise themselves to their hind feet and run like birds. They have baleful, large, dark grey-blue eyes and, when handled, show much fight, gaping and biting with fury.

Another local iguana, this one a hissing, frightening-looking, huge, leathery-skinned, tree climbing variety, known as the "bamboo chicken," sports a large pouch under his chin and is much sought after in Belize for the dinner table. Their meat tastes very much like chicken, the natives say. Specimens up to four feet long have been found on Half Moon Cay in the Lighthouse Reef.

Belize's very active and scientific Forestry Department has been able to isolate and control the malarial-vector mosquito types, making this disease now nearly extinct, but several insects mar this otherwise natural paradise. The common sandflies (Culicoides); "doctor flies" (Chrysops costatus), a yellowish fly that bites hard and long, leaving a large red splotch; and the "bottlas flies," a type of black sandfly of genus Simulium, which swarm in clouds and inflict bites that leave a red area on the skin centered by a small blood blister that turns black, all can make jungle life unpleasant, especially on a hot afternoon when the trade winds subside.

There is a traditional drink in Belize consisting of rum garnished with exactly nine live "wee wee ants." It is supposed to transform anyone who imbibes of it into as energetic a person as this hard-working ant of the genus *Atta*. Commonly known as parasol ant, cutter ant, or wee wee ant, the Atta destroy thousands of dollars of Central American crops yearly and defy extermination. The wee wee ants live in cities of several thousand, interconnected with subterranean tunnels with many sister cities. Each city is a low dome of about forty feet in diameter, about six feet high and sometimes as much as 15 feet deep. They contain a complex of chambers, cross-roads, passages, and deep galleries. Highly organized, this ant civilization has perfected a means of raising its own food, a type of fungus, grown on the decaying leaves of young plants brought to the ant cities for that purpose. Unfortunately the leaves that make the best fertilizer for the wee wee's fungus crop are the Belizean's young, healthy and most valuable citrus trees or, failing this, the fresh shoots of the most valuable timber trees.

From the domed city, radiating out in all directions, are eight or more ten-inch-wide hard-packed "roads" used by the wee wees for their nocturnal leaf-gathering activities. They travel these roads many times a night; each time each ant returns with one leaf carried over its head like a giant parasol. The time required to strip a tree of its foliage is phenomenally short.

The black and yellow Belizean anteater (Tamandua) offers little hope in controlling the proliferate wee wees unless he changes his feeding habits. The anteater is strictly a daytime forager while the wee wees come out only at night.

Of the furry creatures in which Belize's jungles abound, the most common is probably the soft teddy-bearlike kinkajous (Potos flavus). This little relative of the raccoon (raccoons are also found in Belize), very rare in other Central American countries, inhabits Belize in such number that they are considered pests. Called locally "night walkers," they are found in virtually every type of terrain in the country from the mountain forest, the tall lowland forests, area of secondary vegetation, and even in the tall growth of the swampy northern plain. Kinkajous can be house trained, are spotlessly clean, are affectionate, and make ideal pets. Also found is the Honduranean Coati (Nasua narica) and the much rarer Cacomistle (Bassaris sumichrasti), a sharp-faced relative of the "ring-tailed cat" of the southern United States, but so rare in Belize that it doesn't have a local name.

There is no animal that more surely expresses the character of the *terra incognito*, the jungle where man is but a rare and timid intruder, than the "baboons" of Belize. These jet-black regal beasts are really howler monkeys (Alouatta villosa), but have many of the characteristics of their namesakes, the African baboon. Lovers of heights, they ascend the tallest trees and therefrom roar, growl, bellow, and grunt their defiance to the world. There has never been a Hollywood jungle epic yet made that didn't utilize a howler monkey chorus in the soundtrack; a background which gives that rare touch of jungle mysticism. The howlers travel in small groups and are most usually seen in the higher elevations, working their way slowly down to the plains only when certain tree fruits ripen. They are big and black with powerful arms, heavy shoulders, scowling faces, and long prehensile tails which they keep securely anchored to a handy branch. Baboons are often seen in the company of little spider monkeys, whose senseless antics are tolerated so long as they stay well out of reach of their bellicose friends. Having few enemies, the baboon is surely the king of the Belizean jungle and knows it.

Of the few American or European sportsmen that visit Belize each year, some come to fish but a growing number come for big game, and to them that means but one thing: jaguar. This big cat (Felis onca) has been all but eliminated from places like Costa Rica, Columbia, and Venezuela, where they were once common, but they still abound in the unspoiled Belizean jungle. This largest of all wild cats in the western hemisphere reaches a length of six to seven feet and weighs as much as 250 pounds. Locally called "tigers," they are tawny or buff-colored with circular black markings. Pure black ones are sometimes encountered; these are called "panthers" by the natives who highly prize this pelt. Belizeans living in the "back country" have learned to live with, and respect, the cunning jaguar. They rarely attack men, but dogs and livestock are his fair prey. A

Maya guide recounted an incident to the author of a "tiger" entering his thatched roof "pole house" at night and snatching a young dog from its sleeping place at the foot of the guide's bed. He woke in time to see the animal, with the dog, leap through the open door and disappear into the darkness of the night.

Jaguar hunting safaris, under supervision of government-licensed big game guides, may be arranged through several private companies in Belize. They are hunted with dogs, but with the jaguar's superior intelligence and speed, it is not uncommon for a professional hunter to lose half his pack of dogs to the "tiger" on a single expedition. The jaguar does not "tree" as the North American mountain lion does; with increased hunting pressure, they have learned to take to the water, being powerful swimmers and not shunning water, as do most cats. This has made them an even more rare and valued trophy.

Due to the abundance of wild life, game laws in Belize are little observed but in the case of the jaguar the exporting of pelts, a highly profitable venture, has been restricted. In 1974 it became illegal to export a single wild animal pelt of any species. The United States has also enacted laws banning the importation of jaguar and other wild animal pelts. Legal protection has greatly reduced the annual slaughter, but poachers—spurred by continued demand—still kill many of the animals for sale to tourists.

Other wild cats in Belize are the ocelot (Felis pardalis) and the mountain lion (Felis concolor), which are occasionally encountered, and the small, graceful jaguarondi (Felix eyra). The jaguarondi, or eyra, was once thought to be at least two different species, as they have a wide range of color variation. The most common is reddish with metallic, golden-copper tones, but it is also found white and grey spotted, blotched, and solid grey. The natives call them all "tiger cats" and don't care much whether naturalists call them eyra or jaguarondis; "they're all chicken thieves," I was told.

Other big game animals in Belize include the prodigiously ugly and pig-like Tapir (Tapirella bairdi), called "mountain cow." These huge herbivourous, brownish-black animals have short, stout limbs and long flexible snouts with the nostrils near the tip. They reportedly reach 700 pounds!

Somewhat related to the tapir are the three varieties of peccaries, *Tayassu angulatus* being the most common, which crash about the mixed forest areas in "sounders," as groups of peccaries are called, rooting and grunting and otherwise tearing up the landscape. These wild hogs have razor-like prominent tusks which they are inclined to use on anything or anyone that gets in their way. Peccaries are edible, but when frightened they secrete an oily, musky substance which gives them a rank odor.

Also sought, more for gastronomical purposes than as big game, as their small delicate antlers make poor trophies, are the local "antelope," the name by which the local Savannah Deer are known. (There is not the slightest resemblance.) These *Odocoileus truei* —very gentle, small, and timid greyish-brown deer —are frequently found in the mountain pine regions of the Cayo District.

Belize has about 500 species of birds, many of them rare and beautiful. In size they vary from the minute hummingbirds, seen whirring about every flowering bush in Belize City, to the jabiru stork, now close to extinction, whose eight-foot wingspan makes him the largest stork in America.

Driving on the Belize highways at night one encounters nightjars, here called "bullbats," playing in and out of the headlight beams and hears the raucous night cry of the "chachalaca" who Belizeans say can predict a change in the weather. They also claim to be able to tell time in the jungle by the regular whistling habits of the "tinamou" who reportedly sounds off exactly on half-hour intervals.

Belizeans are unusually well-informed and interested in their wildlife in general and their wild fowl in particular. When a young couple to whom I once gave a lift from Belmopan to Belize City learned of my interest in birds, they were able to identify nearly fifty different and unsual species in about the same number of miles. One amusing bird I recall from that trip was the "gaulin bird," a short, white heron-like egret who has recently found a home in Belize. An arrival from the Guianas, this cattle egret was first reportedly only in 1948 and, since the introduction of cattle into the Cayo District, is now found in large numbers. In one field containing about fifty head of wild-eyed rangy cattle, I counted exactly the same number of "gaulin birds," who seemed to have each adopted one steer as its own and accompanied it wherever it went, wobbling along in that drunken way that only egrets can, at the steer's side.

Belizean skies are never free of birds; flocks of hundreds of white herons flying in shifting patterns high over the savannah grass often share the sky with an equally large group of black vultures (Cathartes aura), circling endlessly around in the air, their overlapping formations having a kaleidoscopic, mesmerizing effect.

Fluttering, chattering, vivid green and yellow wild parrots are everywhere seen in the interior, being exceedingly busy doing nothing. Larger parrots, the macaws, come in at least two varieties; the flaming scarlet-colored and the georgeous red, blue and yellow ones. There is also another type of parrot which is all green with a blue head. Besides making a colorful addition to the verdant landscape, the parrot is a choice entree on the Belizean dinner table.

Local gamebirds are the Central American wild turkey, whose opalescent coloring seems to change from blue to bronze to a deep rich gold as light plays along their ocellated plumage, and the curassow. The curassow is a black, turkey-like bird with a large yellow fleshy growth about the base of his bill, small beady near-sighted eyes, and an unkept-looking crest which gives it a constant droll appearance. The shanks of its legs are unexpectedly naked and it struts about with a comic dignity. Of the lesser gamebirds there are partridge, quail, curlew, pigeon, snipe, and many varieties of duck.

THE CAYS

The Belizean cays, pronounced *key* and alternately spelled cay, caye or cayo (Spanish), constitute in aggregate approximately 212 square miles of the nation's territory. These low-lying coral islands string out along the full length of Belize's coastline, lie between ten and forty miles offshore, just inside the Barrier Reef and are of three distinct types. Some are "wet" cays; that is, partially or sometimes submerged and appear, with their dense mangroves growing out of the water, as weird floating forests sailing on the intensely-blue Caribbean. Others are no more than bare outcroppings of white or cream-colored coral, while the third type of cay is typified by miniature Polynesian-like atolls, some with tall coconut palms and lush undergrowth, with white sandy beaches, and are as near to small bits of tropical Paradise as one may find anywhere in the world.

Lying outside the Barrier Reef are two tiers of offshore atolls. The first group eastward is the Turneffe Island group and further out the two groups known as Lighthouse Reef and Glovers Reef. The general outline of these island groups, with their distinctive northeast-southwest axis, results from a block-fault system which is responsible for the form of the shelf and the Bahia de Chetumal. Deep submarine trenches with precipitous slopes separate the two rows of atolls from the Barrier Reef and from each other.

The largest of the cays and atolls are the Truneffe Islands, Ambergris, Caulker, and English Cays. Some have picturesque names as Hut Cay, Alligator Cay, Man-o-War Cay, Blackadore Cay, Hen and Chickens, Monkey Cay and Laughing Cay. Fishermen live on some, coconuts grow on some, some have primitive tourist facilities, while others are yet to be explored.

Giant frigate birds (Fregata magnificens), looking like graceful flying wings, trace the progress of the hundreds of fishing boats which go out daily from Belize Harbor, soaring overhead until their white profiles become lost against the powder-puff clouds of the West Indian sky. The heavy moist air of the mainland becomes more brisk and the sea turns a deep cobalt blue as their captains thread their way through tortuous channels between the cays.

The only sea-charts of these off-shore waters are copies of old British sailing charts, some as old as 1831. They are of small scale and highly inaccurate, with some locations shown as much as one and a half miles off. Some prominent cays are not even shown and some shown cannot now be found. The local captains know these waters in the way Pirate Peter Wallace once knew them and rely little on navigation charts.

Although excellent topographical maps of British Honduras, published in 1964 by the Directorate of Overseas Surveys, are now available at a scale of 1:250,000, they obviously do not provide enough hydrographic detail to make navigation among the myriad islands and shoals a matter to be undertaken lightly by those unfamiliar with the coast.

The nature of these off-shore waters is dramatically stated, perhaps overly so, in a lengthy contract one must sign upon chartering a boat for an exploratory trip from Belize Harbor. Excerpts from it read: *". . . charter group agrees to crew, help handle sails, cook, anchor, and stand watches . . . (the charter company) assumes no responsibility due to accident, death, shipwreck, loss or damage to a guest's person or belongings. . . . all trips subject to weather conditions and the decision of the yacht Captain to "GO" or "NOT GO," at critical passages is final . . . (the area to be covered) is remote, mysterious, exotic, primitive, and unexplored. The very nature of this remote unchartered coast and underwater hostile environment (sharks?) assumes that you take this charter at your OWN RISK."* (Brackets ours.)

St. George's Cay

Sailing out of the Belize River beyond a chain of "wet" cays, aptly named The Drowned Cays, the first cay of any interest, only nine miles northeast of Belize City, is St. George's Cay. Buccaneers were its first inhabitants and it was a favorite place of business for their occasional occupation of smoking, drying and salting turtle and manatee meat for sale to passing privateers, logwood traders, and pirates.

This service of supplying dried meat was indispensable for seafarers in the Caribbean as well as the log cutters on the mainland, and provided the name "buccaneer" to those who dealt in it. It comes from the French term "boucan"; their name for this dried meat. It was later adopted by the British and applied especially to those who supplemented their "boucaniering" income with piracy.

The Spanish, obviously aware of the activities on this cay, named it "Cayo Cosina" (Kitchen Cay) at a very early date. By 1764, the date of the first known map of the Cay, St. George's Cay supported more than seventy houses and other structures and long turtle pens for holding the huge logger-head turtles until they could be butchered.

Today St. George's Cay has a special significance for patriotic Belizeans as it was the scene, in 1796, of a naval encounter between native fishermen and loggers in converted scows and coastal schooners, aided by one British man-of-war, and a massive fleet of thirty-two Spanish Navy ships. The Spanish fleet was decisively defeated and this battle of St. George's Cay marked the last attempt by the Spanish to remove the settlers from the mainland by force.

Until 1961 St. George's Cay and nearby Sergeant's Cay were popular summer retreats for residents of Belize City and for a colony of New Yorkers who maintained summer houses on Sergeant's Cay. Hurricane Hattie turned Sergeant's Cay into a sandbar and sliced the half-moon shaped St. George's Cay into four parts, leaving only two small houses standing and washing the turtle pens, long ago converted to swimming "crawls" (protected swimming areas), far out to sea.

Today, St. George's Cay is all but deserted, visited only by curious visitors wishing to walk in the footsteps of seventeenth century buccaneers or dig for some of the treasure reputed to still be buried there.

Turneffe Islands and the Barrier Reef

Due east of St. George's Cay, and just seaward of the Barrier Reef lies the island group known as Turneffe Islands or Turneffe Reef, some thirty-five miles from Belize Harbor.

Nearing the Barrier Reef, as one approaches Turneffe, the

cobalt blue sea becomes even clearer, the colors change from deep blue to cerulean, and the smooth, gentle flow alters to meandering currents which turn and twist past menacing white and cream coral heads protruding from the reef. Around their edges the colors melt into translucent green, revealing, fathoms down, the whiteness of shifting sandbars, the waving brilliance of undersea foliage, and the flashing fin of a passing barracuda. At times the water appears only a few feet deep, allowing a glimpse of lazy parrot fish browsing on dusky pink coral beds. Spell-bound by the beauty, with the easterly trade winds blowing a salty spray in one's face, it is easy to become attuned to the tranquillity of this great reef whose pristine beauty can be therapeutic for those of us with tensions built up from months of the anxieties of city life. Across the reef, a few miles beyond, lie in the Turneffe Islands.

Turneffe is a sparkling necklace set with thirty-two islands and "wet" cays forming an elongated oval, approximately fifty miles long and ten miles across, protecting a quiet blue lagoon in the center. Hundreds of nameless sheltered coves offer easy protected anchorage. A fishing lodge is located on Cay Bokel, one of the higher reefs on the far south end of the Turneffe chain. This hideaway haven for sport fishermen accommodates thirty guests with sleeping quarters, electricity, good food, and small boats for fishing for bonefish or snook in the lagoon; but the biggest attraction is its reputation for supplying the really large trophy fish, the king mackeral, marlin, and sailfish abounding in the Caribbean along its shores.

Noteworthy cays of the Turneffe group include Calabash Cay, which has a small settlement, and is the center of the island's coconut trade. Here, coconuts are loaded into deep-hulled boats and transported to Belize City for export. Others are Pelican Cay; Crawl Cay, which has a fishing resort; Soldier Cay and Mauger Cay. The latter receives its name from the popular creole word, a corruption of the English "meagre," and means a poor time, when crops wither from the dry heat and activity in general stagnates. Mauger Cay is better known as the site where, in pirate days, woman captives were taken by buccaneers after the sack of Bacalar in the seventeenth century.

The Turneffe Islands were famous at the turn of the century for their bounteous sponge beds. These sponges were wiped out in 1939 by a fungus. In the old days, fishermen started new sponge beds by attaching small pieces of sponge to concrete plates and placing them in the sea bed to grow. Today piles of these plates can be seen throughout the islands.

Lighthouse Reef   Lying due east of Turneffe, even further into the open sea, are the cays and coral heads that make up Lighthouse Reef. Similar to Turneffe, this chain of islands forms an irregular oval encompassing a still-water lagoon. The major islands of this group are Sandbore and Northern Cays at the extreme northern tip and Half Moon Cay and Long Cay at the southern end of the chain.

Long Cay   Long Cay of the Lighthouse Reef group is a favorite of skin divers, offering everything a diver could want: water temperature is ideal, one can stay in the water for hours without getting cold; underwater visibility is a fantastic 200 feet or more; a drop-off provides a variation of depth, within 100 yards of an anchorage, of from 30 to 600 feet. Almost anywhere in the area one can dive in virgin water. The diver quickly becomes charmed by the undersea beauty of this reef; by the absolute charity of the water; the coral bottom dappled by the sunlight patterns penetrating the rolling surface waves, creating an ever-changing light-show while slowly the unwordly scene penetrates the mind and leaves an unforgettable impression. The gently waving yellow and purple sea fans, their delicate lacy surface covered with thousands of darting lemon and black sergeant fish; squid staring with tragic human eyes set in little jelly bodies, jeeting backwards when approached; and even the diver's own magnified human hands and legs reflecting pinkly the filtered light from above, add to the fascination of this quiet suspended Paradise. Rainbows of thousands of little fish skitter out of the way, revealing huge towering brain coral formations. Underwater ravines, caves and drop-offs provide excellent spearfish hunting grounds for 40-pound grouper, roosterfish, jacks and mackerel.

Half Moon Cay   Across Lighthouse Reef's deep lagoon from Long Cay lies the most easterly, and perhaps the most beautiful, of Belize's off-shore islands—Half Moon Cay. Inhabited by only ten people, all relatives of its lighthouse keeper, it is all but unexplored. Until recently, Half Moon Cay was known only to lobster and conch poachers and the rare booby bird which was thought to be extinct until discovered living on this cay. Due to its remoteness, German submarines were able to use Half Moon Cay as a refueling station during World War II without anyone on the mainland being aware. Evidence of this activity has only recently been discovered.

Only a mile and a half long and a half mile across, this little cay has dazzlingly white sandy beaches with a drop-off on the north end and a shallow water lagoon on the south. Untouched by civilization, Half Moon Cay reminds one of the south sea islands in the Tuamotus near Tahiti. It offers the visitor a choice of diving in deep or shallow water, spear fishing, hunting for conch or lobster, or exploration of its reefs and coral caves. The lagoon itself provides excellent light tackle fishing for bonefish, snapper, and grouper. Exploring ashore is worth the trouble and the view from the top of the lighthouse is nothing less than spectacular.

Besides the lighthouse, operated twenty-four hours a day by the National Customs Department, the only buildings on the island are the homes of the lighthouse keeper and his assistant. Many proposals have been made for developing this unspoiled island into a posh vacation resort for tourists, but chances are that they will never be realized, as it is still owned by the far-thinking Belizean government which is inclined to preserve Half Moon Cay as a natural reserve and protect its abundant wildlife and tropical environment from any type of development.

One attraction which brings many adventurers to this off-beat atoll is the search for the fabled Spanish **galleon**, Juan

Baptista, which foundered on the reef on July 21, 1822 with $800,000 in gold and silver bullion aboard. It now reportedly lies in shallow water, about one mile off Lighthouse Reef, but has yet to be located.

Great Blue Hole of Lighthouse Reef Lagoon   Sailing north from Half Moon Cay, inside the lagoon formed by the Lighthouse Reef, one reaches the Great Blue Hole, a natural phenomenon visited yearly by groups of devoted divers from all over the world. The Great Blue Hole was the subject of a Jacques Cousteau expedition by diving saucer, featured in a television special, and since has attracted world-wide attention.

Here, in the middle of a lagoon, with miles of shallow five- to fifteen-foot water, is a round shaft sunk deep into the bottom of the sea. The Hole has a core diameter of about 450 feet and a depth of over 340 feet; an absolutely shear perpendicular drop-off. At about the 140-foot depth the shaft undercuts, revealing a cavern with gigantic stalactites, two to ten feet in diameter, hanging twenty to sixty feet down from the cavern roof. The fairyland configurations of this underwater cavern defy description or explanation, and if that isn't enough, the Hole now has a legend, stemming from some 1970 sightings, of a Loch Ness-type sea monster who reputedly dwells in its depths.

Cay Chapel   Although not one of the largest, only two and one half miles long, Cay Chapel is one of the most beautiful islands in the area. Protected by a solid section in the Barrier Reef, Cay Chapel has always escaped hurricane damage. Its sloping sandy beach stretches out for about two miles, facing the East. The island is one of the highest in elevation, five to ten feet above sea level, and is only sixteen miles from Belize City.

Besides its natural beauty and high elevation, its greatest attraction is its location in relation to the Barrier Reef, which offers it protection from strong winds, and the big-game fish waters of its outer (Caribbean) side, easily accessible by small boat from the cay.

Since 1967 a group of North Americans have done much

promotional and development work on the Cay, but after surveying the island into tracts and lots for homes, clubs, marinas, a nine-hole golf course, and a gambling casino, the venture was dropped for lack of capital. An airstrip was constructed and is still used there and construction of a hotel was started. The Philadelphia development firm is said to have purchased Cay Chapel for 80,000 pounds sterling in 1967.

This latest development scheme for Cay Chapel was not its first. Years ago, a man named Lionel Francis converted the Cay's 300 acres of sand and coral into a prosperous coconut plantation. This operation, too, was eventually abandoned and heavy brush and vines took over, nearly strangling the palm trees. The resort developer's bulldozers cleared away the undergrowth leaving tall coconut palms, which no longer bear on a commercial scale, standing out in bold silhouette against the blue West Indian sky, thus adding a crowning touch of south-sea romanticism to this already beautiful island.

Cay Caulker   Close by Cay Chapel lies Cay Caulker (also called Cay Corker) which has a tranquil little unspoiled village of about 500 people; among them are some of the coast's oldest families. Here, shaded by high rustling coco-palms, villagers walk barefoot down the sandy lanes to the sea where racks of salted fish dry in the sun. They spend many hours mending their nets which gracefully sway in the soft breeze of the trades blowing off the Barrier Reef only 1500 yards away.

The only untoward sound heard is the occasional crowing of a fighting cock or the shrill laughter of healthy young island children splashing in the protected surf beyond the beach.

Tourism has already made an inroad into Cay Caulker. A fishing resort catering to North American tourists is located there and lots have been staked out and sold to foreigners for retirement cottages or vacation homes soon to come.

Cay Caulker village did not escape damage by Hurricane Hattie in 1961. This storm in fifteen minutes demolished nearly every home standing along the former "Main Street" which paralleled the island's eastern shoreline. Today the surviving residents have mostly rebuilt their homes along a new "Main Street" further inland and replaced their public docks, known locally as "bridges," with the aid of government funds. Today there is a new "cricket pitch," community center and hurricane shelter, a concrete hurricane-proof school, fisherman's cooperative warehouse and meeting room.

Typical of the new houses constructed on Cay Caulker (as well as San Pedro on Ambergris) is the little "West Indies Cottage" raised a few feet above the ground on poles brought over from the mainland for that purpose. A simple gabled roof of corrugated metal is left unpainted and drains into "vats" to hold rainwater collected by an elaborate system of gutters and downspouts. Most have a simple shed roof over a small front porch which is decorated with brightly painted "gingerbread" trim. The wood frame structure is sheathed with indifferently-milled vertical plank siding. The large windows are without glass but have shutters for protection at night from inevitable mosquitoes. Cloth curtains are usually preferred to wooden doors for the interior.

The space under the house is used for storing all manner of fishing equipment—motors, dories, masts, sails, riggings, and assorted paraphernalia. It is also sometimes used as a make-shift workshop.

Most of the yards, once carefully tended grass lawns, have been replaced with the more easily maintained bare sun-baked sand, kept grass-free by machete and compacted by constant foot traffic.

Fruit trees, herbs, and ornamental shrubbery are rare. With the exception of coconuts and a few clusters of plantains, there are no crops whatsoever grown on the island. The natives depend entirely on their skill as fishermen to provide themselves with enough cash to produce the quantities of rice, beans, and corn which, together with their own varieties of seafood, constitute their dietary staples. It is said that these island fishermen are so indisposed to anything other than fishing that they even prefer to buy an ordinary mangrove boat pole rather than enter the "bush" to cut it themselves. They have been known to purchase coconuts at the native market in Belize to take back to Cay Caulker rather than take the time to pick them on their own palm-covered island.

Ambergris Cay   By far the largest and best known of the Belizean Cays is Ambergris, whose name bespeaks its whaling origin. Today Ambergris Cay is inhabited by about 500 fishermen and their families, mostly descendants of British and French pirates, as their fair skin and blue eyes attest. Sperm whaling, once a major business here, has since been overtaken in importance by the commercial fishing and lobster industries. Coconuts are raised commercially.

Most of the residents of Ambergris live in the picturesque fishing village of San Pedro at the southern tip of the island. There are no cars; instead of asphalt roads, the village's widely scattered neat little wood frame houses and thatched huts are connected by shady, winding, sandy lanes lined with bougainvillea and palm trees. San Pedro has a primitive air strip served by a local airlines on a once-a-day schedule from Belize City. Tourist facilities are available, but limited. Lots for retirement homesites have been sold to North Americans in recent years, but development is still in the embryonic stage.

The islanders take great pride in their fine cuisine, which includes a local bouillabaisse rich enough to satisfy the most critical French chef, and locally-baked coconut bread. Fresh sea food is caught daily for its one restaurant catering to tourists.

Ambergris is about 35 miles long and varies from a few hundred yards to five miles in width. Much of the cay is planted in coconut palms which fringe the eastern (Caribbean) side for a depth of 300 feet or more. These tall, swaying trees seem to thrive best near the ocean and add to the beauty and romance of its sublime setting of long white sandy beaches (approximately 20 miles of them), intense blue Caribbean Sea, and surf pounding against the Barrier Reef some 500 feet offshore. The reef has channels, or breaks in the coral, that allow the fishing fleet from San Pedro to pass safely to the deep water beyond. The western shore has an equally attractive beach sloping gradually into the still blue waters of the lagoon that separates Ambergris from the mainland, just twenty-five miles away. This long, protected passage has served as a thoroughfare for whalers, pirates, and smugglers trading with Mexico throughout the years, and many ships, victims of freebooters, have driven themselves upon unseen reefs or have become impaled on undersea coral pinnacles. Many wrecks, like *H.M.S. Yeldham* which sunk off Ambergris Cay in 1800, are well known and have been salvaged, but many more lie on the coral sea floor awaiting discovery.

The *Water Witch*, a British frigate, foundered June 12, 1793 just off the southern tip of Ambergris, going down with $2 million in gold and silver bars and specie which has never been fully recovered.

Not all of the treasure is in the sea. Ambergris Cay is one of the sites frequently mentioned in adventure books as likely spots to search for buried gold. One popularly-sought cache is rumored to contain great quantities of gold, church ornaments, and jewels—loot from raids on Spanish mainland settlements—buried by British buccaneers on Ambergris Cay in 1680.

There can be little question as to Ambergris's future as a tourist haven. This island offers everything that could be desired by devotees of sun, sand and surf. The area is perfect for skin diving, water skiing, swimming, boating, and fishing; or just relaxing in its natural Caribbean splendor.

The popularity of skin diving among San Pedranos is a recent manifestation brought about through the introduction of specialized equipment and techniques by a series of tourist-sportsmen who began visiting the area frequently during the past fifteen years.

The Southern Cay   South of Stann Creek the cays string out in an endless chain along the Barrier Reef. Most are rarely visited and some are as yet nameless. Many of them are covered with dense coconut groves that are periodically visited and harvested.

At the extreme southern end of the Barrier Reef are the Sapodilla Cays, one of which, Hunting Cay, has a lighthouse and a good natural harbor which features a huge old anchor, part of the equipment from a vessel whose name has long since been forgotten, which is embedded in the coral sea-floor and serves as a mooring for visiting boats. During the winter months, Belize's famous "northers," bringing little black rainsqualls, make sailing treacherous along the coastal waters where coral heads, inches below the surface, line the narrow, unmarked passages.

Wild Cane Cay, near the mouth of the Deep River, bears signs of an ancient Maya settlement. Here are found mounds and artifacts attesting to the habitation of this island sometime before Columbus. The Mayas traveled along the coast on trading treks to their cities in Spanish Honduras.

Ranguana Cay and Laughing Bird Cay, a long, narrow, sandy Cay studded with palms and as delightfully beautiful as its name, are both inhabited by native fishermen. Slasher Sand Bore, as desolate a spot as its ominous names implies, is surrounded on all sides by dead coral which shelves off abruptly into deep water filled with barracuda and fish of infinite variety.

The Tobacco Cays, first settled by English Puritans who introduced tobacco-raising to Belize in about 1640, lie opposite Stann Creek and just north of South Water Cay. These palm-covered Cays have some very fine vacation homes on them.

English Cay   English Cay, near the Turneffe Islands, guards the passage through the Barrier Reef taken by larger ships. It has a lighthouse on top of several hundred foot banks which rise dramatically thirty feet in the air out of the open ocean. Here, large sea-bass, for shooting with spear gun or underwater camera, are in abundance, in the protection of the sheer banks.

Glover's Reef   South of Turneffe and twenty miles off the coast is the circular chain of bare coral outcroppings called Glover's Reef. Like Turneffe and Lighthouse Reef, it encompasses a spectacular lagoon studded with thousands of tiny coral heads appearing like sequins on a satin sea. Glover is best known for the snapper, grouper, parrot fish, and scrappy bonefish taken from its crystal-clear water.

At the south end of the oval-shaped reef is a remote tourist resort on a tropical atoll. Its huts are built of cabbage bark (a local tree) and widely separated for complete privacy. This resort has hosted such international celebrities as Prime Minister Trudeau of Canada, and is popular for its virtual inaccessibility, as well as its unrivaled natural beauty.

COMMUNICATIONS

There are no railways in the country. Forest and agricultural produce are mostly transported by road, although the rivers are still extensively used for transportation. Buses connect Belize City with Corozal Town and Belmopan.

Shipping

The country's main port is Belize City, but it has no docks or deep-water wharves. Vessels drawing more than five feet have to anchor in the harbor and ships drawing more than twenty feet have to anchor a mile or more offshore. There is a regular service between Belize and Jamaica by small motor ship every three weeks and good shipping connections are maintained with the United States, United Kingdom, and Continental Europe by six private shipping companies. At the Belize Offshore Growers Wharf, ships of ten-foot draught can be accommodated.

There is a weekly Southern Coastal freight, passenger, and mail service. Vessels of the Harrison, Royal Netherlands, United Fruit, Buccaneer, Canada, Jamaica, Caribbean, and "K" lines call at Belize.

The lack of a deep-water port facility is one of the nation's biggest handicaps. All deep-draught ships must anchor a mile or more from the docks at Belize City and are then loaded by any manner of motor launches, sloops, lighters, dories or schooners. This makes for very expensive cargo handling.

The Newport Development Corporation headed by Dan Milan, a Louisiana building contractor who has long been interested in the development of a deep-water port for Belize, obtained one of the first investment survey grants made by the U.S. Agency for International Development (AID) in Belize for a feasibility study to determine the site location and the financial and engineering practicality of such a selection.

After many months of intensive investigation and surveying, this $68,000 grant produced a master plan, to be implemented in phases over a forty-year period, at a cost in excess of $20 million.

Location of the new port, in or adjacent to Belize City, was ruled out early in the investigation as being virtually impossible. Ships that would be using the port would require a water depth of 32 feet. Borings in and around Belize City have revealed a hard limestone bed lying less than 20 feet below the surface. Not until reaching beyond the Sibun River, five miles south of Belize City, did their investigation indicate a proper sea bed and depth. This is the site that the Newport engineers have proposed for the new port facility but the initial phase, calling for a $5 million expenditure, has not yet begun.

Roads

The roads between Belize City and Corozal Town in the north and between Belize City and San Ignacio in the west are partly surfaced. The road from Stann Creek Town has now been extended to Punta Gorda. Traffic makes full use of these roads but, in the wet season, care is needed. The Hummingbird Highway from Stann Creek Town joins the Belize City–San Ignacio Road. Improved roads are an important feature of the development plan, but road construction is a difficult and costly process owing to the nature of the terrain. In 1971 nearly B.H. $4 million was spent on improving the road system.

Belizeans explain their vertebrae-punishing, pot-holed roads this way: *"British Honduras once had the world's worst roads until the British Engineers paved them; now since the chuck holes and wash-outs have appeared, we have the world's second worst roads!"*

All told, there are only 850 miles of all-weather roads, 180 miles of government-maintained cart roads and bush trails. A number of logging and forest roads are usable by heavy duty vehicles, but only in the dry season. In 1970 there were only 29 passenger automobiles per 1000 population. Most of these are Land Rovers and other four-wheel drive vehicles due to the road conditions. There is a total of only 4100 automobiles and 2100 trucks in Belize, but this is substantially more than in 1953 when there were only 500 automobiles in the entire country. Belizeans can accept the discomfort of their road system in the knowledge that work is progressing to up-grade the old narrow roads, built years ago by the British, on roadbeds of crushed rock taken from the thousands of Maya Indian mounds along their right-of-ways. Also, new modern highways are being extended into areas which heretofore were accessible only by light plane or boat.

Road tax for commercial vehicles is B.H. $100 per year and $60 for private vehicles.

Air Transport

Belize International Airport, nine miles from the city, is the main port of entry for the country. It has a runway 6,300 feet long and 150 feet wide and is capable of accommodating medium jet aircraft. The parking ramp is being extended and a new radar tower is being constructed for improved weather information. Aeronautical communications are being improved and advanced landing aids for aircraft are being installed.

Belize International Airport is served by TACA Airlines (Transportes Aereos Centro Americanos) who fly BAC-111 fan-jets connecting Belize City with Miami, New Orleans, Kingston, Jamaica, and the Republics of Mexico, Guatemala, El Salvador, Nicaragua, Costa Rica, and Panama. There are five round-trips a week from New Orleans, four from Miami, eight weekly round-trips to the Central American Republics and two to Jamaica. Flight time from New Orleans is about two hours, from Miami slightly less.

TAN Airlines (Transportes Aeros Nacionales) also operates

between Belize and Miami, four times weekly each way, as well as four weekly flights between Belize City and the Republic of Honduras with connections twice weekly to Guatemala and El Salvador. TAN has one flight a week to Mexico City from Belize via Tegucigalpa and La Ceiba. This airline flies DC-7B's.

In December, 1972, SAHSA, Central America's largest carrier, began regular service to New Orleans from Belize City in addition to their Miami and San Pedro Sula, Honduras flights. Aircraft include BAC-111 and Lockheed Electra jets.

There are also internal air services. Maya Airline (Maya Corporation, Ltd.) links Belize City with all other Districts in the country, providing daily service to Stann Creek Town, Independence, and Punta Gorda and a twice-weekly service to Corozal Town, Orange Walk Town, and Gallon Jug. This airline also provides charter service to all the landing strips in the country or to towns in the neighboring republics. Maya uses twin-engine British-built Britten-Norman Islander aircraft.

Two other charter services operate in Belize. Central American Transport, Ltd. provides a daily scheduled flight to the village of San Pedro on Ambergris Cay in addition to its charter business. Chemicals, Ltd. also provides planes for charter. This latter company reports the use of aerial spraying of insecticides and fertilizer is coming increasingly into use.

There are some twenty-eight landing strips throughout the country, some government-maintained and some private, available for use by private pilots. One is being built in Belmopan.

Navigational Services for the country are handled by the Central American Corporation for Navigational Services which is under Government contract to provide, operate and maintain the fixed aeronautical telecommunications and air navigation facilities located at Belize Internal Airport. Its equipment includes V.H.F. teletype links between Belize City and Tegucigalpa.

Pilots of private aircraft are required to have their documents inspected upon arrival at Belize International, and for on-going flights, must file the normal flight plan. An informal briefing is given by the local civil aviation authorities concerning the use of landing strips while in the country. Landing fee at this moment is U.S. $6.00 and parking fee of $1.00 per day.

Telecommunications

Cable and Wireless, Ltd. provides radio telephone service overseas through Miami and Jamaica and telegraph through Miami, Jamaica and Mexico City. A telex service is available to any part of the world. At the moment only Belize City and the new Capital at Belmopan have modern telephone service but on January 22, 1971 the government concluded arrangements with General Telephone and Electronics International, Inc., a New York-based firm, for a new $5 million telephone system which, when completed, will more than double the number of telephones in the country and provide service to all district towns. Until its completion, Belize has but 11 telephones per 1000 inhabitants.

Radio

Since its founding in 1952, Radio Belize, the nation's only radio station, has become a national institution. This government-operated, semi-commercial station transmits 17 hours a day, in Spanish and English, and is an important factor in the country's progress. It has provided a lifeline to all the people in the remote outlying districts and, in the absence of telephones, devotes time for personal messages (mostly of an emergency nature) and keeps Belizeans everywhere informed on current events in their country. It also provides something for everyone in the way of entertainment. "Disc jockeys" must be versatile enough to blend Calypso, popular Mexican numbers, and the current "top forty" in the U.S. into their programming.

Since October, 1967, Radio Belize has belonged to the Commonwealth-Caribbean-Canada broadcasting group (CCC) and world news coverage is excellent. In 1971 there were 59,931 radio receivers in use in the country, or one for every two people. There are a number of television sets, but they can only be used on rare occasions when weather conditions allow reception from one of the stations outside the country. In 1967 there were less than 7000 radios in the entire country.

The Press

There are two daily newspapers in Belize and four weeklies, including two Government Newsletters. The paper with the largest circulation is the daily *Belize Times*, the unofficial party organ of the reigning Peoples United Party, and the most influential of the nation's newspapers. As with all the country's tabloids, the *Times* is written in a very informal colloquial manner and contains a large amount of local gossip and editorial opinion and little international news. Its rival, the *Belize Billboard*, is published by Lindberg Goldson on a less-than-regular basis.

The independent weekly, *The Reporter*, now strongly supported by the conservative minority political party, U.D.P., is perhaps the best of the nation's papers. In addition to full coverage of local news, its editor, Harry Lawrence, an unsuccessful U.D.P. candidate in the 1974 elections, contributes to his readers' knowledge and appreciation of Belizean history and folklore with a regular column each week on some aspect of Belize's past. The second weekly paper in Belize is *The Beacon*. The government publishes the *Government Gazette*, its official weekly; the *Weekly Newsletter*, published by the Government Information Office; and the quarterly, *The New Belize*.

The Amandala is the most recent addition to the country's news media. It is the voice of the vociferous Black Power Movement in Belize. It was an article in the *Amandala* demanding an end to "economic colonialization" that caused two members of the United Black Association for Development, U.B.A.D., to be charged with seditious conspiracy in 1970.

Another politically sponsored weekly, *The Liberal*, ceased publication in 1974.

Land of the Mysterious Maya

Archaeologists, anthropologists, writers, and explorers have been at work for years in Central America attempting to scientifically reconstruct the history of the Maya Indians, one of man's most remarkable civilizations which flourished in the millenium before Columbus and rivaled that of the Egyptians and the Sumarians at its height. Without a doubt, more study has been devoted to these mysterious people than to any other in the aboriginal New World, yet still today very little is known of their origins.

The application of arithmetic, one of man's most brilliant achievements, is attributed to the Maya people for they utilized a numerical system long before its arrival in Europe and even before the Hindus. Their schools, highly moral social code, agriculture, temples and crafts were a high point ·in human achievement. Then, sometime between the ninth and tenth centuries A.D., the advance suddenly stopped and the people abandoned their great temple-cities. Why? . . . The subject has baffled scientists for years.

The Maya are hardly a lost people; today they number over two million and inhabit a well-defined area that includes all of the Yucatan Peninsula, Guatemala, British Honduras, parts of the Mexican states of Tobasco and Chiapas, and the western portions of Honduras and El Salvador. The Mayas still form a high proportion of the population of this area; speak their native tongue, although many speak Spanish as well; and retain much of their old way of life. A short, stocky, and extremely broad-headed people, with dark skin, straight black coarse hair, and high cheekbones, the Mayas have resisted with remarkable tenacity the encroachments of European-oriented civilization on their life-style.

The Maya language group today includes some twenty diverse, but related, dialects. Geographically, the 550-mile-long by 350-mile-wide area inhabited by these people is subdivided into three distinct regions with corresponding cultural differences. Even with their cultural integrity and extraordinary cohesion, these divisions are easily discernible.

The southern third of the Maya rectangle is a highland; a land of great beauty, plateaus and lakes, and cool temperatures. The central area, which includes most of Belize, is typified by tropical rain forest. Today most of this region is covered with a dense, almost impenetrable, forest and is uninhabited, except for woodcutters and chicle gatherers. This hot, low-lying, limestone country once contained the greatest of all the Maya centers. The third division includes the Yucatan Peninsula, where less annual rainfall changes the natural vegetation from rain forest to dry scrub. This lack of rainwater forced the Mayas living in this region to construct *cenotes*, or wells, reservoirs and cisterns whose remains are still in evidence.

It is not known when the first inhabitants entered the Maya area, nor precisely from whence or why they came, but we can assume that these first people were hunters and gatherers, or possibly horticulturists, and much more dependent upon wild plant foods than were their agricultural descendants. The roots of Maya civilization are so deeply buried in time that they are seemingly unrecognizable, and even the earliest archaeological remains yet found are those of already-settled groups in possession of a comparatively elaborate culture. In the Guatemalan highlands, the earliest materials found date from as early as

1500 B.C., while in the central rain forest of Belize they date from only 600 B.C., although evidence of earlier habitation, often consisting of little more than bits of pottery and an occasional burial, lies deeply buried beneath later construction, and its discovery is almost always a matter of chance.

EXPLORATION AND DISCOVERY

Maya civilization had passed its peak and its great "cities" had been deserted and forgotten long before the Spaniards conquered the area (1520–1545). Smallpox, hookworm, and malaria brought by the Conquerors took their toll on the remaining Maya population. The Mayas survived the conquest but, with the suppression of their pagan customs, the remains of the ancient grandeur of their civilization was lost and the ruins of their old cities and temples were disregarded. Today one finds traces left by an ancient advanced culture throughout the jungles of Belize. Ruins of cities and pyramids, deserted and covered with tropical growth, with here and there a monument marking some early event, bear mute witness to a once-great era of Maya history.

Unfortunately, most of the few native written records, called codices, which might have shed some light on the origin and history of these people, were demolished at the destructive hands of Spanish priests during the Conquest. In an attempt to suppress the pagan Indian religion and substitute Christianity, the multi-colored hieroglyphic-covered Maya documents were burned, and with them, the only written record of whatever literature and history that remained of the ancient people. A few original records found their way to European museums, though they are very incomplete. The Chilam-Balaam books are of interest to students of Maya history. They were written in European characters by Mayas educated by the priests, and are translations of some original hieroglyphic records of Maya families. The Popol-Vuh, a book of the sacred writings of the Quiche Mayas, has been translated into French by Brasseur du Bourbourg. This great epic relates a story of the creation similar to the Old Testament, together with many legends and history of that tribe.

Rediscovery of the ancient culture began with the exploration of the ancient city of Palenque in Chiapas, Mexico by the Spaniard, Antonio Del Rio in 1785; but it was not until the 1840's, when John L. Stephens wrote a two-volume popular travel book covering his visits to many forgotten Central American ruins, that the attention of the outside world was drawn to the Mayas. Stephens, an American diplomat and attorney and his companion, the British artist Frederick Catherwood, were the first to attribute the ruined "cities" that they visited to the actual inhabitants of the area—the Maya Indians.

It was so difficult to imagine that the simple illiterate Indian farmers living near the ruins were actually the descendants of a people capable of erecting these structures and creating such artwork as was found, that the construction of the jungle edifices had previously been credited to such diverse and unlikely origins as the lost tribe of the Israelites, wandering Welchmen, Druids, and even Tartars by European "authorities." The Maya peasants that Stephens encountered in 1841 were as puzzled by the ruins as were the explorers, for they had long since lost all knowledge of the meaning of the elaborate hieroglyphics and pictorial records embellishing their crumbling stone architecture.

Stephens explained this phenomena by assuming that these peoples' forefathers had in some way come in contact with Egyptian, Sumarian, or travelers from some other advanced culture across the Atlantic; a theory still popular, although not supported by scientific evidence. To date, no object manufactured in the Old World has been unearthed in any Maya excavation site so, except for some unnerving similarities between ancient Mediterranean culture and the Maya, there is no evidence to support a trans-Atlantic migration theory—"RA-type" expeditions to the contrary.

Stephens and Catherood had no way of even roughly estimating the age of the jungle-covered ceremonial sites that they visited. It was not until the Maya calendar "code" was finally broken by Ernst Forstermann, a Saxon librarian, from studying Maya inscriptions published by the Englishman, Alfred P. Maudsley, at the turn of the nineteenth century, that a breakthrough in Maya chronology was achieved. At about the same time, large-scale expeditions began in earnest, starting with the Peabody Museum of Harvard's expedition and followed by ones sponsored by the Carnegie Institution of Washington, Tulane University, the University of Pennsylvania, and the Institute of Anthropology and History in Mexico. Much work has been done photographing, excavating, and mapping, yet only the surface has been scratched. Due to the nature of the unexplored regions of the Maya country, important new sites are continually being discovered as the areas are opened up by loggers, chicle-gathering "chicleros," and more recently, by oil exploration firms.

The dating of the ancient civilization now rests on four lines of evidence: archaeology itself, the strata of soil in which the cultural artifacts are found; radiocarbon tests, in use since 1950; historic native traditions gleaned from post-Conquest materials such as the Chilam-Balaam writings and the correct correlation of the Maya with the Christian calendar. With all the scientific endeavor, neither archaeology nor tradition has been able to reveal much of Maya origins. Tribal memories are weak and a combination of inacessibility and unfavorable geological conditions have made the search for truly early remains difficult. It is hoped that some of the limestone caves and rock shelters common in Belize, suitable for habitation by primitive hunters and gatherers, might yet reveal traces of an age far earlier than the pottery and artifacts that they have yielded to date.

The most valuable records left by the Mayas are contained on tall, slender, elaborately-carved stone monument slabs, called *stelae* (plural of stela), found throughout the Maya area and inscriptions all over the ancient cities of the central and northern regions. The ten foot or taller stelae are generally carved with dates of historic events on one side and with gods of scenes from Maya life depicted on the reverse. Correlating the dates on the stelae with our own calendar was a complicated task. The

Maya calendar used at the time the stelae were carved is referred to as the Maya "Long Count" which is an absolute day-to-day calendar which has run like a giant clock from some point in the unknown past. The Maya calendar was made possible by a knowledge of astronomy, mathematics, and years of acute observation by scientists lacking modern scientific instruments. There are eighteen months in the Maya calendar, each month being twenty days long, with five dreaded "unlucky" days left over every year. The months were called Pop, Uo, Zip, Zotz, Tzec, Xul, Yaxkin, Mol, Chen, Yax, Zac, Ceh, Mac, Kankin, Muan, Pax, Kayab, and Cumhu. The five extra days were called Uayeb. The accuracy of the presently used correlation formulated by J. Eric S. Thompson has now been successfully checked by radiocarbon tests of timbers found in Maya ruins. The Maya dates recorded on the stela for the date of construction of the structure in which the timbers had been employed, translated by the Thompson correlation and the estimated dates arrived at by the radiocarbon tests coincided, proving Thompson's work substantially correct.

From this breakthrough, we are able to classify history by periods for more concentrated study. The *Formative Period* (1200 B.C. to A.D. 300) is the earliest date that traces of their existence have been found. It was marked by an emergence of agriculture, a rise of a ruling class, and the construction of early ceremonial centers (cities). The most important period, called the Classic Period (A.D. 300 to 900), was the peak of the civilization when the more important ceremonial centers were constructed. These were abandoned about 900 A.D. *The Interregnum* (900 to 1000) was a period of decline with cultural levels returning to that of the Formative Period. This was the age of the unexplained migration of the Mayas living in Belize and the rest of the Central Maya region to Yucatan, abandoning their cultural centers, homes, and farms.

The period from about 1000 to 1200 A.D. is referred to as the *Mexican Period* because Mexican warrior groups from outside the Maya Region dominated both the southern Guatemalan Highland area and the northern Yucatan area of the Maya

homeland. The central area containing Belize remained uninhabited. New religious and social ideas developed and the city
of Chichen Itza became most important. Gradually the Maya
region became split into two distant factions: that of the north,
dominated by the city of Mayapan, and the Guatemalan Highland dominated by the Quiche Mayas of that area. This period,
1200 to 1450 A.D., is usually identified as the *Mayapan Period*
and was characterized by militarism. After 1450, until the
Spanish Conquest in the early 1500's, the Maya civilization
underwent a complete disintegration with the destruction of
central government and the consequent breakup into many
warring states. Mayan Civilization eventually degenerated culturally to the state of intellectual decay that was observed by
the first European conquerors upon their arrival.

The Formative Period (1200 B.C. to A.D. 300)

Little is known of the centuries of development leading up to
the apogee of Maya achievement reached in the first millennium
of the Christian Era known as the Classic period. The Mayas
were not the only peoples inhabiting the region defined as
Mayaland. The Mayas shared their vast territory with other
tribes of semi-nomadic hunters who also shared common dress,
hair style, superstitions, and knowledge of agriculture. It was
during the period referred to by Maya history scholars as the
Formative Period that the differences between the Mayas and
the others began to be discernible. By about the first century
A.D., Maya culture was sufficiently differentiated from neighboring cultures to be called Maya.

Agriculture, without which civilization is impossible, reached
full development in this period with maize (evolved from teo-
cintle, a windgrass raised by prehistorical indians), being the
most important crop. Also of importance were cotton, beans,
squash, and fruits such as avocado, papaya, and probably cocoa.

The life-style of the Mayas began to assume the shape that it
was to sustain for many future centuries. The so-called cities,
actually religious and community centers, began to be built and

the priesthood, which certainly existed since very early times, took on more and more importance to the Mayas and slowly emerged as a very dominant ruling class. At this time, as later, the people lived in thatched huts in small clearings scattered throughout the forest living off the produce of their small farm plots, but they attended regular religious ceremonies at cen- trally-located ceremonial centers. These centers consisted of thatched temples set high upon large stone pyramids with stone-faced platforms flanked by "palaces" (lower, multi- roomed residential buildings) surrounding vast lime-plaster paved courtyards. Tikal, in Guatemala, the largest of these centers yet discovered, covers a square mile and is encircled by smaller, detached groups of structures covering much more additional area. Besides religious use, these centers were used as markets where produce was traded in the huge courtyards, and as centers for the civil administration of the area and for courts of justice.

Except on market days and times of great religious festivals these centers were empty, with the possible exception of a few priests and novices who retired there for prolonged periods of fasting and continence preceding important festivals. The build- ings in the centers were of local limestone quarried near the site. The small quarries were usually modified for continued use as rainwater catch-basins for storage of drinking water. The build- ings themselves were built without windows and had only a small doorway to each room covered with a cotton curtain. Some were roofed over with wood beams and mortar, some were simply thatched, but the more important temples were generally supplied with a corbelled vault.

Maya architects never achieved a true vault but the two soffits were inclined inward until the gap between them became narrow enough to bridge across with a row of capstones. Thus the width of rooms was limited, usually no more than 12 feet. The absence of chimneys and hearths indicate that the buildings in the ceremonial centers were never intended to serve as permanent residences, and elaborate carvings on the stone lin- tels and panels portraying high priest-rulers seated on daises, apparently holding court and administering justice, suggest that this is the primary use for the corbelled chambers.

All of the major temples found today are actually the remains of not one building, but several. The Mayas, for reasons not as yet understood, seem to have believed that temples had a definite life span; that is, they could be used for various cere-monial purposes for a time and then had to be modified in some major way, or covered over entirely with a new structure. For this reason, most of the temples began as buildings of moderate height, and grew to their present heights, The "Castillo" at Xunantunich near Benque Viejo in Belize is 127 feet tall, and one in Tikal measures 229 feet in height as a result of successive building additions over the centuries.

In all cases, the basic form of structure was the same; a solid pyramid which served as a sub-structure for the support of a chambered building or an altar on top. The pre-Classic pyramids did not serve the function similar to those of Egypt in that they did not usually contain burial chambers, but were rather a simple mass of boulders and soil, faced with hewn limestone blocks, and capped with a thick layer of burnt-lime stucco. Similar structures in the Classic Period have been found to serve this purpose, however. The pyramids were often topped with a thatched roof comb to form a backdrop for the high priest who performed his "magic" on a masonry table, or over a ceremonial fire, for the benefit of the worshippers gathered in the stucco-paved courtyard below. The pyramid temples were sometimes demolished or remodeled and another architectural "layer" added to their height as often as every fifty years.

The cyclic destruction of objects is a unique characteristic of the Mayas and helps explain why nearly all artifacts found, including simple every-day pottery, have been broken when unearthed. One practice that is known to have existed was the extinguishing of household fires at the end of the year and the kindling of new ones. This probably included the breaking of existing household ware as well. On a small scale, this relates to their periodic destruction and reconstruction of buildings. But its full significance is as yet a mystery to Maya students.

The Classic Period (A.D. 300-900)

The greatest achievements of the Maya were made, not in the southern highland region with its excellent climate and superior natural resources, but in the central lowland region of Belize and Guatemala where the people were required to expend a great effort in hacking out an existence in an inhospitable jungle region. The northern highland Maya formed a wealthy group throughout Maya history and some of their centers were large and important, but they had little or no part in the development of hieroglyphic writing or of the distinctive styles of sculpture and architecture which we now know as Maya. These were a contribution of the Mayas of the low rain forest belt which extends in an arc from the Bay of Campeche across the Mexican states of Chiapas, Tobasco, Guatemalan Peten Department and British Honduras. This was the cradle of the Maya civilization which reached cultural fruition in the Classic Period and lasted for 570 years.

The Classic Period is characterized by greater architectural development and artistic embellishment; artistic climax in stone sculpture, painting and pottery decoration; perfection of hieroglyphic writing; advanced arithmetic including the concept of completion, or zero, and a position notation of numbers; highly developed science of astronomy; complex calendrical calculation by use of the "Long Count" system of time reckoning; and the worship of dieties not directly related to the powers of nature. Maya sculpture, usually in low relief, is now acclaimed as one of the great art styles of the world. The full extent of intellectual achievement can only be estimated from the few remaining traces of the culture; the stone stelae with their historical notations; forest-covered and weather-eroded remains of temples and pyramids; and hieroglyphic texts carved on stone monuments, on buildings, and on pieces of wood, jade and shell that we are capable of translating only in part.

One of the three major Maya books to survive, the Dresden Codex, gives a clue to the unusually advanced state of learning of these ancient people. It contains tables for accurately determining the date of eclipses, though they did not even know that the moon revolved around the earth and the earth around the sun. The book reveals that the Mayas had ascertained the average synodical revolution of the planet Venus with extreme accuracy; their error was one day in 6000 years! When the Maya language is finally fully understood (it contains approximately 850 characters, most of whose meaning is still unknown) perhaps even more of their accomplishments will be revealed.

SOCIAL AND POLITICAL ORGANIZATION

The subject of the Maya social and political structure during the Classic Period is one of speculation and conjecture. It is likely that the major ceremonial centers served as administrative capitals for independent states. These city-states served perhaps an area of 100 square miles. The largest of these centers, and the only one which has yet been completely surveyed, is Tikal. At Tikal, the central core of the "city" covers approximately six square miles and contains about 3000 structures, ranging from lofty temple-pyramids and massive palaces to tiny thatched-roofed huts which served as homes for servants. The total population of Tikal during the Classic Period is estimated at only 10,000 or 11,000 people. The peasant farming community was widely dispersed around the center in a highly unorganized and unplanned manner, with an increase in frequenty and size of houses becoming evident as one moves closer to the heart of the center itself, where the homes of the bureaucrats and aristocrats were more splendid.

Districts outside the perimeter of the major centers were served by minor ceremonial centers corresponding in some way to our county seats, and usually contained a temple-pyramid and several "palace" buildings which provided a focus for religious and civic activities. It is estimated that for every 50 to 100 dwellings in the Central Area, there was a minor ceremonial center of some type with a dependent cluster of supporting structures. The bulk of the population lived in unplanned hamlets built in hacked-out clearings of 200 to 300 yards square in tiny pole-and-thatch huts.

Awe-inspiring as the great Maya "cities" are, there is little indication that any planning went into their arrangement. Rather, the typical ceremonial center appears to have grown by accretion as temples, palaces and entire complexes were built and re-built over and over through the centuries.

More is known of the physical make-up of the government than of the form of the Maya government itself. It is certain that the church and state were one, and it is assumed that the great power that a relatively small aristocracy held over their subjects for so many centuries was one of religious rather than of economic or militaristic basis. Though convenient to term its leaders "priests," it is not altogether correct as the leaders were not celibate theologians but very powerful hereditary elite; the top strata of a complicated hierarchy whose privileged positions came from one's genealogy. The keeping of genealogical records was therefore of grave concern to the Maya aristocracy.

The very title given the high priests, Ah Kin (He of the Sun), suggests that preoccupation of the priests was as much with astronomy and the calendar as it was with religious rites. In addition, the priests apparently had firm control of all Maya learning as well as of ritual. Their duties included the computation of the days, months, and years; the supervision of festivals and ceremonies; administration of the sacraments; observance of the fateful days and seasons; the preservation of methods of divination, prophecies, events, and the cures for diseases as well as all other antiquities including the ability to read and write with the Maya letters and characters. The priests also kept the all-important genealogies.

The exact political relationship between major ceremonial centers, between major centers and minor centers, and between Mayas living in one geographic region and another is not understood, but the marked homogeneity of their writings, calendrics, architecture and art testifies to a rapid and free-flowing communication of knowledge between the peoples greatly beneficial to the intellectual progress of their civilization. Close religious communion—the gods were pan-Maya, with no local dieties—seems to indicate much travel and communication between the ruling priests of the various communities, and would even tend to indicate an arrangement for the exchange and common training of priests, and possibly of skilled artisans as well. By whatever manner achieved, the Maya gained a high degree of cultural solidarity—the sort of unanimity of outlook which encourages the growth of formality in religion and art.

We cannot rule out the possibility of tribal warfare between various Maya groups during the Classic Period, as we know they maintained standing armies and often used captives from other villages as sacrificial offerings in their rituals, but military might did not hold the scattered Maya "nation" together, nor were they controlled by a central government. Each community appears to have been a sovereign dominion within a loosely defined federation of minor states. Each community had a "high priest," or ruler, but the duties of ruling the state were shared by all members of the small ruling class. The office of the high priest never took on the significance of a king or dictator, as one might suppose. This remarkably smooth-running, yet informal, style of government must have depended upon a placid and well-adjusted citizenry, who held an unusually unanimous opinion as to proper behavior.

There is little evidence of massive conscription of labor. Maya public works, the largest of which are massive acropolis-like platforms of the major centers, in no way rival the Pyramid of Cheops of Egypt in size, for instance, and did not require the millions of manhours of hard unskilled labor to create. The renown of Maya architecture does not rest on its mass or size. On the other hand, the proportion of skilled labor to unskilled is much higher than in architecture of other civilizations and the quantity of outstanding stone sculpture work bears favorable comparison with that of any of the world. This would indicate that the Maya stonemasons and sculptors were fulltime specialists and that levies on the peasant population were largely in food rather than in unskilled labor.

If we were to attempt to analyze the factors which shaped the success of the Maya civilization, some become obvious. A deeply religious spirit, an appreciation of beauty and order, a desire for moderation in all things, an attitude of "live and let live" and the innate advantages of determination and discipline had to be governing factors. Without these, the Maya could not have overcome the threats of nature and built great "cities" in a most inhospitable jungle and adorned them with such beauty. This same spirit contributed to their achievements in astronomy and arithmetic, for the Maya sought to master the rules which they saw as governing the movements of the stars and even their gods. The great flowering of culture in the Classic Age marked the triumph of these best attributes.

Maya Thought and Customs

Religion, except in the final decadence of the Maya culture, was the single most important factor in the life of the Maya. Their dieties were many, the chief ones being the rain gods, the sun and the moon, and the creator god. There were four rain gods, called Chacs, each assigned a geographic direction and a color. They had evolved, supposedly, from snakes, which in many parts of the New World are believed to announce rain. The chacs were seen as storing rain in great jars, sprinkling it on the earth when needed; or hurling stone axes to earth to cause thunderbolts and lightning when angered.

The sun god and his mate, the moon goddess, were the first inhabitants of the world and the progenitors of the entire human race. Mayas living in Belize today often refer to the sun and moon as "our father" and "our mother." The sun is the chief god of hunting; the moon is the goddess of soil, birth and fertility. The Mayas paid little heed to the creator god; he was too far removed to be interested in mere man.

Mayas envisaged the sky supported by trees and by the upraised arms of gods called Bacabs at the four points of the compass. The sky was comprised of thirteen layers, lowest of which was thought of as a celestial dragon decorated with the symbols of planets, stars, night and darkness. Beneath the earth were nine underworlds, in the lowest of which dwelt the skeletal death god.

Occasionally, when a religious rite called for it, human sacrifice was necessary. At this time young boys, mostly orphans or bastards, became victims of the Nacom, a functionary of the priests, who opened the unfortunate's breast cavity and removed the heart. The body was then flung down the sloping face of the pyramid-temple to the courtyard below. Before and during rituals, food taboos and sexual abstinence were rigidly observed, and self-mutilation was carried out by jabbing needles and sting-ray spines through ears, cheeks, lips, tongue and penis, the blood being gathered to annoint the idols. In the later Classic Period, animals were substituted for humans in the sacrificial rites.

Throughout the year, agricultural rites and ceremonies were held for the benefit of various groups such as hunters, bee-keepers, fishermen, and artisans to entreat the gods to increase the game, or to provide an abundance of honey and wax, etc.

Young men lived apart from their families until they became married and learned the trade or art of their caste. Their free time was spent in gambling, entertaining prostitutes, or in practicing the ceremonial ball game common throughout Maya culture. The purpose of this soccer-like game is not fully known. It had certain religious significance and it is said that, when played in earnest at a religious festival, the losing team paid for their lack of skill with their lives. A double standard was obviously present, as the young girls were brought up in a very strict manner by their mothers and were punished severely for lapses of chastity. Marriages were arranged for with much care and rigidly governed by rules concerning genealogical lineage and status. Polygamy was allowed for only the highest nobility and adultery was punishable by death.

Ideas of personal beauty varied somewhat from ours. Both sexes had their frontal teeth filed in various patterns, and some even had them inlaid with small plaques of jade. Until married, young men painted their bodies black in the manner of professional warriors of the time, and tattooing and otherwise scarifying the body with decorations was popular for both married men and women. Slightly crossed eyes were held in great esteem by the nobility; parents attempted to induce this condition by hanging small jade beads over the forehead of their children.

Death was greatly dreaded as the person's future residence in the Cieba tree-shaded Paradise was in no way a certainty, even for priests.

TABLE 4

Archaeological Sites in Belize

Ceremonial Centers

Altun Ha	The most extensively excavated Classic center, 35 miles north of Belize City, the largest and most important site yet discovered in Belize.
Lubanntun	Large late-Classic site northwest of Punta Gorda, studied and surveyed in 1970.
Pusilha	Older center on Moho River near Lubanntun.
Caracol	Classic site noted for rare use of giant date glyphs on circular stone altars. Covers five square miles. Little of the site has been excavated.
Actun Balam	Located near Caracol in the Cayo District.
Xunantunich	Ancient center noted for elaborately carved stone and stucco friezes, located at the headwaters of the Belize River near the Guatemalan border at Benque Viejo. Xunantunich means "Maiden of the Rock," but is probably not the ancient name.
Cahal Pech	"Place of the Ticks," former center near San Ignacio in the Cayo District.
Tzimin Kax	"Mountain Cow" in the Cayo District.

Other sites of Maya Ruins and Populated areas with
Evidence of Maya Activity

Cayo District

Tzimin Kax, Mucnal Tunich, Baking Pot, Barton Ramie.

Orange Walk District

San Jose, Mun Diego, Kaxil Uinic, La Milpa, Indian Church,
Nohmul, San Estevan.

Stann Creek District

Pomona.

Maya Settlements

The ceremonial centers classified as "major" are Palenque and
Yuxchilan in the Mexican state of Chiapas; Tikal, Uaxactun and
Piedras Negras in the Guatemalan Department of Peten; Copan
in Honduras; and Uxmal and Labna in Yucatan. None of the
major centers is in Belize, but a number of important Classic
Age secondary centers have been located throughout the country and more will inevitably be found.

Not included on the list is the late post-classic center of
Santa Rita at Corozal whose superior murals in the Mixtec
fashion have been the subject of much study since they were
first investigated by the Carnegie Institute in 1939, but are not
typical of Classic Maya culture.

Archaeological work by Gordon R. Willey in the 1950's in
the Belize River Valley has shown a kind of settlement pattern
previously unknown in the Maya area during the Classic age.
These settlements, located on river terraces, are house-mound
clusters, ranging from a dozen mounds to more than 300. In
each cluster appear larger mounds thought to have been bases
for pyramids and palace-like buildings common in ceremonial
centers. Domestic refuse from areas flanking these house-
mounds have yielded poly-chrome and figure-painted ware and
vessels with elaborately carved design. Fine pottery was found

in association with burials and one Late Classic burial. was accompanied by a fine jade gorget and several objects of polished stone. One of these, a monolithic axe, bore an Ahau glyph.

These discoveries seem to indicate that, in this area at least, the gulf between major ceremonial centers and rural village was not as great as once imagined and the village dwellers apparently possessed some of the finer material items, participated in religious and ritual life, and at least knew and appreciated the intellectual attainments of the urban centers to a much larger extent than was supposed.

In 1964, Dr. David M. Pendergast of the Royal Ontario Museum, his wife, and a small team of Maya and Creole workers began excavation of a jungle-covered site 35 miles north of Belize City known as Altun Ha. Their work over the next several years revealed an important ceremonial center of the Classic Period surprisingly rich in archaeological treasure. This center apparently was an important trade center linking the Caribbean shore with Maya civilization of the interior. The Mayas of Altun Ha supplied the peoples of the inland settlements with pearls, shells, coral, and possibly fish bones and stingray spines—things that were ritually valuable. In return they received such things as jade and obsidian which are not available locally.

Typical of the Classic Maya centers, Altun Ha has a central ceremonial courtyard with its major pyramid, temples, smaller palace-structures and a reservoir which provided water for its ancient inhabitants. Still hidden under dense tropical growth are myriads of smaller mounds, some of which cover remains of ceremonial buildings, while the majority conceal the former residences of upper and middle class residents of Altun Ha. Within a square kilometer area surrounding the central court are more than 275 such structures, as yet unexplored. The remainder of the site, including at least a part of the sustaining area (the region in which corn, beans, squash and other crops were grown for the support of the settlement) covers roughly an additional 5 square kilometers and contains an additional 250 to 300 visible structures plus, very probably, a large number of house floors and smaller mounds now covered by brush and accumulated soil. Since the exact boundaries of the site cannot be traced with any precision and because the count of mounds is incomplete, there is no solid basis for an estimate of the population of this ancient settlement at its height. It is estimated, however, that at least 8,000 (and possibly as many as 10,000) Mayas resided in the immediate area with only 2,500 or less within the central square kilometer.

There is some evidence that a fairly substantial settlement existed here from very early times, perhaps by 200 B.C. By the first century B.C., if not earlier, its inhabitants had begun to construct permanent structures, with the major concentrations near the principal reservoir east of the present center. The reservoir is of artificial construction, in part, with a clay lining and dam at the south end, and it is probable that this construction was the initial effort at the site. Other small rainwater catch-basins around the site are apparently quarries for limestone which were adapted for this use.

The beginning of the second century A.D. saw a settlement of sufficient size and stability to undertake its first major construction effort in the form of a temple near the main reservoir. This appears to have been the focus of the ceremonial life of the center in the Pre-Classic and Proto-Classic times, lasting until about A.D. 250 when the period of the full flowering of the Maya civilization, the Classic Period, began. Probably at or near this time work was begun in what was to be the central precinct of the center for some six centuries, the effort culminating in the group of temples, priestly residences, and other buildings that are seen on the site today. Construction began with a northern plaza with four temples facing it which served as the ceremonial center until about A.D. 550 when the center was extended southward with the building of a fifth temple and a second plaza was added. Construction and reconstruction of at least some of the temples continued at Altun Ha until near the end of the ninth century A.D., though for possibly as much as a century and a half prior to this the size and quality of the new building had been declining. All construction ceased sometime prior to 900 A.D.

Graffiti scratched on the walls of one of the temples, showing a figure of a ball player, indicates that the ancient Maya game was known at Altun Ha. One broken and uncarved (or unfinished) stela has been found, but the absence of a number of stelae which one would expect at a center of the importance of Altun Ha suggests that this was a community in which the erection of such monuments played no major role in ceremonial activity. An unusual insight into the type of ceremonial activities that were performed by the priests was revealed, however, by the discovery of altars atop the tallest of the pyramids, called the Temple of the Masonry Altars, bits of jade, resin and charcoal, revealing that copal resin and jade objects, including beautifully carved pendants, had been smashed and thrown into the ceremonial fire as propitiatory offerings to the gods. Incense urns were found in concealed niches to add to the unearthly performance.

Of the important discoveries resulting from Pendergast's work at Altun Ha, most revealing were the priestly interments found to have begun here in very early times and to have continued in evolution of a unique tomb form, characteristic of Altun Ha throughout the six centuries of the Classic Period. Here Egyptian-like important personages were buried in concealed chambers deep within the temples. Of all the tombs uncovered, the most striking was the earliest tomb built into the Temple of the Masonry Altars and dates from A.D. 600 to A.D. 650. This burial, found in 1968 hidden deep within a huge stair block at the top of the pyramid, proved to be the richest yet discovered at Altun Ha and perhaps in the whole Central Lowland Region of the Maya civilization. It bore the remains of an elderly priest, accompanied by an array of jade objects including the largest carved jade artifact ever recovered in the Maya area: a giant full-round head of the sun god, Kinich Ahau, standing 6 inches high and weighing 9¾ pounds. In this region in pre-Columbian times jade was one of the most valuable materials. The head was fully carved, green and polished, in a way grotesque with a bulbous nose and crossed eyes so favored by the Mayas, but with a beauty both magical and mysterious.

The discovery of this artifact clearly established its former owner as a priest of Kinich Ahau, and the other artifacts found in the crypt must therefore be regalia identified with a priest of the Sun God. Also, if these assumptions are correct, perhaps this tall altar-topped pyramid was erected, not for mundane sacrificial use, but for the worship of the sun, a much more important and prestigious use. No other structure containing sacrificial altars of the type of The Temple of The Masonry Altars has been found in other Maya sites. With each new discovery, many more unanswered questions help to point out the tremendous gaps which still exist in our knowledge of the ancient Maya.

Decline of Maya Civilization

The Maya civilization of the central lowlands did not gradually decline. It came to a sudden and abrupt end. One day, some-time between the year 900 and 950 A.D., all writing, carving, building, erection of stelae, and astrological calculating ceased. The reason has been the subject of speculation for over a century by Maya historians, but it has only been in the past decade that any real evidence has been found to indicate the reason for this event.

For possibly as long as a century and a half prior to this time, the quality of the new buildings and of the artwork had been declining, probably the result of a general weakening of the organization which had bound the society together. Perhaps the building and rebuilding, without respite, of the ceremonial buildings had become objectionable to the common people from whose ranks this immense effort was required. Hundreds of tons of rock and soil for pyramids and platforms had to be carried on the backs of men, women, and children drafted for this work; huge numbers of goodly-sized trees had to be felled with stone axes for burning in lime kilns to produce the immense quantities of lime used as mortar and plaster for the structures   ᄀ for pavement of courts and walkways. By the late-Classic times, perhaps in part as a result of the increasing number of priests and in the gulf separating them from the middle and lower classes, discontent began to gnaw at the social structure, and is now thought to have brought about the collapse of the civilization which had thrived for possibly 2000 years in this inhospitable land. Excavations have revealed evidence to affirm that it was not an epidemic, a military invasion, pestilence, famine, or any of the other causes heretofore offered by way of explanation, but a violent popular peasant revolt against the priest-rulers that brought the sudden downfall to the Classic Maya society.

Many aspects of the fall of the Maya civilization remain unclear due, in large part, to the fact that an event of this sort, and of processes leading up to the event, leave little or nothing in the way of archaeological evidence. The same can be said of occurrences following the collapse, though here, some parts of the picture can be pieced together from scattered data.

In the first place, a body of a priest has been found, unburied, with a crushed skull. Three existing priestly tombs at Altun Ha show unmistakable signs of having suffered desecration, involving destruction of contents, burning of portions thereof, filling of the crypt with soil, and tossing of the roof slabs, which had been removed to uncover the tombs, back on the pile. Such activity, clearly not the work of looters, could only have taken place at the time of the final collapse of the civilization and is an indicator of the violence therein attended.

Historians have thought for many years that, following the downfall of the civilization, all the Mayas abandoned their settlements and fled to Yucatan. This may be partly true, yet we now know, from evidence found in Altun Ha and elsewhere, that at least a portion of the population remained after all ceremonial and traditional activities ceased. From large masses of refuse found at the base of one of the temples at Altun Ha, it looks very much as though the early post-Classic inhabitants (probably lower class peasant — farmers) lived on, in or around the ceremonial centers, dumping their garbage on what had once been sacred ground. This is logical, as all advanced learning

and knowledge of nearly all functions other than the agricultural cycle had been proprietary characteristics of the priest-
ruler class, and there is no reason to believe that there would
have been any disruption in the everyday activities of the lower
class in the absence of the priests. Architecture, sculptural art,
astronomy, and hieroglyphic writing, which had never formed a
part of their lives, died with the aristocracy. Simple ceremonies
still may have been held in the ceremonial centers, but gradually
the forest crept in and engulfed the unattended structures.

We know that there were people living in the lowlands as late
as the 13th and 14th centuries. Refuse found indicates that
they had been reusing buildings built during the Classic times
for their own residences and barns. There is some strength to
the belief that they did eventually all migrate north into Yucatan; at least it is certain that even the stragglers had all abandoned lowland centers by the time the British began settlements
in Belize.

Recent archaeological field work of a British expedition
working near San Estevan Village in Northern Belize indicates
that this area was occupied by the Mayas several centuries
earlier than had been thought. Both the size and density of the
Maya centers in the area between the New River and Rio
Hondo, north of Orange Walk, have been found to be much
greater than previously recorded. Among the expedition's discoveries are a "factory" for making flint axes and other tools,
and a human effigy vessel dating from before 300 A.D.

The expedition, which concluded the first phase of its work
in July, 1973, is sponsored jointly by the British Museum and
the University of Cambridge. Work is planned to resume in
1974 and there is speculation that this site may provide some
important clues to the processes involved in the mysterious
collapse of Mayan civilization, as evidence has been discovered
here of a continuity of occupation from pre-Classic times to
well after the ceremonial activities had ceased in the ninth
century. In fact, one building excavated was of the Mayapan
era, built as late as the twelfth to fourteenth century.

MODERN COMMUNITIES

The Mayas living in Belize today belong to three separate and distinct groups, speaking three different Maya dialects (related somewhat the same as Spanish is to Italian), and living in three widely separated areas. All are relative newcomers to Belize and only one, the Mopan in central Belize, are descendants of Maya peoples who once lived in this country. The infiltration of Mayas from Yucatan and Guatemalan Peten Province has only been since about 1850.

These Mopan Mayas speak a version of the Cholan dialect, the language of the priests who wrote the codices and inscribed the stelae of the Classic Period. The Kekchi Maya, who have taken a dominant role among the various Maya tribes since Spanish Conquest times, have expanded from the Alta Verapaz region of Guatemala to colonize southern Belize, once a Chol-speaking area, and the Mayas of northern Belize are Yucatec Mayas who are recent arrivals from Mexican Yacatan.

The Mayas today cling steadfastly to their Indian identity, although their life is an unusual mixture of ancient tradition and European customs. The ancient Maya calendar still governs the annual ceremonial cycle, though the "long count," astronomy, and means of notation are unknown. The Mayas, especially the Kekchi Mayas, have an unusual passion for cleanliness. They bathe at least twice a day, perhaps a carryover from the Classic days when they ritually attended the steam baths common in every center. Their art survives in boldly colored textiles, but they no longer paint murals, frescoes, or do stone sculpting.

The Mayas in Belize remain a rural people living in small isolated villages surrounded by cornfields. Their social-political-religious unit, the village, though embedded in the larger economy of the country, holds the allegiance of its inhabitants, thus making incorporation into the mainstream of Belizean life difficult as yet. The universal religion of the Mayas today is Roman Catholic, though their own folk heroes and ancient gods are so intermixed with the Catholic saints and religious and civic officials, and ceremonies so interchanged as to be unrecognizable by either the national government or the church. In recent times, great improvement has been made in raising the standard of living for the Mayas, with required school attendance for the children and improved health standards and economic level.

The Belizean government recognizes the value of preserving Maya traditions and folklore. Belize considers all Maya relics a part of the national patrimony and has begun enforcing strict laws to protect Maya archaeological sites from vandalism and looting, and makes every effort to keep artifacts from leaving the country. It supports a national museum for exhibiting pre-Columbian Maya artwork and Maya history is taught in the schools.

Land Of Pirates and Loggers (1600-1800)

Europeans first sighted the coast of Belize one day in 1502 as Christopher Columbus passed on his fourth and final voyage to the New World. His view of the Cockscomb Range, rising from a misty green jungle and framed between the white coral heads of the Barrier Reef, could not have been more spectacular than one has today, approaching Belize International Airport. Nothing has occurred in four hundred and seventy years to alter the peacefully dramatic setting of this quartzite and granite mountain range which has served as a landmark for travelers since Sir Walter Raleigh and Henry Morgan played a game of "Hide and Seek," for real lives and Spanish gold, among the thousands of tiny coral cays along the Belizean coast: the Spanish Main.

Since the first sighting of the Caribbean coast of Central America in 1502 and the subsequent explorations by Spaniards (Cortez may have passed through a portion of British Honduras in 1524), no attempt was made to settle any of this region by the Spanish until 1531. At this time Davilla, acting under the instructions of Montejo, Governor of Yucatan, founded an outpost at Chetumal (then called Payo Obispo) located in Quintana Roo, Mexico just a few miles north of the present Mexico-Belize border. The coast of Belize was visited by exploration parties from Chetumal but pronounced "unsuitable for settlement" and virtually abandoned by the Spanish who had an unusual fear of its dense, forbidding jungles and unhealthy climate.

Spanish priests based at Chetumal, however, conducted missionary efforts among the apostate Indians of the upper Belize River. These Indians ostensibly had been converted to Christianity by Dominicans from Vera Paz in the 1550's.

On May 14, 1603, Peter Wallace, a Scotsman and privateer, left England with six ships and King James' blessing, bound for the Gulf of Honduras in search of Spanish treasure ships. No novice, Wallace had served as Sir Walter Raleigh's lieutenant on many similar ventures and he himself had previously been Governor of the island of Tortuga, the infamous pirates' lair northwest of Haiti, before it became French in the 1650's. Wallace spent some time, in 1617, encamped with eighty men in a mangrove swamp at the mouth of the Belize River where the City of Belize is now located. This may have been the first landing on Belizean soil by an Englishman. Some give credence to the belief that the very name Belize is a corruption of the name Wallace (pronounced in Spanish Valeese and eventually Belize), but there are several probable theories for the origin of the name of this country.

First Settlement—1638   Wallace's hideout may not have constituted a Settlement, but in 1638, in search of a cargo of logwood, a crew of English seamen became shipwrecked and took refuge here. The city of Belize, at least, dates her founding from that time. They took up residence in a few houses surrounded by a crude wooden fence left by Peter Wallace and his crew in the general area where the national warehouses now stand. They were joined that year by another group of seafaring settlers from Jamaica, and in the next decade privateers from several nations made their base of operations at St. George's Cay in Belize, carrying out raids against the homeward-bound Spanish plate fleets heavy-laden with New World gold and silver.

Piracy

The Belizean coastline is as if created for piracy. Everywhere the coral reefs and sandbars provide protection behind which the pirates' shallow-draft sloops could escape their heavier pursuing men-of-war. Among the pirates and privateers plying these waters were Dutchman "Pegleg" Jol, who operated off of the Turneffe Islands, and Piet Heyn, a Dutch admiral who, in 1628, captured an entire fleet of bullion-transporting galleons, homeward bound, near Cuba. A French surgeon, Alexander Olivier Exquemelin, joined a crew of twenty-eight buccaneers against a large fleet of Spanish ships and succeeded in capturing the largest and heaviest galleon. With his plunder he returned to France and wrote a book, published in 1678, of his and his companions' exploits in the Caribbean. This book drew an immediate influx of new adventurers from all over the world to the West Indies to seek an illicit fortune during an age of exploration and discovery, adventure and romance, carnage, plunder and exploitation without precedence.

The great shortage of gold in Europe, due to the hoarding by national treasuries and the lack of new production, helped to arouse a gold craze unrivaled by even the California Gold Rush of 1849. It drew violent, rugged individualists from all walks of life; sons of rich noblemen in search of adventure and angry renegades from the poverty of Europe's slums, with a lust for gold and an obsession for revenge against society.

Spanish trade was carried on in a very orderly and routine way. Every year in the springtime a fleet of ships, *La Flota*, set out from Cadiz, Spain for Vera Cruz by way of Santa Domingo. In the autumn a second fleet, *the Galleons*, sailed from Cadiz to the mainland, making for Porto Bella by way of Cartagena. Every year the ships followed the same route. They could sail only from Cadiz, and could call only at certain ports. After some months in Porto Bello, the Galleons, having taken on their cargo of silver bars, chests of gold, hides, tallow, corn, wine, indigo, and spices, set out on the return journey to Spain. Sometimes stopping at the mouth of the San Juan River, they sailed north by way of the Yucatan Straits to Havana where they waited for the *Flota* from Vera Cruz. The whole fleet, bound for Cadiz, then crossed the Atlantic together. This routine was as well known by pirate captains as the Spanish admirals themselves, and they laid in ambush along the route in fast sloops manned by armed and desperate renegades anxious for the first sight of the slow, heavy galleons and frigates, their sides swollen with rich treasure, ripe for plundering.

Soon after the Discovery of America, Pope Alexander the Sixth, with a view toward settling an impending dispute between Spain and Portugal, issued his famous decretum by which he gave Spain the whole of America with the exception of Portuguese Brazil. Thus began an era of attempted Spanish exclusion from the Americas and the Caribbean islands of all foreigners, and the prevention of trade by other nations with the Americas.

Great Britain, with an eye toward breaking Spanish monopoly and its domination of the New World, condoned and even commissioned piracy in the West Indies. Three distinct strata in the social structure of this violent profession developed with subtle and rather academic distinctions (difficult to discern by their victims, to be sure). They were the buccaneer, the privateer and the pirate.

The buccaneer considered himself a soldier in the service of his country, and most often raided mainland settlements, plundered, and retreated to the safety of the sea. These guerrilla tactics were part of a general scheme to demoralize and loosen Spain's hold on the native population. The most noteworthy buccaneer, Sir Henry Morgan, captured the Spanish fortress of Porto Bello by sending defenseless priests and nuns up the scaling ladders, to their certain deaths, ahead of his men. Once inside the walls, the buccaneers destroyed the churches and tortured the priests and civic leaders.

The attack on Porto Bello yielded 300,000 pieces of eight; that on Marcacaibo a few months later produced 280,000, and he came away from the capture of Panama in 1670 with 780,000 pieces of eight. Morgan worked out of Jamaica, which had been taken from Spain in 1655. Sir Thomas Modyford, the

Governor of Jamaica, encouraged Morgan and the other British buccaneers, who made their base of operations Port Royal on that island, to raid the Spanish strongholds on the mainland. Gold began to flow into Port Royal and into Modyford's pockets. Port Royal's narrow alleys were crowded with lines of black natives carrying casks of gold from the ships at the wharf, gentlemen in fine brocade hurrying to Littleton's tavern, and seamen with ears heavy with rings of gold swaggering up Thames Street.

The strength of the buccaneers and their presence in Jamaica guaranteed Britain's hold on that island and also offered some security to the British settlers in Belize and Campeche on the mainland. Buccaneering continued until after the treaties of 1667 and 1670 in which Britain promised its suppression. Although Sir Henry Morgan had been commissioned, knighted, and made Lt. Governor of Jamaica for his fearless buccaneering as pacification to Spain in 1670, he and Governor Modyford, were called to England and imprisoned in the Tower of London for having commissioned buccaneering and profited therefrom, for a brief time before being freed.

Captain William Kidd, a Scotsman born in 1645, was a merchant ship owner in New York before serving with England in King William's War with France. After the war he remained at sea in his own ship, commissioned as a privateer to prey on ships of unfriendly nations. The spoils of these raids were his compensation. Kidd voluntarily surrendered to face charges of piracy and murder in 1701. He was subsequently found guilty and hanged at Execution Dock, London, on May 23 of that year. Many think he was sacrificed in an effort to appease nations demanding an end to officially-sanctioned piracy at sea.

The third and lowliest class of seagoing hijacker was the common pirate who acknowledged loyalty to no one and took his treasure where and when he found it. Of these the most notorious was surely Edward "Blackbeard" Teach, so nicknamed because of his greasy black hair which covered most of his face. He was distinctively repulsive and the stereotype for the pirate of fiction with bulging eyes, deformed ears, and broken nose. He spent most of his time in a state of drunken-ness. So feared was Blackbeard that on one occasion in April, 1717, sailing off the Belize Coast in the Gulf of Honduras, he overtook a fleet of four sloops escorting the ship *Protestant Ceasar* from Boston; upon recognizing his personalized version of the dreaded "Jolly Roger" flag, all the crewmen of the merchant ships abandoned their ships and fled to shore, leaving ships and cargo for his taking. Being more braggart than villain, Blackbeard did not deserve the legend that has grown up around him. He died in hand-to-hand combat with a British Naval Officer named Maynard on November 22, 1718.

During the hurricane season in early fall, when all shipping in the Caribbean stopped, buccaneers, privateers and pirates alike, tied up in ports like St. George's Cay, the low mangrove island opposite Belize City's waterfront, to spend their free time in merrymaking and debauchery. One senses a spirit of swash-buckling adventure in Belize even today. It is not unusual to hear whispered talk of buried treasure and one of the week-end pastimes of natives, and tourists as well, is digging on any of the many off-shore cays for what "Pegleg" Jol or Peter Wallace may have left behind. Rotten hulls of pirate ships, lying in the clear cerulean water of the bay amid a coral forest, still give up an occasional piece-of-eight or gold doubloon to a modern-day buccaneer with air tank and flippers.

Logwood Discovered

While the Belize Settlement in the mid-seventeenth century was not officially recognized, it was loosely governed by Sir Thomas Modyford, the Governor of Jamaica. On May 23, 1667, Great Britain signed a treaty with Spain. Spain granted Britain free-dom of trade, if Britain would suppress piracy. Humanitari-anism was not the chief motivating factor in Britain's agreement to end piracy, however. The need for trade and the discovery of logwood (Haematoxylon campechianum), used as a fixing dye, had opened a whole new industry in the West Indies. The value of this tropical wood, also improperly called "Brazil Wood," soared when a Dutchman discovered a method of fast-setting the dye in 1660. While logwood dye had already been introduced to Europe by the Spanish, this new technique created a great demand and logwood was being sold in England for $500 a ton. Early British buccaneers had not fully appreciated the value of logwood, highly prized by the Spaniards, until the chance sale in Europe of a logwood cargo brought over by one Captain James. James's windfall opened great possibilities to later privateers when the policy of suppression began to make things hot for their piracy in the Caribbean.

Governor Modyford was quick to realize that the Bay Settlement of Belize was a ready source for this material and urged his government to officially recognize the Settlement as a colony and begin exploiting this resource. From this point on Great Britain began to take an interest in the Belize Settlement, but it wasn't until over a century later that any real effort was made to officially govern it, other than rare communications made through the Governors of Jamaica.

By 1670 the population of the Bay Settlement had reached seven hundred, bolstered by refugees from the Bay of Terminos and other British settlers forced out by the Spanish, and by Mosquito Indians who moved in to cut logwood. Many of the Baymen became loggers. Mature logwood trees are approximately two feet in diameter with short, irregular trunks. They sometimes reach a height of fifty feet. The trees are cut down and stripped of their sapwood in the forest, then the logs are transported to a dye mill where the important dye substance is extracted by boiling the reddish-brown heartwood chips in water. Originally used solely as a dye and stain, it was later used in making ink, and today is used in certain vegetable food coloring products. Loggers handling this wood daily soon acquire an almost permanent red stain on their hands.

Trade with the United States in logwood was started by the Settlement, but not without difficulty. Spain declared that the trade agreement did not extend to logwood and confiscated all ships, other than her own, carrying this product. The British pirates-turned-traders found themselves, in a reversal of roles, being the prize for marauding Spanish *guarda costas*,—patrol ships sent to hunt foreign vessels. Logwood trade remained the most important Belizean industry until it reached its peak in the second half of the nineteenth century, after which logwood dye was largely replaced by synthetic dyes, and loggers turned their attention to mahogany and chicle.

Godolphin Treaty—1670

An important treaty was concluded between Spain and Great Britain in 1670. Called the Treaty of Madrid, or Godophin Treaty, after one of its authors, Sir William Godolphin, K.B. of England, it confirmed to Great Britain: "*sovereignty, dominion, possession, and propriety in all the lands, regions, islands, colonies, and places whatsoever, being or situated in the West Indies, or any part of America, which the said King of Great Britain and his subjects do at present hold and possess.*" . . . The wording of this treaty has led to much controversy.

There is a question as to whether British Honduras was considered a colony at this time, as it had neither Governor nor constitution, and had not been formally established as a colony by any British authority. Spain later contended that the treaty was meant to include only those areas recognized diplomatically at the time of its writing. There is an article incorporated by footnote in the treaty that lists a number of the territories to which it refers; the Honduras Bay Colony is not listed. The treaty did assure British possession of Jamaica, Belize's nearest friendly neighbor over six hundred miles away, which Britain had captured and governed since 1655.

Even Godolphin, reluctant to offend Spain over this tiny frontier colony surrounded by Spanish territory, acknowledged the Spanish contention, but suggested that the settlers be allowed to continue wood-cutting in the area. The colonists were left to their own devices, without legal rights, while England offered ineffectual diplomatic effort on their behalf. The only form of government in Belize was their own magistracy, democratically elected at annual "town meetings" similar to those in early New England. The upshot of this was that Belize developed from early democratic origins and has remained, due to this, the least "British" of all the British colonies on the West Indies, and the most culturally independent.

The logical outcome of the new policy of appeasement of Spain was the recall of Governor Modyford from Jamaica and his replacement by an administrator who would at least try to enforce the new policy. As has been mentioned, Modyford and Henry Morgan were brought back to England, lodged in London Tower for appearance sake, and subsequently allowed to return to Jamaica without ever being brought to trial or deprived of any of the loot they had acquired from their cooperative buccaneering. Modyford later died in Jamaica, an honored and respected gentleman. Morgan swaggered about Port Royal living grandly off the gains of ten years of lustful rapine. Modyford's successor, Sir Thomas Lynch, made a strenuous effort to carry out the new policy, though without an armed force he could do little to suppress piracy. Henry Morgan was drafted as Lt. Governor on the dubious theory that "it takes a thief to catch a thief," and charged with the assignment of putting an end to the very pillaging and destruction which had been his forte.

Morgan's role as a "policeman of the Caribbean" was ludicrous at first. In 1677, six British buccaneering ships sacked Santa Marta without being reprimanded and Captain John Coxon, his old shipmate and protege, raided the ports of the Gulf of Honduras in 1678. When he landed in Port Royal with his ships loaded with cochineal, indigo, and cocoa, Morgan allowed him to refit his ships before sailing to New England, the best market for stolen goods at that time.

Upon his return to the West Indies on March 23, 1679, Coxon joined a group of eight privateering captains in launching an ambitious large-scale attack on the Spanish settlements on the Pacific side of the Isthmus of Panama, reached by marching overland. They seized Spanish ships and sacked many small harbors before Coxon and his men returned, on foot, to their anchorage in the Caribbean, laden with treasure. The remainder of the party, led by Captain Bartholomew Sharp, returned home by way of Cape Horn. Not only were the deeds of this last desperate act of organized piracy outrageous enough in their own right, but the raid was ill-timed, taking place precisely when England was negotiating a treaty with Spain in Windsor. Both the West Indian business interests in London and the local merchants in the Antilles were determined to legally establish trade with Spain, which could only be accomplished with the cessation of such hostilities.

One concession which Britain was willing to make to Spain in negotiating a Caribbean trade agreement was the peaceable removal of her woodcutters from the mainland (Campechy and the Honduran Bay Colony), whose existence had always been a grievance to the Spanish monarchy. For this purpose the infamous Captain John Coxon was recruited by Governor Lynch, at Morgan's suggestion, in 1682, and was commissioned to proceed with a small fleet of ships to the Bay Colony to remove all British citizens from their mainland enclave.

Fortunately for the colony Captain Coxon's crews, unhappy in having to serve on this mission for seamen's wages with no booty to share, mutinied enroute, put Coxon ashore at Belize, and proceeded with the King's vessels on a pirating venture of their own. Rather than return to Jamaica under these circumstances, and fearful of punishment for the Panama raid which had aroused public opinion against him even in Jamaica, Coxon remained in Belize as a permanent resident, working as a logwood trader the rest of his life. By this time, every Governor in the West Indies had been alerted to apprehend the perpetrators of the Panama "outrage." Coxon's crews were hunted down and brought to Port Royal in irons, where three of his mutinous Captains were sentenced to "swing and sun-dry" by Sir Henry Morgan. Coxon died in Belize in 1689, where he had lived quietly among his Mosquito Indian friends in his final years.

That was how Governor Thomas Lynch described the "Coxon incident" in an official communique to Secretary Sir Leoline Jenkins, but there are several versions of this event cited by historians, and Captain Coxon has been reported to have taken part in buccaneering exploits after the time he supposedly "retired" in Belize.

By 1685 Morgan had a small British Navy frigate squadron at his disposal and waged an effective war on pirates, most of whom left the West Indies, or became legitimate logwood shippers. As if to mark an end of an era, Sir Henry Morgan died in 1688, and his old Port Royal—wicked, opulent, and shabby—paid the price for its sins, or so the pious believed, and disappeared beneath the sea in the great earthquake of 1692.

The end of the age of buccaneering was not, of course, the end of Caribbean fighting; it merely introduced a new, more formal policy of organized warfare fought by admirals instead of free-lance freebooters. The West Indies, from the beginning of the eighteenth century, became more under the direct influence of European conventions of war, peace, and diplomacy.

Britain's primary goal in the Caribbean was that of "forcing a trade," to allow her to trade freely and completely in the slave trade bonanza shared by the Dutch and the French. By the seventeenth century a trade agreement with Spain, called an *Asiento*, had come to be regarded as so valuable a concession that its grant acquired all the characteristics of an international treaty. It loomed large in Spanish-Anglo foreign policies.

It took a war, fought largely in Europe, to eventually enable the British to extract from Spain an *Asiento* for legalized trade in the Caribbean. The Treaty of Utrecht in 1713 granted an *Asiento*, together with other trading rights in Spanish America, to the South Sea Company, a private British firm founded expressly for the purpose.

Only exhaustion and defeat could have induced the Spanish Government to consent to these concessions. The Spanish crown still claimed lordship over the Americas, but that was, in reality, an empty pretense. Great tracts of land and forest remained unoccupied and unexplored, hostile tribes of Indians occupied large amounts of the mainland claimed by Spain, and many of the islands were already irretrievably lost to the Dutch, French and English. But Spanish claims were not thereby abated; according to Spanish statesmen, what Spain had not expressly granted to others was still theirs by right.

As for commerce, if Spain was unable to prevent foreign settlement, as in the case of the Baymen of Belize, still less could she prevent the foreign settlers from trading with their own colonial subjects. But in the face of facts, Spanish diplomats insisted on an exclusive monopoly of trade and the right of regulating all seaborne commerce in the Caribbean. Such still being the official Spanish Caribbean policy, Spanish statesmen especially smarted at the concessions forced on them by the victorious British at the Treaty of Utrecht. For a time at least Britain could trade openly, in the guise of the South Sea Company, while its competitors had to continue their illicit smuggling, running the risk of attack of the *guarda costas* and the confiscation of cargoes.

By the terms of the *Asiento*, Britain had the right to supply Spanish colonies with Negro slaves and to send one ship of 500 tons each year to Porto Bello and Vera Cruz. In the hands of the South Sea Company the concession was regarded as doubly valuable as, in addition to the legal trade it assured, it also offered opportunity for a heavy increase in the dealing in contraband which speedily came to permeate every phase of the company's activities. The result was that a great stream of illicit traffic was carried on surrepitiously under the cover of the South Sea Company's legitimate trade. This, in addition to the already steady illegal commerce carried on by private traders operating from Jamaica, Barbados, and the other English West Indian Islands, brought wholesale complaints and outright attacks from the Spanish patrols.

Britain had far from free sailing in the Caribbean. Peaceful and lawful traders were seized, condemned, and sold in prize in frequent incidents. Two brief wars, in 1718 and 1727, tested the validity of the *Asiento* leading up to the resolution of the British House of Commons in 1738 that stated "it was the undoubted right of the British subjects to sail their ships in any part of the seas of America." British seamen claimed 95,000 pounds sterling for depredations to their shipping by Spain, and in 1739, war was declared between Britain and Spain. It was nicknamed the "War of Jenkin's Ear," and merged the following year into "King George's War." Central America became deeply involved in the European conflict as the British pushed their "trading and raiding" activities along the entire coastline from Compeche to Costa Rica.

Start of the Spanish Conflict in Belize—1718

The presence of a foreign community in the heartland of New Spain had been a constant source of irritation to Spain. In 1725, Antonio de Figueroa Silva was appointed Governor of Yucatan, and was charged with the express assignment of ridding the Mexican Peninsula of all "logwood-stealing foreign trespassers." First dealing successfully with the British settlements of Luguna de Terminos in the Gulf of Campeche and in the Cape Catoche areas, he turned to the Belize Settlement with threats of sending all her citizens to the Mexican mines. Spanish diplomats communicated similar threats to London in 1722, and again in 1728. Meanwhile, Figueroa had the City of Bacalar rebuilt as a fort and garrisoned it with troops to serve as his base of operations against the Bay Settlement.

The first encounter had already occurred in 1718, the year of a brief Anglo-Spanish War, when a large force of Spanish and Indian soldiers entered the colony from Guatamalan Peten in an attempt to dispossess the woodcutters of Belize. Being intimidated by the strong determination of the Englishmen, they contented themselves with building a fort on the northwest branch of the Belize River, near Spanish Lookout, occupying it for about four years and accomplishing little.

In Bacalar, Governor Figueroa began large-scale preparations for a combined land and sea expedition against Belize, which he hoped would result in its complete destruction. Learning of this, the Baymen prepared for resistance by importing a large number of friendly Indians from the Mosquito Coast to help them. Believing aggression to be the best line of defense, the intrepid woodcutters set out by sea to Ascension Bay and attacked the Spanish city of Chuhuhu, which they sacked and pillaged before being driven back to their ships by a large force of Figueroa's soldiers. In retaliation, in 1730 a Spanish man-of-war entered the Belize River and sank seven logwood freighters.

In anticipation of the attack they knew to be imminent, the Baymen strengthened their fortifications at the mouth of the Belize River and mustered all available manpower to the city, including the Mosquito volunteers and Negro slaves recently arrived from Jamaica. This at best, could only have amounted to a few hundred men. It wasn't until February 22, 1733 that the Spanish fleet finally sailed out of the Bay of Esperitu Santo with over seven hundred soldiers, bound for Belize.

Figueroa's plan was to land his troops on the coast north of the mouth of the Belize River and, while the fleet engaged the enemy from the sea, the soldiers would attack from the flank. This proved successful. The Spanish forces advanced as far as Haulover Creek, captured the city, burned many vessels, took captives and razed most of the city. Figueroa left, believing that his mission had been accomplished, but this time, as always, the Baymen returned to rebuild their city, more determined than ever to hold on to their tiny isolated empire in the Caribbean.

Logwood harvesting was still very profitable, but since the woodcutters had to rely on the rivers for transportation, only those areas near the water could be logged. As the crop was harvested, the loggers had to range over an increasingly larger area each year. This required more and more time and manpower. The answer was provided by enterprising entrepeneurs who imported African slaves to the Settlement from various West Indian communities where trade in slaves had flourished since 1518. It is estimated that there were over 15 million Africans introduced into the Americas in a period of three hundred years. While those Africans, brought to Belize to provide the additional labor required in extending the logging operations, were technically slaves until their emancipation in 1838, they worked shoulder to shoulder with their masters and fought the Spaniard with equal zeal. They proved to be courageous and loyal allies and the sense of comradeship shared between the British settlers and the newcomers, unique in American history, has lasted to the present day in Belize which is nearly free of racial tension.

Another Spanish-Anglo war in 1739 spread to the Caribbean, and once more Belize became one of the chief areas of conflict. British warships were needed at sea, and those at Belize were withdrawn, leaving the Settlement with little defense. The settlers petitioned Britain for recognition as a crown colony and for protection. Before an answer could be received, Spanish troops marched on the logging camps along New River, destroyed them, and were proceeding toward Belize City when the war came to an end. The truce of 1748 was followed by two years of diplomatic negotiations, much of it concerning the future of Belize, but no understanding was reached. The British refused to recognize the Settlement as a colony, yet defended their right to its mahogany and logwood. Meanwhile, Spain reinstituted her campaign for the expulsion of the woodcutters.

Skirmishes with the Spaniards became so frequent and demoralizing that many of the families of the Bay Settlement retreated for a time to the British-held island of Roatan, the largest of the Bay Islands, but a victory of two hundred and fifty machete-wielding loggers over a Spanish force of fifteen hundred from Peten on April 5, 1754, near Labouring Creek, gave the settlers renewed confidence and several months of peace. Peace was sharply broken the following year, however, when taken by surprise by a large Spanish force, they were again forced to flee down the coast, leaving their homes to be burnt to the ground. As the Spaniards withdrew from the ruined city, the Belizeans moved back, to once more rebuild their homes, cheered only by the fact that the Spaniards had not destroyed a large stock of mahogany logs left on the "barquediers." Once their homes were rebuilt, a Public Meeting was held at which it was decided, in spite of official British objections, to fortify their town. Toward this end, a military engineer was hired to direct the erection of a fort on Haulover Creek. The stockade was armed with cannon and swivel guns, and a guard of forty soldiers was posted there full-time. These soldiers wore civilian dress, "like Baymen, in frocks and trousers," so as not to be conspicuous to the Spanish.

The Treaty of Paris

During the Seven Years' War in Europe, which began in 1756, Britain, endeavoring to induce Spain to join her against France, offered among other things to abandon all logging camps established by her subjects in the Bay of Honduras and the Mosquito Coast since 1748. Thus again Britain was using Belize as a valuable "hold card" with which to bargain with Spain. By the subsequent Treaty of Paris written on February 10, 1763, which concluded the war, Spain guaranteed the British the right to cut, load, and carry away logwood unmolested, and to erect all necessary buildings for this purpose, as well as granting the right to build and occupy homes within those districts. In return, Britain agreed to demolish all fortifications (this meant losing the stockade at Haulover), and acknowledged Spain's right, as sovereign, to periodic inspection.

The Treaty of Paris, as written by the Spanish commissioner, the Marques de Grimaldi, was not a well-conceived document and opened the way for future complications. It was a virtual recognition of British right to occupy, indefinitely, a portion of Spanish territory. Although Spain resolutely reserved her sovereignty in the soil, no limits were made to the encroachments of the woodcutters, nor were they in any way made subject to Spanish rule. The settlers in Belize, however, were disappointed in the treaty. It spoke of logwood cutting but did not mention other species. Mahogany had begun to be an important trade item. The demand for mahogany resulted from a recent increase of the popularity among English cabinet-makers for mahogany in making fine furniture. During the eighteenth century mahogany nearly replaced walnut, which had until that time been widely in use. The cabinet-makers preferred it because of the wider widths that were available, and the general public liked its lovely grain and rich coloring. The possession of mahogany furniture became a status symbol in Britain, an indication of a person's success and prosperity. Their most serious objection to the Treaty was to the British agreement to the demolition of their stockade in Belize City. They knew that, without the fortification and soldiers, they would again be vulnerable to attack in case of another war with Spain.

Spanish colonial authorities from Bacalar made yearly visitations to the logging camps to insure that the various obligations and restrictions of the Treaty of Paris were being carried out. A major disagreement between these Spanish envoys and the Belizeans living along the Hondo River, the northern boundary between Mexico and modern Belize, grew so heated that Governor Estenoz of Yucatan ordered all loggers to be withdrawn from that region and woodcutting confined to the area between the Belize and New Rivers, and no further than 20 leagues from the coast. The woodcutters petitioned Governor Lyttleton of Jamaica in April, 1764 for help in this crisis. After six months of diplomatic exchanges and threats between Spain and Britain, Governor Estenoz did rescind his order and allowed the settlers to reestablish their camps in the north. To insure their safety, Admiral Sir William Burnaby, commander-in-chief of His Majesty's fleet in the West Indies, was dispatched to Belize with four war ships.

Burnaby's Code—1764

During the several months spent in Belize, Sir William Burnaby worked with the Baymen in drafting a democratic constitution, a formalization of their existing system of government by magistrates popularly elected by vote at Public Meetings. Thus the country's first codified set of law was completed in 1765 and Burnaby returned to Jamaica, leaving the Settlement to its own self-protection and self-government.

Burnaby's Code, as the new constitution was called, was a uniquely practical document based on the "customs of the Bay" and dealt with such immediate problems as fines for personal misbehavior and for the kidnapping of sailors for use as woodcutters. (One amusing exception was that the code allowed the kidnapping of any steersman, since they were so badly needed, but only for one trip.) The code went further than establishing rules of good conduct. It provided the means for the making of new laws, collecting taxes, and administering justice. It provided for a Public Meeting, an assembly of all free residents, to vote on all laws. At this Public Meeting two Magistrates were to be elected, together with five other citizens, to act as judges in settling civil disputes and imposing penalties. Another body of seven Magistrates were elected to serve as civil servants and carry out the decisions of the Public Meeting. These persons so elected by the assembly served without pay and were, in fact, fined if they did not carry out their duties after being elected.

Renewed Hostilities with Spain—1776–1783

While heavily engaged in the American War of Independence, both France and Spain took the opportunity of declaring war on Britain. This development presented a severe menace to the determined settlers of Belize. They began at once to refortify the mouth of the Belize River and St. George's Cay where many now had their homes. An expedition was sent out from Belize in an attempt to surprise the Spanish and capture Bacalar. The new Yucatan governor, Don Roberto Rivas Vetancur, had anticipated this move and was waiting for the Belizeans with eight hundred men. Rivas drove the Baymen back over the Hondo River and then proceeded on, with a fleet of fifteen small armed vessels and one schooner, to St. George's Cay which he easily captured and destroyed.

The City of Belize was saved from another ravage only by the chance arrival of three British warships, one the brig *H.M.S. Badger* under command of the nineteen-year-old Lieutenant Horatio Nelson, in his first command. Since July, 1777 this squadron had been working out of Jamaica, protecting local trade and patrolling in search of American privateers. Since the War of Independence, trade with the former North American Colonies had been prohibited. Passing close to the Belizean coast, they had become aware of unusual activity on St. George's Cay and diverted their convoy to Belize to investigate.

The Spaniards had enough warning to escape ahead of the approaching British warships. The Spaniards made off with 140 prisoners: men, women and children taken from their homes on St. George's Cay, and other loot, including many small vessels. Rivas continued into the interior, sailing up the New River toward the River Hondo, burning homes and destroying camps along the way. Once across the Hondo, the prisoners who survived the cruel treatment to which they were subjected on the way, were forced to march all the way to Merida from where they were shipped to Havana and imprisoned in dungeons until July, 1782. Those settlers fortunate enough to escape capture fled down the coast or retreated into the jungle, too reduced in number to resist the Spanish army and without many of their leaders captured by Rivas. Belize City, for a time, was totally deserted. Reinforcements, in the form of settlers from the British colony of Roatan Island, arrived shortly with Colonel Edward Despard to help rebuild Belize. By the time the war ended in 1783, the city had been restored to near normalcy.

The first immigration to the Bay Settlement from the United States occurred during this time. Several families with British loyalties left the American colonies during the Revolutionary War and some found their way to Cay Caulker, where today reside many of the colony's oldest families.

Treaty of Versailles—1783. By the Count of Aranda & The Duke of Manchester

Peace returned with the signing of the Treaty of Versailles on September 1, 1783. This time, the treaty defined the limits of the territory and the rights of the woodcutters. The boundaries, now fixed as unalterable, were the Belize River on the south, the Hondo River on the north, and the frontier of Peten Itza on the West. Navigation on the Belize and Hondo Rivers was to be open to both countries; the exact location for the erection of woodcutting camps was to be subject to approval of the Spanish commissioner; and it was provided that the foregoing stipulations should not be "considered derogating in any wise" to the rights of Spanish sovereignty. All British subjects living without the prescribed district were to retire within before the expiration of eighteen months; fishing rights were granted on the cays, but no "establishments" could be made there.

Once more the people of Belize were disappointed. The treaty again made no provision for mahogany cutting; while fishing rights were included, no provision was made for catching turtles; St. George's Cay had become a favored place of residence in recent years, as it was more healthy, and the treaty forbade living there. The new boundaries would mean that many cutters working in Peten would have to withdraw, as well as those in the logwood-rich area between the Sibun and Belize Rivers. Several meetings of protest were held in which the Baymen voiced their indignation to Britain. Three years later, Britain met with Spain to discuss easing the restrictions and "to prevent even the shadow of misunderstanding of the treaty which might be occasioned by doubts."

At a treaty convention in London on July 14, 1786, it was agreed to extend the boundaries as far south as the Sibun River; mahogany could be cut; St. George's Cay could be occupied by homes, but not fortified; farming would be permitted, but not on a "plantation" basis; and last, two commissioners were to be appointed, one from each of the governments, to visit the country twice a year to assure that the provisions of the treaty were being carried out. For these concessions, Britain had to pay dearly. She had to agree not to establish any colonial government in Belize except "that necessary to maintain law and order," and she had to give up the Mosquito Coast lands. This area (now the coast of modern [Spanish] Honduras, as far south as Costa Rica) had been acquired by Britain in 1739, when the King of the Mosquito Indians placed himself under the protection of Great Britain. The Mosquito Indians who, generations before, had mixed with Negroes from Jamaica, removed themselves to the Bay Settlement by the middle of 1787. These black Indians were called "Sambos" by the settlers. They were mostly of the "Waika" tribe who had befriended Belizean settlers who had temporarily fled to Roatan and the Mosquito Shore during the 1739–1748 War with Spain. They are thought to have originated from the survivors of a slave ship carrying Negroes from the Samba country in Africa, and Amerindians, much like the origin of the Black Caribs of St. Vincent.

The Settlement's First Superintendent—1784

Colonel Edward Marcus Despart had enjoyed a distinguished military career before coming to Belize, having served with Lord Nelson in San Juan, and had been commandant of the Island of Roatan in the Bay of Honduras. Somewhat of a British West Indian hero, he had led an expedition of settlers from Cap Gracias a Dios on the Honduran-Nicaraguan border, escorted by a small force of artillery regulars, into the Spanish-controlled Negro River valley and had been successful in securing the area for British settlement. He received official commendation from the King and was made a Colonel of the Provincials.

When Belize City was destroyed in the war which ended in 1783, Despard was directed by Jamaica to take reinforcements from Roatan Island to the Bay Colony and direct its rebuilding. He was, at first, so successful in negotiating concessions from the Spanish for the raising of small crops and for the limited use of the Cays for residences that, at a special request of the Bay settlers themselves, he was appointed by Jamaica's Governor Campbell to be "Superintendent of His Majesty's financial affairs" there on December 1, 1784. The appointment of a "Superintendent" was the first step toward the eventual establishment of a crown colony with a Governor, which was now expressly prohibited by the treaty.

Almost as soon as Colonel Despard assumed his new duties as Superintendent, his efforts were met with opposition and resentment from the original settlers, of which only about 700 now survived. With the appointment of a Superintendent the Settlement's democratic constitution was invalidated. This was disputed vehemently by the disenfranchised, popularly-elected magistrates. Not the least of the ironies of the anomalous development of the Belizean government is that now, as it gained its first small degree of legal colonial status it had so long demanded, the price was to be forfeiture of the free democracy which had been established by a few hundred sturdy adventurers in the heart of a hostile foreign land and defended with the lives of countless of her patriots.

The old settlers, led by a Robert White, sent a number of communications to the House of Assembly in Jamaica complaining of Despard's preferential treatment of the Sambos, the 2000 Indian-Negro logcutters from the Mosquito Shore, and charged him with "cruel and illegal actions" in several specific incidents. These accusations were largely ignored, or dismissed as frivolous, by Jamaica.

Despard, also serving as commissioner to represent Britain in the treaty administration, began a survey of the territory accompanied by his Spanish counterpart, Colonel Enrique de Grimarest, early in 1787. They found many treaty infractions. Logging was being carried out far beyond the boundaries established in the treaty. These loggers were compelled to abandon their long-established camps and relocate within the boundary limits. Charging him with "complaisancy in dealing with the Spanish government by yielding on issues injurious to the Settlement's interests," the settlers asked Lord Grenville for Despard's immediate removal and demanded reinstatement of Burnaby's Code, the old constitution which had made no provision whatsoever for a Superintendent.

Lord Grenville, newly appointed secretary of state for the colonies, agreed with the settlers. In 1790, Colonel Peter Hunter replaced Despard as Superintendent; under his aegis, the old constitution was partially restored. Britain informed Spain that the removal of Despard did not indicate that infractions of treaties were condoned by His Majesty's government and measures were now being taken to discourage them. They also assured Spain that no attempt would be made to establish anything resembling a colonial government in Belize.

Colonial Edward Marcus Despard was deported to England where he protested his loss of appointment so persistently, and demanded his reinstatement (with due compensation), so violently at the Secretary of State's office in London, that he was imprisoned on two separate occasions during the following years. A soured and embittered man, he became involved in an improbable plot to seize the Bank of England, capture the Tower of London, and to assassinate the King. The entire affair was so ridiculous that his sanity should have been suspect, but Despard was subsequently arrested, tried with twelve Irish fellow-conspirators, found guilty of high treason, and was "hanged and beheaded" on the 21st of February, 1803.

The Battle of St. George's Cay—1798

In a battle lasting only two and a half hours, the Bay Settlement won her final and lasting victory over the Spanish. St. George's Cay, the tiny island lying nine miles northeast of Belize City, the former capital of the Settlement and the port-of-call for trading ships throughout the Caribbean, was the scene of this important encounter. In October, 1796, England declared war on Spain and in a too-familiar pattern of events, the Governor of Yucatan, Arturo O'Neill, made preparations for the capture of Belize City. In September, 1798, an imposing Spanish force set out for Belize with thirty-two ships, including two Spanish frigates, five hundred seamen, and two thousand soldiers.

Colonel Thomas Barrow, a very capable leader, had just become Superintendent of Belize. Upon learning of the impending attack he called an emergency meeting of the Assembly, which all the public attended, where it was decided to remain in Belize and face the superior power of the Spanish forces with as much might as they could muster on short notice. Three companies of the West India Regiment were brought in, together with one hundred and seventy-one slaves from Jamaica who had volunteered to fight for Belize in exchange for their freedom after the war. Under the direction of Colonel Barrow and Captain Moss, Commander of His Majesty's sloop *Merlin*, which was in Belize at the time, all the available scows and small boats of the Settlement were fitted out as gunboats and their owners made "Captains." They waited in readiness, a motley, but determined, crew.

On September third, the imposing Spanish fleet arriving in

Belizean waters was met head-on by Captain Moss of *H.M.S. Merlin*, with a crew of only fifty, and numerous small boats manned by the loggers and fishermen of Belize. An attempt by the Spaniards to thrust over Montego Cay Shoal to effect a landing was successfully repulsed. The fleet regrouped and tried to gain passage at Long Cay, and were again driven back. Their large frigates proved useless in the shallow coastal waters and returned to Yucatan. After hovering for several days off the coast, on September 10 the main Spanish fleet attacked St. George's Cay with all its force. An American sea captain named Osmar, who happened to be on St. George's Cay after losing his ship on a reef, took command of a riverboat, and in two encounters turned away five Spanish gunboats on the first wave and seven on the second to help stem the onslaught. The Belize settlers, friends, and slaves successfully defended their island and the great Spanish fleet was turned away, never to return.

This engagement, known as the Battle of St. George's Cay, has long been celebrated in Belize as a national holiday, observed on September tenth each year. This was the last attempt to dislodge the British from Belize by force and is often offered as a basis for the British claim to sovereignty in Belize by right of conquest.

Speaking of life in the colony after the victory at St. George's Cay, Professor Arthur Newton, D.Litt., in his foreward to the *British Honduras Archives* in 1931 said, "It was not until the last quarter of the 18th century that the colony was launched upon an unthreatened life wherein its inhabitants could put forth their energies, after a struggle for existence of nearly a hundred and fifty years, without the fear that they might be sacrificed to imperial interests elsewhere."

CHAPTER SIX

Land of Eternal Conflict (1800-1900)

Freedom from open hostility from its Latin neighbors allowed the Bay Colony to turn its attention, in the nineteenth century, inward to problems of her own government. The system of rule by absentee British ministers inattentive to the concerns of the Settlement, acting through Superintendents sent from Jamaica, was not palatable to independent-minded Baymen. In exercising their power of office, the Superintendents did so in direct antagonism to the democratic constitution of the Settlement, which did not provide for this office. Preferring the old Public Meeting form of government, the spirited colonists opposed such a radical departure from this form of self-government. Equally irritating to them was the fact that, although subjected to British regulation and dictates, they had no representational vote, and were steadfastly denied the colonial status and identity which they felt they justifiably deserved as a British colony. Although challenged by a coalition of new commercial business houses and the crown-appointed Superintendent in 1830, the real political power remained with the local lumber interests, which had held a dominant position in the country since the last century.

The ever-expanding area covered by Belizean woodcutters in

quest of mahogany wood had increased, until by 1821 the territory occupied by English-speaking settlers had grown to over three times greater than that allowed by the treaties of 1783 and 1786. The northern boundary, the Rio Hondo, was well watched and maintained by Spanish colonials of Yucatan, but the southern and western borders opened onto vast unexplored jungles rich with mahogany and cedar.

In the west, the woodcutters' ambitions for driving deep into El Peten (now a Department of Guatemala) were thwarted only by the extreme difficulty encountered in transporting logs by pack mule through the trackless and hazardous bush. They succeeded in penetrating only as far west as Garbutt's Falls on the Belize River.

Since mahogany trees grow sparsely interspersed with other species, a great area is required for their harvesting. The popularity of this wood, used in fine furniture in England, reached its peak in the 1820's and its production in Belize was never greater, except perhaps during a shortlived British railway boom in 1830 and another in 1840 when mahogany wood was used extensively in railway coach interiors.

Long before 1821, in defiance of Spain, British loggers had established camps far south of the Sibun River designated in the treaties. Southern expansion was much easier along the seacoast. Loggers had reached the Deep River by 1800, the Moho by 1814, and by 1824 were logging along the Sarstoon River. Speaking for the Settlement of Belize in June 1825, Mr. Marshall Bennett publicly decreed the boundaries of the Settlement to be the Hondo River on the north, the Sarstoon on the south, and Garbutt's Falls on the west: her present international borders.

Spain's inability to control her empire during the Napoleonic years allowed British expansion beyond the Bay Colony to the Bay Islands and the Mosquito Coast south of the Belize Settlement. Here the Indians were friendly to British settlers and even claimed to have lived under British protection since the days of Charles I, based on the fact that their chief (later styled "king") Oldham bequeathed to his son, Jeremy, an old

British laced hat and a worthless piece of parchment as evidence of this status. Actually, an early act of friendship between a buccaneer sea captain named Wright, who lived on St. George's Cay, and a Mosquito Indian boy sealed this curious alliance against the Spaniards. Wright's crew took up with the Indian fisher-boy, trained him to hunt turtles, taught him English, dressed him in European clothes, and called him "John Gret." John Gret became their chief interpreter and a very valuable negotiator between the British settlers and the Mosquito Indians, whom they were able to persuade to ally with the British against the Spanish monopoly.

In answer to Spanish protests over the increasing encroachment on their territory, the British Government asserted that the Bay Settlement and Mosquito Coast were not officially occupied areas, and they therefore had no control over their expansion.

At the same time, British interest in the Bay Settlement, in fact, increased. In 1919 the local courts of the Settlement, with their locally appointed judges, were declared by London to be void of authority, and a British Supreme Court and criminal court were established in their stead by an act of Parliament, although British judges did not actually fill these positions until much later. Parliament also directed that appointments to the Superintendency of Belize were henceforth to be by Royal Letters Patent, giving that office additional power and stature.

The increased stature of the superintendency did not, however, prevent the settlers from having an unpopular superintendent removed from office in 1822. Superintendent Colonel Sir George Arthur was accused by the local magistrates of reporting untrue incidents of the mistreatment of slaves and Indians in the Settlement in his dispatches to Jamaica. Arthur, who later became a baronet and a lieutenant-general, claimed credit for having suppressed a serious slave revolt in Belize which the Baymen said had never taken place. They charged him with fabricating entire incidents for inclusion in his communications with the Colonial Office to substantiate his claim to expertise in dealing with problems of slavery in the West

Indies, a subject with which he had become obsessed during the last of his eight-year term in Belize. A formal complaint filed by the magistrates led to his subsequent recall to London, termed a "leave of absence for the purpose of furnishing his government with further information on the subject of emancipation." After two years of idleness in London, he was finally assigned as commandant of a penal institution.

The Central American Federation   1823–1838

Spain, weakened by the Napoleonic Wars, could no longer hold onto her American colonies. In 1821 Mexico gained independence, and Guatemala was annexed to the short-lived Iterbide Empire of Mexico. In 1826 Britain successfully concluded a treaty with Mexico, recognizing her existing boundaries in the Belize Settlement and providing for the same terms of occupation as those granted by Spain. Prior to this, however, in 1823 a Central American Federation had been formed, styled after the United States form of government, with Guatemala as a nucleus.

From the turn of the century until the Mexican and Central American independence of the early twenties, the mercantile community in Belize had enjoyed dramatic growth. Spain's inability in her twilight years of American empire to control commerce afforded shippers in Belize the opportunity of supplying European goods to the Spanish-American communities, which Spain was no longer capable of supplying and, in exchange, acquiring much-needed livestock and agricultural produce for their colony.

This trade between London and Central America, by way of the Belize Settlement, continued to expand even after Central American independence. The new Federation allowed the British to import and retail on the domestic market in spite of challenges from local merchants, who claimed that the British had two competitive advantages that would be the ultimate ruin of their establishments: sheer volume, and the freedom from payment of most of the local taxes which they were forced to pay. So long as the British were allowed to retail goods on the local markets, the local merchants could not survive. The British trade must be limited to wholesale, they declared; but the new Federal Government, for a time, turned a deaf ear to the protests from the provinces.

The Bay settlement welcomed the establishment of the Federation, seeing in this turn of events a chance for free legal trade with the new Republic and economic development of their own Settlement as a result; equally promising was the possibility of obtaining recognition of their boundaries and wood-cutting rights, if not their own sovereignty.

The National Assembly of the Federation met in Guatemala City in April, 1823, and at this meeting, in a surprise move, the members decreed the abolition of slavery. This was a radical move at this time in history and done, the Belizeans thought, to deliberately encourage the defection of Belizean slaves who, by this time, constituted a large percentage of the work force of the lumber industry and represented an extensive capital investment. A delegation of lumbermen from Belize met with representatives of the Federation to discuss ramifications of this law, but after heated debate were unable to resolve their differences. To be sure, many Negro members of the logging crews working near El Peten did seek refuge and free-status across the border in the new Republic, but they were few and, in fact, many returned to their old jobs after finding it difficult to make a living in the backward villages of Spanish-speaking Guatemala.

The results of the anti-slavery legislation were more of a political nature than humanitarian. After all, the Latin Republics had no slaves to free. What did result from this law was renewed hostilities, with the Bay Settlement and the Federation engaging in economical warfare by levying huge taxes on each other's products. The Belize Government claimed the reason that they imposed additional customs duty on goods deposited there for Central America was that Belizean slaves were being allowed to remain in El Peten, and the Federation began to display, after 1825, an increasing awareness of the threat of territorial encroachment by the British Settlement and a strong desire to contain it.

Based on their position as Spain's successors and heirs, the Republic now began threatening the Settlement with the withdrawal of wood-cutting rights in Belize, a preoption they claimed to have inherited from Spain stemming from treaties of 1783 and 1786. "These loggers are merely trespassers," it was stated at the Federal Assembly, "and, at most, the Belize Settlement can only be considered as a province of the new Federation of Central America."

Britain did not seek formal diplomatic relations with the Federation because London felt "they could not operate efficiently in the midst of the civil turbulence which characterizes the Central American Federation." Britain did, however, send a very skillful plenipotentiary, Minister Frederick Chatfield, to represent her rights with the Federation.

Refuting the Federation's claims to Belize, Chatfield pointed out that the Central American Revolutions were "acts of populations rather than of juridical areas; hence the rebellious peoples obtained rights only over the lands which they actually possessed or occupied at the time of their independence. Furthermore, the settlers of Belize have a claim to their land by right of effectual and continuous occupation of an undeveloped land, claimed but never settled by Spain. The English have been in Belize nearly two hundred years before Central American independence was attained."

The need for commercial trade agreement at this time was vital to Belize in order to maintain her trade, and to protect British investments in the new Republic. Frederick Chatfield was directed, as minister, to negotiate a commercial treaty for Britain with the Federation. In this endeavor he labored relentlessly, though thwarted by belligerent Federalists bent upon breaking the hold of the little foreign colony in their midst, and by the Belizean magistrates themselves, who held out tenaciously against even the smallest compromise with the Central American Federation. Chatfield's patience and perseverence bore fruit, as he was able to convince the 1837 Federal Assembly to drop their tax levy against Belize and to repay some of the debts owed to British bondholders.

Just one year later the Federation, Central America's experiment with a united republic of all the Central American states, officially perished in February, 1839; a dismal failure. The memory of this Union has endured to the present date, and in fact a movement, carried on by idealists from all the Central American Republics, is at work even today attempting to recreate a United States of Central America. The failure of the Federation had many contributors, not the least being petty rivalry between various greedy opportunistic *caudillos*, but the favorite scapegoat for the failure at the time was Great Britain's "eternal agent," Frederick Chatfield. Most historians can agree today that this was a baseless charge as he was, in fact, a positive force in forwarding the union. Chatfield only became a foe of the Federation when its eventual failure became obvious, and only after it seemed destined to endanger his nation's holdings.

Abolition of Slavery

Slavery was abolished throughout the British Colonies in the West Indies in 1834. Although Belizean slave-owners did not benefit from the British government's program of compensation for all ex-slaveowners, the Bay Settlement did voluntarily follow in 1838 by making all slaves free "apprentices," a half-step toward complete freedom. Slavery was completely abolished the following year.

By this time, the Black population in Belize numbered four thousand, or two-thirds of the entire population. Most of the Blacks were employed in gangs as mahogany cutters. Their position had been, even before the act of abolition of slavery throughout the British dominions, more as that of indentured servants than slaves, and many were already freemen while others had never been slaves.

According to the *Honduras Almanack*, a chronicle of the times, the lifting of the last nominal yoke of bondage was voted and passed upon at a public meeting of all proprietors on

August 31, 1839, a year before the act had stipulated, and was celebrated throughout the Settlement by religious ceremonies, processions, and rallies attended by all the residents of the Settlement.

John L. Stephens, in writing of his stay in Belize in 1839, describes in detail life as it was at that time in the Bay Settlement. Speaking of color he observes, "In Belize, in political life there is no distinction made whatever, except on the ground of qualifications and character; and hardly any in social life, even in contracting marriages." He continues, "Before I had been an hour in Belize I learned that the great work of practical amalgamation, the subject of much angry controversy at home, has been doing on quietly for generations; that color was considered mere matter of taste; and that some of the most respectable inhabitants had Black wives and Mulatto children, whom they educated with as much care, and made money for with as much zeal, as if their skins were perfectly white."

The MacDonald Era

Since 1833 magistrates in the Settlement had not been popularly elected, but were elected by nominees appointed by the Crown and did not have the confidence of the citizenry. Also, unfortunately at this critical time of uneasy peace with her neighbors and great internal unrest, Belize was governed by a contentious and arrogant Superintendent—Colonel Alexander MacDonald. The bellicose Colonel MacDonald stood over six feet tall, was thickly built, and had an imposing military bearing acquired from a lifetime of military service, having entered the service at the age of eighteen. He was a veteran of the action in Spain, of the "Twenty Years War," the Peninsula War, and had commanded a regiment at the Battle of Waterloo where, for his outstanding leadership, he received the order of Companion of the Military Order of the Bath from the King of England and was made a Knight of the Order of St. Anne by the Emperor of Russia. All his connections and associations before this assignment had been military; his brother, Sir John MacDonald, was

Adjutant-General of England, and his cousin was Marshall MacDonald of France. He was not well-suited for the civilian post he now held in Belize, which required thoughtful diplomacy and infinite patience.

MacDonald assumed power to legislate by proclamation; he personally took full control of the nation's treasury. He assumed power to punish anyone who questioned his authority or obstructed his mandates. Not being satisfied to limit his dictatorial powers to matters of local government, he turned in 1836 and 1837 to foreign affairs; specifically to the expansion of British rule in the Mosquito Coast and the Bay Islands. This brought immediate protest from the Central American Federation and served to negate much of the work Chatfield had done in mediating their disagreements with Belize. In a counter move, the Commandant of Honduras blocked all British shipping between Roatan, the largest of the Bay Islands, and Belize. In April, 1839, British warships arrived in Roatan and occupied the Island. The harm done to British relations in Central America by this act is untold.

Walker–Caddy Expedition

In December, 1838, Lieutenant John Herbert Caddy arrived in the colony assigned as a gunnery officer of the small Royal Artillery garrison quartered on Fort George. He soon became harbormaster of Belize, but it is his paintings and writings which survived that are of interest. While carrying out his duties as harbormaster, Caddy had the opportunity, probably to combat the sheer boredom of his job, to set down in his diary descriptions of the Settlement, its capital, and the "fort" as he found them in 1839. He also made sketches and paintings of the Settlement which attracted the attention of Superintendent MacDonald and established himself in the Settlement as an accomplished artist. Only two paintings from that period, both views of Belize City, have survived. His diary, however, provides a good picture of the Settlement and its people at that time.

Late in the year 1836 Mr. Thomas Miller, keeper of the

records and clerk of the courts of British Honduras, succumbed to an attack of the fever, the ever-present tropical scourge. Lord Glenelg, Secretary of State for the Colonies, recommended in February, 1837, James Walker to succeed Miller. Walker, who had for some years held a position with the colonial office, arrived in Belize on April 15, 1837, accompanied by his younger brother, Patrick. James was immediately sworn in as clerk of the courts of British Honduras and keeper of the public records, as well as one of the judges of the Supreme Court. He served with distinction until April of the following year.

On April 28, 1838, Superintendent MacDonald advised Lord Glenelg that James Walker had returned to England on "urgent private affairs" and had been granted a leave of absence for "a few months." Lord Glenelg refused to sanction such a leave after so short a duration in his assignment; however, Walker had already departed for England and never returned to British Honduras.

Prior to leaving, James Walker had seen that his brother Patrick was sworn in as assistant keeper of the public records and as assistant clerk of the Supreme and lower courts. Patrick, then in his early twenties, had no background for public service, but made up for this deficiency with a great deal of talent and energy. His zeal sufficed to make him a logical successor to his brother's positions, and on May 8, 1838, he assumed the duties of keeper of the records and clerk of the courts *pro tempore.*

Patrick Walker's enthusiasm in office brought him an increasing number of duties and positions. On June 28, 1838, he was made one of the Supreme Court judges, while simultaneously serving as clerk of the courts. He made himself an indispensable member of the government; Colonel MacDonald, in a dispatch to the Secretary of State for the Colonies in August of the same year wrote: "Walker is talented and energetic, I have ever found him a firm friend and faithful counselor." MacDonald sent Walker on an expedition to the Mosquito shore, after which he compiled a thorough report for Her Majesty's Government on "the habits, dress, customs, and economy of the Mosquito Indians."

Walker became a landed gentleman with the acquisition of two landgrants from Superintendent MacDonald in 1839, one on the New River Lagoon in February and one on the south bank of the New River later in the year.

With an insatiable desire for expansion of his activities, Walker became a member of the staff of the Prince Regent's Royal Honduran Militia in 1839, in which organization he served as "Inspector and Keeper of Arms, Clothing, and Accoutrements." In February of that year he became a major of the militia, and took on the additional duties of aide-de-camp to the commander-in-chief of British Honduras, a title held by Colonel MacDonald. In June he became both the advocate for the Crown in the Settlement and the magistrate of the Bay of Honduras.

Expanding his field of interest from military and legal professions, he became public treasurer for a time, and by mid-1839 had added the title and office of colonial secretary, a position second in importance to the Superintendent in the Settlement, to his portfolio. Meanwhile, he served on the committee of management for the Regatta Club and was rector, and later churchwarden, of St. John's Church.

Reporting on Patrick Walker's qualities to the Colonial Office again in 1839, MacDonald stated, "From the testimony I have already borne of the value of Mr. Walker's services, I need not now repeat anything in his praise in a public point of view. As for his private conduct, I may, with safety, add that he is one of the most exemplary young men I have ever met." The Superintendent's appraisal of Walker did not reflect the opinion of all of the Settlement, apparently. His quickly-acquired power and position in the Settlement had made enemies, and there existed some confusion and disagreement among the residents regarding the legality of some of the titles and positions he held. Considering their proliferation, this is almost inevitable.

On October 30, 1839, the brig *Mary Ann* brought two distinguished travellers to Belize: John Lloyd Stephens and Frederick Catherwood. The former was the recently-appointed *charge d'affaires* for the United States, and his companion, an

English architect and artist, was renowned for his pen and ink
drawings and depictions of archaeological finds throughout the
world. Their mission was the exploration and recording·of the
little-known and unreported ancient cities of the Maya Indians.

Stephens and Catherwood spent several days in Belize
(Stephens called it "Balize" in his writings) as the guests of
Superintendent MacDonald. During this time they discussed in
detail with MacDonald and Walker their proposed expedition,
which would begin in the Honduran ruins of Copan and include
the fabled Maya city of Palenque in the State of Chiapas.
During his stay, attorney Stephens had the opportunity of
sitting as a judge in the Belize court with Walker. His account,
recorded in his book, of the informal trial procedures is quite
amusing, he being the only person present with any legal training.

Colonel MacDonald, competitive person that he was,
decided immediately that Britain, despite her reputation for
scientific research, was about to be upstaged by the *parvenu*
former colony and that the honor of British science was at
stake. Since the resources of the Settlement were insufficient to
sustain an expedition of the magnitude planned by Stephens, he
reasoned that a British exploratory expedition could proceed
directly to Palenque while Stephens' party was occupied in
Honduras, and would be there well before the Americans and at
little expense to the colony.

To lead this expedition, MacDonald turned to his right hand
and confidant, Patrick Walker, who had little interest in relics of
lost Indian civilizations, but on whose enterprise and persever-
ance he knew he could rely. To play "Catherwood" to his
"Stephens" the logical candidate was the Settlement's only
artist, John Caddy.

Without waiting for a reply from his communique to Lord
Russell apprising him of the undertaking, MacDonald authorized the two men to proceed with preparations for the trip. It
was the worst of times to undertake an expedition through the
uncharted interior, especially one which was to commence with
the passage up the Belize River in the face of the rainy season,

which could bring a deluge at any time. The river was in flood stage already, and its strong current and floating debris made it even more treacherous. With the community's interest aroused in the "race to Palenque" and MacDonald's keen sense of urgency pushing them, Walker and Caddy could do little but strike out on their ill-prepared, and what proved to be extremely difficult, journey on November 13, 1839. After a long and tortuous trip up the Belize River, through the Peten District by way of Flores, they arrived at Palenque, where they spent two weeks producing the first scientifically accurate depictions of the ancient Maya city.

When Stephens and Catherwood arrived at Palenque, they found the names of Walker and Caddy inscribed high on a wall of one of the buildings, in the time-honored custom of early explorers. They received this news with mixed emotions; relieved that the British pair had not been "speared by Indians" as had been rumored, but a little put upon at having to retrace the steps already taken by the earlier party.

Upon their return to the Settlement, Walker and Caddy set about to prepare their report, illustrated with Caddy's drawings and watercolors, to send to the Colonial Office for eventual publication. With it they sent an accounting of their expenditures, amounting to $1000 advanced by Superintendent MacDonald, and an additional $600 expended by Walker of his own funds. The report was sent to England in late 1840, but a reply wasn't forthcoming from Lord Russell until February 1841. In his dispatch to MacDonald, he admonished Walker for certain political opinions expressed in the report concerning the Mexican Government, and had the report and illustrations sent to the Geographical Society and the cost accounting to the treasury department.

The "race" was ultimately lost when, later in that year, John Lloyd Stephens published his famous two-volume *Incidents of the Travel in Central America, Chiapas, and Yucatan* with its brilliant description of Palenque and many other heretofore-unknown ruins. It was an immediate sensation throughout the world and permanently squashed any hope of fame or fortune

Walker or Caddy may have still held stemming from the publication of their works.

The crowning indignation arrived by dispatch, stating that the explorers' request for reimbursement for their expenses was denied, the reasons given in part: "I fear that it is quite certain that the Treasury will not pay them, especially since the expedition was undertaken without their sanction, and it has really proved no use at all. An American named Stephens made the same journey, and has published a full account of Palenque with drawings, etc., far more complete than any which were made by Captain Caddy (he had been promoted to 2nd Captain upon his return to the Settlement) and with far more extensive range of general observation. I fear, therefore, that nothing can be done with the dispatch but to lay it aside." Another functionary in the Colonail Office appended his own comments to the dispatch, saying, again in part: ". . . Colonel MacDonald, Mr. Walker, and Captain Caddy executed this scientific mission with no previous sanction from the Treasury. The motive was merely that we might not be outstript, in this case in scientific zeal, by the Americans. This was not very wise, and the result is that we have been bested by these new rivals in scientific research, who will now boast over our inferiority instead of having to boast only over our comparative inactivity. After all, the Drawings and Travels have not been published, and now it is hardly to be supposed that any bookseller would hazard their publication. In short, the whole affair has been a blunder, though a very well-meant one."

Following the suggestion of this dispatch to lay the matter aside, the British Government filed it away and never did reimburse the parties for the expense of the expedition. It was only in 1967 that Professor David M. Pendergast, assistant professor of anthropology at the University of Utah, collected and edited the hitherto unpublished accounts, including John Caddy's diary, and published *Palenque: the Walker-Caddy Expedition to the Ancient Maya City, 1839–1840.*

Captain Caddy, after accepting a military assignment in Canada, eventually retired there, took up painting, taught art, and died at the age of 83.

Patrick Walker resumed his career of staggering plurality of offices in Belize, becoming a councilor of the Executive Council and, in 1841, a magistrate. He was hereafter referred to as The Honorable Patrick Walker.

In order to strengthen his stand against the local advocates of democratic representation in the governing of the colony, Alexander MacDonald, on the second of November, 1840, officially "set aside all local laws and 'usages' of the country, heretofore abiding," and declared that, "from said date the law of the Settlement or Colony of British Honduras should be the law of England and that local laws and customs repugnant to the spirit of the law of England, or opposed to the principles of equity and justice, shall be null."

In May of 1841, Walker was commissioned to represent the Settlement in discussions with the Governor of Jamaica concerning these and other proposed changes in the structure of the Settlement's government. The general feeling as to the superintendent's choice of representative is seen in the first of two important petitions filed by the local residents in 1841 to the Governor of Jamaica. This petition, in the form of a letter, was designed to underline the general feeling of discontent with the policies of Superintendent MacDonald by criticizing his representative, and was timed to have the effect of minimizing Walker's effectiveness in the discussions with the Governor. In their communique, signed by local merchants, one of whom had been the defendant in a lawsuit brought by Walker some time before, begins by averring that they had no wish to state anything disrespectful of any party, and goes on to comment: "We regret that H. M. Superintendent should have deemed it advisable to appoint Mr. Walker for this mission as no individual less qualified by general experience or local knowledge or from the whole tenor of his public conduct more obnoxious to the inhabitants could possibly have been selected . . ." As Professor Pendergast commented, "One can only be grateful that the gentlemen said nothing which they thought disrespectful of Walker!"

Although Walker generally was well-respected in the Settlement and held in high esteem by the Governor, it was felt apparently by all but himself and MacDonald that he was spreading his talent a little too thin. A Select Committee appointed to review salaries of public officials summed it up thusly:

". . . Your Committee has come to the conclusion that it will be unwise to continue in one individual such a plurality of offices—they consider it quite incompatible with the duties of Secretary of H. M. Superintendent that he should at the same time hold the office of Queen's Advocate as well as Keeper of Militia Arms and Clothing. Our present Superintendent may be pleased to permit his Secretary to hold these offices, but his immediate successor may at once disapprove of the time of that Office being occupied in any but his legitimate duties and as it is certain that the public interests do materially suffer from want of attention in some of the departments, your committee recommends the (Public) Meeting to address His Excellency, Her Majesty's Superintendent, on the subject, requesting that the person holding, in future, the situation of Keeper of the Militia Clothing shall receive the appointment at the recommendation of the Officer Commanding the Militia, satisfied that the person held responsible by that Officer will be more likely to perform well the duties of the appointment than one over whom he has no control and who considers this Office as a sinecure."

Obviously little attention was given the recommendations of this committee, as Walker soon assumed, in addition, the appointment as commissioner and treasurer of the Mosquito Nation now under British protection, and was advisor to the Mosquito King. These positions he held along with his others until in May, 1843, when he was granted a nine-month leave to return to England. This was prompted, in part at least, by the worsening of relations between the MacDonald administration and the local inhabitants, and perhaps he had prior knowledge of MacDonald's imminent demise as Superintendent.

Walker never returned to British Honduras. When he did

return to the West Indies, he was assigned by the Colonial Office to the Mosquito Shore and, while serving there, drowned during a military skirmish with the Nicaraguans in 1847.

After many informal complaints to the Colonial Governor concerning the political situation in Belize had gone unanswered, the colonists drew up a second formal petition in 1841 to be sent to Jamaica, requesting "the right to cultivate the soil, freedom of discussion, right of enactment of local laws for their own internal government, and the control of their own finances." Until a reply was received, the Assembly (Public Meeting) refused to transact business.

Sir Charles Metcalf, the Governor of Jamaica, finally replied in 1843, stating: "A Public Meeting is authorized by Her Majesty's Government to exercise its legislative powers, harmoniously (if it can) with the executive, each taking 'usage' as the rule by which their respective powers are to be defined." This was a bitter pill for MacDonald who, defeated and humiliated, was soon recalled from the colony.

Colonel Charles St. John Fancourt was appointed Superintendent on June 10, 1843, and arrived in the colony on June 15, 1843, after being instructed by the Governor of Jamaica on the line he was to follow which was to skillfully withdraw from the Public Meeting its recently acquired constitutional powers and privileges, and to subvert the influence of the people in the government. Colonel Fancourt, a diplomat by training and well-versed courtier, knew well how to conceal the iron hand of arbitrary authority under a silken glove of a benevolent and courteous manner.

For the first time, the office of Chief Justice was filled when Robert Temple arrived from Jamaica with Fancourt. Chief Justice Temple proved to be less popular than the new Superintendent, but he was able to initiate a policy of registration of aliens which is the antecedent of modern immigration laws in the colony. Before this British court was finally established, justice had been administered by a local "Grand Court" consisting of seven judges, one of them the Colonial Secretary; the others being merchants, mahogany cutters, or other tradesmen.

None were attorneys and there were no attorneys to represent plaintiff or defendant in the many civil cases it heard daily. Being a place of large commercial transactions, contracts were made and broken daily, requiring the mediation of this tribunal to interpret and compel their fulfillment. The judges sat on a raised platform around a massive circular mahogany table in heavy mahogany chairs with high backs and cushions. The proceedings were conducted in a familiar and colloquial way; the parties being more or less known to them in this close community, the judges were greatly influenced by their prior knowledge of general character. So satisfactory had this system proved that only one case in twenty-two years had ever been appealed.

The War of the Races—1847

In 1847, the Maya Indians in Yucatan revolted against their Spanish (Mexican) landlords. With a force of over seventy thousand, the Indians descended upon white settlements throughout the peninsula, intent upon killing off every person of less than pure Indian blood. There were, at this time, approximately twenty thousand European and half-breed peoples living in Yucatan. Over one-third of the entire population of the Mexican peninsula was annihilated in this War of the Races. All of the Yucatan Peninsula, at one time or another, was captured by the Mayas with the exception of the City of Merida, which was besieged. Southern Yucatan soon became an anarchic Indian domain from which most of the rudiments of European civilization had been torn away. Thousands fled for their lives into the Bay Settlement. These Spanish refugees, most of them "Mestizos" with mixed Spanish and Indian blood, added yet another ingredient to the racial blend of today's Belizean.

This rush of mass immigration offered immediate administrative problems, but according to Superintendent Frederick R. Seymour in a communication to Lt.-Governor Bell of Jamaica a few years later, it created a long-term opportunity:

"Surrounded by Republics in a state of dissolution where all the evils of tyranny and anarchy subsist simultaneously, British Honduras has in the last few years appeared as if it was intended as an experiment to see what can be made of the Spanish Americans, who, though not useless individually, seem to have proved their inability to manage successfully their own public affairs. In our territory several thousands of persons—in Corozal alone three thousand—have found a home where, under a tolerably strong and abundantly liberal Government, they come and go and do as they please. At first political refugees were the principal Immigrants, but when it was found that those who crossed the frontier, hoping for better times, and a more favorably disposed Government, did not return when their wishes were fulfilled and the party opposed to them overthrown; the attractions of Corozal, San Estevan, Puerto Consego, and other villages became known in Yucatan and persons of no particular political bias began to emigrate to a country where there was no military conscriptions, arbitrary taxes, revolutions and shootings; but where, on the contrary, they can enjoy personal freedom and the full benefit of the fruits of their industry."

A Maya raiding party followed the stragglers into Belize in March, 1848, and drove as far south as Hill Bank before being routed by the old Jamaican Regiment dispatched from Belize City. This all-black "Queen's Gentlemen" Regiment, normally stationed at the "Old Barracks" still standing in Belize City, had been enlisted at various British recruiting stations in Africa and were extremely tall and athletic. With their red coats, on a line, bristling with steel, their ebony faces gave a peculiarly warlike appearance. However warlike their appearance, there were only one hundred of them and, together with thirty or so civil police, constituted Belize's entire defense force.

Communication was established between Superintendent Charles St. John Fancourt and the Indian leaders. As a neutral, Fancourt was asked by the Mexican Government to act as intermediary between themselves and the Indians. A meeting attended by the Maya leader, Jacinto Pat, Fancourt, and a representative of the Mexican Government on November 15, 1849, at Ascension Bay came to no agreement. A second such meeting held in Belize four years later resulted in a Mexican-Indian truce which was immediately broken.

After the 1848 raid, the Indians respected the neutrality of the Bay Settlement and confined their raids to the northern side of the Hondo River. This was largely due to the fact that they were able to purchase lead, gun powder, and rifles from neutral British merchants and smugglers in Belize. These opportunitists, native Belizeans, Yucatan refugees, and British businessmen alike, did a brisk trade in gun-running from Belize City to Ascension Bay, dodging Mexican patrol boats in their coastal schooners and shallow-drafted "pit pans." The Indians purchased the goods from them in loot taken from a hundred captured cities.

The Mexican government objected strenuously to the furnishing of guns and ammunition to the revolted Indians, but it was Fancourt's contention that this was a civil war between two political factions, not a racial matter, and as a neutral nation Belize was free to trade with either. It appeared at the time that the Indians might well be able to hold onto the southern Yucatan Peninsula, which would be to Belize's advantage, and anyway Fancourt saw little difference; both were equally "non-British." Also, Fancourt had received instructions from Jamaica several years previously to "take a benevolent and protective interest in the Indians; the British Government has no wish to interfere in their affairs."

The immediate question facing Frederick Seymour when he assumed his duties as the superintendent of Belize in 1857, was how to protect his colony against the rampant barbarism of the Santa Cruz Mayas. The residents in the northern districts of Belize lived in constant terror that the pillage, rapine, and massacre perpetrated by these unpredictable Indians would spill over the Hondo River while the small British constabulary force on the border was no match for their superior numbers and vicious tactics. The Santa Cruz, supported by a fanatical religion which, in a perversion of Christianity, included the worship of a "talking cross" that directed its followers to commit all manner of atrocities in the name of God, had overcome all rival Indian tribes in southeastern Yucatan and now ruled, as Superintendent Seymour put it, "as predators; spoiling all that they touch." Yet the arms trade went on, unhampered by Seymour's administration.

Bacalar, the last Mexican stronghold in southern Yucatan, contained a garrison of Mexican troops employed there in an attempt to impede Indian trade with Belize. This citadel, located on a lagoon just north of the Rio Hondo, fell under a surprise attack in the spring of 1858 and most of its inhabitants were massacred by the Santa Cruz. Both private and official commissioners were sent from Belize to treaty with the Santa Cruz chief for the lives of the remaining Mexican prisoners. Their efforts failed and the prisoners, mostly women and children, were sentenced to death by the tribe's oracle, the "talking cross," unless the British commissioner would deliver up the Mexican Commandant at Bacalar who had fled to Corozal. The commissioner was unable to make such an arrangement and the large wooden cross, through some means of dissimulation, "spoke," condemning all the prisoners to death. That night the captive women and children were butchered with machetes within earshot of the commissioners.

The commissioners returned to Corozal convinced of the need for British troops on the Hondo for the colony's protection. A request by the Mexican Government for Belize's help in mounting a punitive expedition against the Santa Cruz in retaliation for the Bacalar massacre was turned down by the Superintendent due to lack of troops, but also from dread of a prolonged campaign against the powerful Indians, if provoked. For the same reason, he refused to grant the Mexican Government the use of the Colony's territory (Ambergris Cay) from which to land and stage their assault against the Santa Cruz. Seymour even refused British aid when Mexico offered final cessation of Mexican claims to Belizean territory as a *quid pro quo* for such cooperation. Colonial officials agreed that the interests of the colony would be best served by mounting a strong guard to exercise constant surveillance of the border while maintaining strict neutrality.

Relations grew tense between the British and Mexican governments. The Mexican Imperial Commission for Yucatan issued a decree proclaiming Mexico's southern boundary to be the River Sarstoon, thereby annexing Belize *in toto*. Britain reminded Mexico through diplomatic communications of the treaties of 1783, 1786 and 1850 which had clearly outlined the Settlements' national limits.

Fearing that the San Pedro Mayas living within the colony might join the tide of Indian rebellion and join with the Santa Cruz, Superintendent Seymour sent an urgent request to Jamaica for British regulars. His call was answered in 1858, when *H.M.S. Leopard* arrived in Belize City Harbor with men of the Second West Indies Regiment, who were immediately dispatched to the north to relieve the ill-equipped Citizen's Militia near Corozal Town.

This display of force had its effect, and an uneasy quiet settled over the northern district from the Fall of 1858 until well into the 1860's. Indian violations of Belizean territory continued intermittently, but were minor and usually provoked by disagreements over broken agreements with British gun-runners and traders upon whom the Indians had come to rely as their only ally and source of aid against the Mexicans.

The political situation became further complicated by Mexico's claim to Belize territory and the cessation of boundary-marking efforts by the Belizeans in 1861. This encouraged the Santa Cruz Indians to believe that the British had serious doubts about their right to lands near Blue Creek and the upper Hondo. Rumors of a separate treaty between the Mexican Government and the Icaiche Mayas, and of an impending Mexican assault against the Santa Cruz to be staged from Belize, were all contributing factors in arousing them.

In 1864 the Icaiche and Santa Cruz Mayas raided Corozal Town, killed three people and took twenty-four hostages. They returned in April, 1866, in another surprise raid on Qualm Hill on the Rio Bravo and successfully demanded ransom for some seventy woodcutters, after destroying their mill. In January, 1867, arriving from the headwaters of the Blue Creek, an

Icaiche raiding party advanced well into the heart of the Settlement, destroying a mahogany bank at the junction of the Belize River and Labouring Creek, and making off with another group of woodcutters. The Icaiche moved on to San Pedro village where they were sheltered by the Maya inhabitants there, and forwarded a ransom note to Belize City. The 4th West India regiment was sent to dispatch the Indians, but in a comic opera-like encounter in which the unit's commander, Major McKay, was later charged by the press with cowardice, after only firing a few rounds both forces fled the battlefield, each thinking the other to be in hot pursuit. The Indians appeared again in 1870 taking Corozal Town, which they succeeded in holding for ransom again before retreating across the border.

In 1872 the Icaiche leader, General Marcus Canul, launched a massive force across the Rio Hondo at Paintings Landing near Corosalito. His hordes advanced through August Pine Ridge as far as Orange Walk, where they were engaged by the West India Regiment. After more than six hours of fierce fighting, in which the smaller group of Black soldiers found themselves completely surrounded, General Canul was killed and his Indian troops retired from battle, receded across the border to Yucatan and did not return.

With the loss of the tacit support of the British, the Santa Cruz lost what remained of their hope for an autonomous existence in southern Yucatan. The Mexican Government's eventual expedition against them, with reluctant British cooperation, effectively terminated an era of fear and apprehension in Belize. Belizean economy had been so devastated by the cost of maintaining armed troops to defend the Colony against the Indians that the first land tax had to be levied. While fear of Indian uprisings were laid aside in 1874, the dispute with Mexico over the British aid to the Indians during their revolution was far from forgotten.

Constitutional Reform—1854

Charles St. John Fancourt had been a firm, well-respected

Superintendent during his eight years in office. He remained for a time after his term to complete a book on the history of Yucatan, and was given a testimonial dinner in February 1853, at which the people of the colony presented him with a silver centerpiece. He retired to Cheltenham in 1854, and was succeeded in office by Sir Philip Edward Wodehouse.

By 1851 the Bay Settlement had outgrown the old Public Meeting form of government, and the manner in which recent Superintendents had made laws by proclamation and appointed their own magistrates had not been popular with the people. Colonel Wodehouse successfully gained support of the magistrates through his work on financial and fiscal reform. Before leaving Belize to accept an appointment as Governor of British Guiana in 1854, he established a Legislative Council which consisted of the Superintendent, eighteen popularly elected and three crown appointed members. Membership in this council was restricted to holders of property valued in excess of 400 pounds, which is high, bearing in mind the low value of land in the colony at the time. This property qualification has been continued until the present date. The right to vote in a public election required an income from property rental of at least seven pounds per year, or a salary of 100 pounds per year. While being far from the democracy of the old Public Meeting government, this did restore some responsibility for their government to the people.

Clayton-Bulwer Treaty—1850

In 1847 the United States, becoming interested again in affairs in Central America, sent its first consul to Belize to administer the growing commerce between the two countries. Cornelius Vanderbilt had organized a profitable system of transporting Americans from the East Coast of the United States across Nicaragua to the Pacific Ocean, from where they could make their way to the California gold fields; United States investment dollars were beginning to be spent in Central America.

Differences between Great Britain and the Republic of Nicaragua over the boundaries of the British Mosquito Coast territory led to U.S. intervention in the name of the Monroe Doctrine to protect U.S. interests there. The United States, like Britain, was interested in building an international canal to link the Atlantic and the Pacific. To avoid future misunderstandings, Sir Henry Lytton Bulwer of England met with the United States representative, John M. Clayton, to draw up a treaty concerning this proposed inter-ocean route. The resulting Clayton-Bulwer Treaty of 1850 was to be an assurance that the proposed Nicaragua Canal would not be the exclusive property of any country nor controlled, fortified, or colonized by any one nation.

The treaty held broader implications. The first article of the treaty stated simply that neither party was to exercise dominion over *any part* of Central America. Before it could be ratified, Bulwer and Clayton had to exchange declarations to clarify that this wording had been meant to apply to all territory *exclusive of British Honduras.* It was clear, however, that Britain gave up any further claim to the loosely defined area of the Mosquito Coast. This treaty became ratified by both countries although the canal, of course, was never built.

The Clayton-Bulwer Treaty may have averted a major confrontation between the two great nations, as the United States had been, since the Monroe Doctrine was promulgated in 1823, adamant in her position that no European power was to acquire new territory or expand present holdings in the Americas. This treaty effectively blocked British expansion in the areas of the Islands in the Bay of Honduras, the Honduras Mosquito Coast, and the Port of San Juan del Norte (Greytown) in Nicaragua. The United States, as a result of this diplomatic victory, acquired the image of protector and champion of the small young Central American republics, until a few years later when the menace of the Yankee filibuster expeditions gave them occasion to question American intentions.

The term "filibuster" originated from the unsuccessful attempt of the French to pronounce "freebooter." The British added the slang term "filibuster" (the way it sounded when pronounced by the French) to their vocabulary; its origin was soon forgotten, but the word has survived. Of the filibusters, the most notorious was William Walker, a doctor and lawyer from Nashville, Tennessee who, from 1855 until 1857, made himself virtual dictator of Nicaragua, after having been thrown out of Baja California by Mexico's Santa Anna and driven out of Nicaragua twice before. He was eventually killed in Honduras.

Dallas-Clarenden Agreement—1856

Since the failure of the experiment with democracy by the Central American Federation in 1838, the Republic of Guatemala, one of the successor states, had taken up the claim to the territory of Belize, although by the same basis Mexico had equal claim based on inheritance of former Spanish sovereignty. Be that as it may, when the United States and Great Britain drew up the Dallas-Clarenden Agreement on October 17, 1856, it included this paragraph concerning Belize:

> "That Her Britannic Majesty's settlement, called Belize or British Honduras, on the shores of the Bay of Honduras, bounded on the north by the Mexican Province of Yucatan and on the south by the River Sarstoon, was not and is not embraced in the treaty entered into between the contracting parties on the 19th day of April, 1850; and that the limits of the said Belize, on the west, as they existed on the said 19th day of April, 1850 shall, if possible, be settled and fixed by treaty between Her Britannic Majesty and the Republic of Guatemala, within two years from the exchange of the ratifications of this instrument, which said boundaries and limits shall not at any time hereafter be extended."

Upon learning of this, Guatemala protested, for among other things, this document set out the southern boundary shared with Guatemala without her knowledge or consent.

Anglo-Guatemalan Boundary Treaty of 1859

Fearing filibuster activity in Belize, the British Government recruited men and vessels to stand a constant watch for expeditions in that country. The acts of the filibusters had made such an unfavorable impression on Guatemala that her government began to consider framing a treaty with Britain, from which they saw the possibility of gaining British friendship and protection from freebooters from the United States. Also, Guatemala was apprehensive over the possible intervention by the U.S. government in their border dispute with Britain, as in Nicaragua, and apparently was now ready to discuss settlement of the Guatemalan-Belizean boundary lines with Britain.

At Guatemala's request, on April 30, 1859, His Excellency Rafael Carrera, President of Guatemala, negotiator Don Pedro de Aycinena, and Charles Lennox Wyke, Frederick Chatfield's recent successor, held a boundary convention to establish, for all time, common bounds between Belize and Guatemala.

Wyke's prime objective was to secure recognition by Guatemala of Britain's sovereignty in British Honduras within definite, well-defined boundaries, something which Britain had never been able to obtain from Spain. The Guatemalans wished to gain from the treaty the assurance against further encroachments by acquisitive Belizean lumbermen, and at the same time avoid becoming a pawn in a possible dispute between Great Britain and the United States.

Wyke, a capable negotiator, realized that Britain's hold on this last remnant of her empire in Central America depended upon his being able to quickly and quietly secure this agreement with Guatemala in the face of world criticism, especially from the United States. He was very careful to make clear by the wording of this treaty that no acquisition of territory was involved, but that it was a mutual recognition of existing boundaries which were in existence at the time of the Clayton-Bulwer Treaty.

It was under this pressure that Charles Wyke, apparently without consulting London, agreed to cooperate with Guatemala in the building of a cartroad between the Settlement of Belize and the Guatemalan capital. The purpose was to re-establish trade between Great Britain and Guatemala. This agreement was included as Clause VII in the Anglo-Guatemalan Treaty of 1859, although no stipulation was made as to the time of commencement or conclusion of the road's construction, nor its possible cost to either party. Clause VII stated:

> "We mutually agree conjointly to use our best efforts, by taking adequate means of establishing the easiest communications (either by means of a cart road or by employing the rivers, or both united) according to the opinion of the surveying engineers, between the fittest place on the Atlantic Coast near the Settlement of Belize and the Capital of Guatemala; whereby the commerce of England on the one hand, and the material prosperity of the Republic on the other, cannot fail to be severally increased at the same time, and the limits of the territory being now clearly defined, all further encroachments, by either party, on the territory of the other, will be effectually checked and prevented for the future."

The construction of a road through unexplored jungles and over mountains ranging up to five thousand feet in elevation would have been a difficult task, but not impossible for a country with the capabilities of Britain in the nineteenth century. Although no estimate of cost is mentioned in the treaty, it was believed that the cost to Britain would have been on the order of 50,000 pounds sterling, not an excessive cost for the world's greatest commercial nation to pay for the uncontested sovereignty of this valuable territory. The remainder of the treaty accomplished everything for which Britain had hoped. It established the boundaries as they were demarcated in the Dallas-Clarendon Treaty; i.e. from Gracias & Dios Falls on the Sarstoon River, north through Garbutt's Falls on the upper reaches of the Belize River and on to the Mexican Border.

The United States was quick to react when this treaty was signed. Protesting through their Legation in Guatemala, U.S.

diplomats insisted that Britain could not gain sovereignty in
Belize in this manner, as to do so would be an infraction of
their Clayton-Bulwer agreement. Britain disregarded the protest.

The Chamber of Representatives of Guatemala approved the
Boundary Convention on the thirtieth of May, 1860. At that
time, their Foreign Minister addressed the Chamber as follows:

> "Though Guatemala regards herself as having inherited
> the rights of Spain, these territories (Belize) have been
> abandoned by Spain herself. They have never been in the
> actual possession of Guatemala, nor has she exercised
> any act of sovereignty over them. Britain's occupation,
> on the other hand, began even before Central America
> became independent and it is impossible to determine
> what had been occupied before that date and what after.
> In any event, the territorial loss to Guatemala is trifling
> compared to the importance of defining the boundaries
> of the Belize Settlement and putting an end to Anglo-
> American discussions, and also to Guatemala's interest in
> possessing as her neighbor in the Gulf of Honduras, a
> great and responsible nation instead of what would have
> become, had Great Britain withdrawn from Belize, a nest
> of irresponsible adventurers and pirates impossible to
> control."

The British Foreign Office, seemingly intent upon fulfilling
its obligations under Clause VII of the treaty, sent Major Henry
Wray of the office of the Royal Engineers to work with Manuel
Cana Madraza of Guatemala to conduct a survey. The joint
survey commission spent a year preparing plans for the route to
link Guatemala City with Izabel, a Guatemalan village on the
Golfo Dulce on the Atlantic Coast. These plans, together with a
final estimate of the project's cost (145,465 pounds sterling),
were submitted to London and to Guatemala City. With this
work done, the party proceeded to Garbutt's Falls with the
intention of surveying the entire Belizean-Guatemalan border.
Working south only six miles before becoming hopelessly bog-
ged down in the dense jungle, they returned to the Falls and

began to extend the line northward. They had gone but ten miles when Wray received orders from London to suspend operations until further notice, which never came, and he returned to England. The line was later completed north to Blue Creek in 1864 by others.

The commissioner's estimate of the cost of construction of the road was thought to be excessive; it had originally not been expected to exceed 100,000 pounds sterling and Guatemala subsequently undertook to investigate the possibility of another, less costly, route.

After studying the treaty obligations, the Colonial Office came to the conclusion that a cartroad (Railroad) with a terminus in Guatemala would not prove a stimulus to Anglo-Guatemalan trade, and in fact might hurt rather than aid the commerce of the Belize Settlement. They forwarded their report to the Treasury who flatly stated that implementation of the treaty obligation acquired by Wyke was impossible, as the Parliament could never sanction such an expenditure. The road was never built.

A copy of a dispatch contained in the Government files in Belize, written by Charles Wyke to London after the treaty was framed, reveals his attempt to explain why such an unusual article as Clause VII came to be included in a boundary treaty. In this letter, widely quoted by Guatemalan historians today, Wyke expresses his personal belief that Britain's claim to sovereignty in Belize was tenuous, and therefore he had agreed to the terms of Clause VII to assure ratification of the treaty by Guatemala. A quite different version of this dispatch was published in Britain in 1867.

The non-fulfillment by Britain of this obligation, incurred by the Boundary Convention of 1859, has been the cause of dispute between the two countries to the present day. An effort by British Minister George B. Mathew in 1862 to settle the matter by compensating Guatemala the sum of 25,000 pounds sterling was rejected by President Carrera. A supplementary convention held in 1863 failed to be ratified by either government. The question has never been satisfactorily resolved.

The Belize Settlement Becomes a Colony—1862

In 1861, the Legislative Council in Belize again requested their recognition as a colony, and pressed their plea until the Law Officers of the Crown conceded that the Settlement of Belize was indeed *de jure* as well as *de facto* a part of Her Majesty's Dominions. On May 12, 1862, Britain finally declared Belize, which had suffered two hundred years of ill-defined status with questionable boundaries and confusing government structures, a British colony. The current Superintendent of Belize, Frederick R. Seymour, was appointed Lieutenant-Governor of the new Colony of British Honduras by the Queen. He was to work directly under the Governor of Jamaica. The timing of the colonial recognition was especially opportune as the United States, who certainly would have objected, was now involved in her own Civil War and could hardly be expected to attempt to enforce the Monroe Doctrine in Central America with her own country fighting for its very life at home.

British Honduran economy had undergone a rather drastic decline in recent years, primarily from depletion of her important timber resources from over-exploitation, and had lost its unique trading position. Without an agricultural industry to broaden their economic base, the Colony was hardpressed to find ways of compensating for the failure of its prime timber resources and by the dislocation of trade routes. A temporary solution to their economic problems came from an unexpected source—the Civil War in the United States. This war proved to be the greatest single influence for the internal development of British Honduras in the nineteenth century.

Belize and the Blockade, 1861–1865

The Federal Government in Washington attempted to establish a naval blockade of the South in order to cut off its exportation of cotton, its basic exchange commodity. This was an impossible undertaking from the offset, as the Federal Navy was far too under-equipped to effect a blockade of 3,500 miles of coastline. The Federalists concentrated their blockade efforts at four critical points along the southern coastline, and had to be satisfied with this arrangement as an effective blockade. The British Honduran trading community was the immediate beneficiary of this situation, which greatly stimulated internal growth in the Colony. Colonial opportunists could easily carry on an active trade with the Confederate States by running the loosely-woven network of Federal ships and exchange European-manufactured guns, boots, and gunpowder for agricultural commodities.

Belize was the nearest British port to the markets for this contraband. Belizean merchants had over a half century of experience in coastal trading and their flat-bottomed, shallow-draft vessels could hug the coastline all the way south from Louisiana in relative safety from pursuit of the larger deep-drafted Federal men-of-war. The British Hondurans knew every angle in the complex occupation of gun-running, and were not slow in exploiting the opportunity it afforded them.

Early in the war years, when the South was at high tide, there was every indication of the imminent recognition of the Confederacy by the British Government. Every ruse and trick was used to camouflage the trade with the South. One typical rebel sympathizer, a James McNab, operated a successful gun-powder export busuiness from his "groggery" in Belize City. His establishment served as a meeting place for blockade runners. Captains of ships from the Confederate ports could "sell" their vessels to McNab, thereby obtaining British registry and allow-ing them to sail under the British flag. McNab became owner *pro forma* of over twenty ships in this manner, which he kept fully outfitted and furnished their captains with cargoes of contraband gunpowder and shot packed in flour barrels from his grocery store located adjacent to his tavern, marked as other commodities such as coffee and dry goods.

Civil War in the United States was too important an event to be ignored in British Honduras. While most of the colonists sympathized with the Confederate cause, the Federalists found some strong support among the humble classes. Feelings became so pitched that at one time a violent riot broke out between the Black soldiers stationed at the Old Barracks and the local citizens, which lasted for three nights. One life was lost and a large number were seriously injured in the fighting. All the white women in the Colony were housed at the fort for their safety, while every white man was notified to prepare to defend his life on a moment's warning. Pistols, guns, dirks and all manner of weapons were employed by either side, but no other casualties resulted.

As the tide of the Civil War changed, less contraband activity was possible. The efforts for its suppression by the commercial agent for the United States in Belize, Dr. Charles A. Leas, began to take effect, especially when Lt.-Governor Seymour agreed to cooperate in discouraging this clandestine trade. By the end of 1863, Leas was able to report to Washington that all contraband shipping, except for an irregular stream of blockade runners putting into Belize with illegal cargoes of southern cotton, had stopped, and no more war goods were being shipped from Belize to the South.

Even before the war between the states had concluded, a movement was on in Belize to attract immigration of newly-freed Blacks to British Honduras. Governor Seymour saw in the North American Blackman, who had been trained in the arts of agriculture, a vehicle for opening up the vast fertile interior of the country to the cultivation of cotton, rice, sugar and tobacco. It was thought that the better-trained and more ener-getic American Blackman would do much better in this endeavor than those from the West Indies whom they com-plained were indolent, lazy and unenterprising—"suited only for the fugitive arts of cutting logwood and mahogany."

Neither the government of British Honduras nor the largest landowner, the British Honduras Company, who had their own plan for colonization of the country with American ex-slaves, were willing to guarantee even the minimum requirements to assure that the prospective emigrant would be any better off in British Honduras than at home, or that he would not, in fact, find himself another indentured servant of the British Honduras

Company. After much consultation between Mr. John Hodge of the British Honduras Company and the United States Government in Washington, the Lincoln administration turned down his immigration proposal, due to a large extent to the counseling of Dr. Leas, the U.S. agent in Belize.

Dr. Leas wrote to Secretary of State Seward in 1863 concerning the proposed emigration:

> "Do they propose to share the profits of labor with the colored emigrant? Do they propose that he be a co-
> -laborer in the great and glorious work of subduing and opening up the vast wilderness, and developing its full agricultural and commercial capabilities! And afterwards, to enjoy in common the great social, political and moral reward, that naturally flows from honest and well-directed toil! No, by no means, they intend him for quite a different purpose. He and his posterity are only designed as hewers of wood and drawers of water."

Contemporary with the interest in the colony for immigration of the freed slaves was the desire in Belize to attract Confederate "emigres" who began to flee the New South, when it became obvious that the doom of the Confederacy was imminent. This movement was with the approval and aid of the U.S. government. As early as 1864 Dr. Leas had suggested to the State Department that Confederates who wished to escape the "reconstruction" should be allowed to enter British Honduras. He assured them that they would be welcome and that he considered it the humane thing to do.

By the end of 1865, the economic decline in British Honduras had reached crises proportions. Depleted mahogany reserves, lost markets, corruption of absentee landlords and the stark isolation of the colony, without even the federal blockade smuggling windfall of the past years, had left British Honduras with only one alternative—the development of agriculture. Immigation from the southern states was seen by many as their greatest hope for the future.

Governor John Gardiner Austin reportedly admitted to Dr.

Leas that he considered American immigration the only hope for the colony's economy, and he saw in this immigration the means by which the colony would some day achieve independence from Britain.

For more than three years after the conclusion of the Civil War, the port of Belize City was alive with prospective southern settlers looking for land on which to settle in British Honduras. In spite of the acute awareness on the part of the colonial government in Belize of the great importance of Confederates to their future, few concessions were offered them as incentives to stay. Land prices remained uniformly high, even for undeveloped land far from the coast.

There is some evidence that the large landowners, particularly the British Honduras Company, collaborated with the Colonial Office in London in maintaining the high price of land. Whether because they feared future competition from the newcomers or used these monopolistic tactics in an effort to reap high profits isn't known, but the effect of their tactics was that thousands of would-be settlers by-passed British Honduras in favor of any number of Latin American nations from Mexico to Brazil who were bidding eagerly for the Southern immigrants. Some, like Brazil, were offering free land to the settlers.

Private immigration companies were somewhat more successful over the next decade in enticing immigration, but by 1869 more were returning to the U.S. than were immigrating to British Honduras. Cotton growing had proved to be unsuccessful in Belize, and many immigrants yearned for the conveniences of the United States.

Guatemalan Dispute Revived—1884

British treatment of the subject of the road construction obligation, the key to the ratification of the Boundary Agreement of 1859 with Guatemala, was a story of evasion and delay. Since construction of the Panama Railroad in 1855, the commercial importance of British Honduras in the eyes of the Foreign Office had been reduced, so that by the 1880's the value of a cartroad (railroad) between the Atlantic and Guatemala City seemed remote and insignificant.

Lord Grenville had responded to a Guatemalan proposal to "arrange the controversy by the honorable and civilized method of arbitration" by replying in August, 1880, that Britain was "exonerated from all obligations arising from the Treaty of 1859."

Except for some sharp exchanges in 1882 between U.S. Secretary of State Frelinghuysen and the British Secretary of State over British Honduras—at one juncture Frelinghuysen advised Lord Grenville that in his country's opinion, the control which Great Britain exercised over British Honduras was illegal—after the 1850's, United States diplomacy mostly ignored the colony.

In 1884, tired of rebuffs and delay, Guatemala's minister in London, Grisanto Medina, announced the end of his government's pursuing tactics. Guatemala, he stated, had exhausted all diplomatic means of broaching the subject, and Britain still declined to discuss it. In these circumstances, Guatemala filed a protest in the form of an ultimatum: either the entire treaty of 1859 was in force and must be carried out, or it was totally null and void and the situation would remain as it had been before the treaty.

Britain needed three things that this treaty, if ratified, would give them; unquestionable sovereignty in Belize, clearly defined boundaries, and a trade agreement with Guatemala. Yet the Colonial Office spent the next two decades in internal wrangling and weighty discussions without drawing the debate to a conclusion. Guatemalan diplomats returned again and again to the task of opening negotiations on the road question, but such negotiations held a progressively low priority and were easily set aside for future consideration.

Anglo-Mexican Treaty—1893

All attempts by the British minister in Mexico, P. Campbell Scarlett, to extract a permanent boundary settlement from Emperor Maximilian's shaky government, before its collapse, were unsuccessful. When Benito Juarez regained power in Mexico and the French puppet, Maximilian, was ousted, he promptly terminated diplomatic relations with Britain in 1867 for having taken part in his political demise after the Mexican War of Reform. That year, in the midst of chaos on her northern frontier, Great Britain commenced a unilateral survey of the colony's boundaries.

The Mexican Empire fell without ever disavowing its claim to Belize and to El Peten District of Guatemala since it first made the claim in 1864. The lack of diplomatic relations between Great Britain and Mexico made negotiations difficult. British feelers concerning a possible solution to the northern boundary problems were answered by President Juarez's Government with a four-hundred-page letter accusing the British of having perpetrated the War of the Races and having prolonged it by the sale of arms to the Indians, and questioned Great Britain's very title to Belize.

On June 8, 1878, Lord Salisbury replied by briefly stating that his government would not discuss its title to British Honduras, which title it considered good and sufficient, having been fully established by conquest (at the battle of St. George's Cay) long before Mexico's existence as an independent state. He warned that they would be compelled to take all measures necessary to preserve order and security on their northern border.

Intense pressure upon the British cabinet to protect British investments in the North was brought by a group of firms, headed by the powerful British Honduras Company, after the last raid by Marcus Canul on Orange Walk in 1872. These firms, despite lack of diplomatic relations, traded sharp exchanges with the Mexican Government and pressed for compensation for damages incurred in the Indian raids.

At the close of the 1870's, Mexico's attitude began to change in regard to the problem, and she appeared more willing for a settlement in order to control the Yucatan Indians, yet diplomatic relations were not restored until 1884.

By 1882, Mexico agreed to a meeting with Guatemala to

discuss the Mexican-Guatemalan boundary dispute. Held in New York City in August of that year, this meeting resulted in an agreement between those two countries. Mexico conceded that in demarcation of boundaries, actual possession should serve as the basis of deciding claims, and Mexico dropped her claims to Guatemalan Peten.

Encouraged by the success of this meeting, Britain was able to restore diplomatic relations in 1884, and initiated negotiations which ultimately resulted in the signing of a boundary treaty between the two nations on July 8, 1393. This treaty had four articles as follows:

Article 1.   The international boundary between Mexico and the Colony of British Honduras is to be a line, beginning in the strait which separates the States of Yucatan from Ambergris Cay, running thence in a defined course south to the Hondo River, following the Hondo in its deepest channel, continuing up Blue Creek until it crosses the meridian of Garbutt's Falls at a point due north of the point where the boundary lines of Mexico and British Honduras intersect and thence due south to latitude 17 degrees 49 minutes (the boundary line between Mexico and Guatemala).

Article 2.   The exportation of arms and ammunition for sale to Indian tribes is prohibited.

Article 3.   Mutual aid shall be given in the prevention of Indian incursions into each other's country.

Article 4.   Free navigation is to be guaranteed merchant vessels using the water between Amergris Cay and the mainland.

The Mexican Senate hesitated in ratifying this treaty, but were convinced by their Prime Minister who pointed out, "The historical evidence of Mexico's claim to Belize was by no means clear, British occupation had become legalized by lapse of time, and the question is now purely one of practical politics."

This treaty was the first clear recognition by an American state of British sovereignty over the colony. Thus, as one historian has observed, "The history of Belize is a fine example of how successful buccaneering can lead to territorial encroachments, to settlements, to a sphere of influence, to a protectorate with expanding boundaries, and finally to actual sovereignty."

The boundaries so established have never since been disputed by Mexico, and it is difficult to see on what valid grounds the question could ever be re-opened. In 1930, when Guatemala renewed her claims to Belize, Mexico made it known to all parties that should the status of Belize change, Mexico would not allow Guatemalan claims to any territory north of the Sibun River, but would, in this eventuality, consider this major portion of Belize to be Mexico's.

INTERNAL PROBLEMS OF THE COLONIAL GOVERNMENT

By 1869, pressure had been building to convert British Honduras to a "Crown Colony"; that is, one directly administrated by the Crown through a Governor. This was in keeping with British policy throughout the West Indies at the time, and would allow the Imperial Government to allocate what was necessary for defense against the Indians on the northern border without having to be voted by the Legislative Council who had been hesitant to appropriate monies for defense of Corozal while they themselves enjoyed the relative safety of Belize City. The elected Legislative Council in recent years had been plagued with poor attendance, and general remissness in their duties. There was strong opposition to such surrender of self-government, but in 1870 the Legislative Council abolished itself, paving the way for Crown rule.

The new constitution inaugurated in April, 1871, became a point of bitter controversy in British Honduran politics for the next twenty years. It was very difficult for the colony with a tradition of self-government to accept despotism, however practicable it might be, as the solution to their problems. Even though only approximately 8 percent had been eligible to vote under the old system, local people had enjoyed the benefits of the political training their involvement in the government afforded. The new constitution was soon regretted and ultimately proved to be a grave set-back to the colony.

The able Lieutenant-Governor Cairns saw the colony through the constitutional change of 1870–71 and managed to pour enough oil on the troubled waters of local discontent to be able to leave his post in 1874 to become Governor of Trinidad without leaving too many enemies.

Cairns was replaced in Belize by Major R. M. Mundy. He and his colonial administrator, Captain C. B. H. Mitchell, completed arrangements for military defense so badly needed on the northern frontier. Mundy seemed unable, however, to stem the tide of economic depression, and in 1875 imports fell off by $306,000 and exports by $72,000. He admitted to his successor, "the general stagnation of trade has been severely felt in the colony."

Into the doldrums of the late 1870's came one of the few truly outstanding governors of British Honduras, Sir Frederick P. Barlee. With twenty-two years of experience as colonial secretary for Western Australia behind him, Barlee came to Belize with the knowledge and equipment to deal with the complex problems facing the colony. He began his tenure in office with an exhaustive tour through the entire colony, from the northern frontier to the jungles of the South, in order to fully inform himself as to the existing conditions. Back in Belize City, Barlee launched a program to develop the entire colony.

Barlee's plan had five parts, or changes he saw as needing implementing: (1) Change the mail route from Jamaica to New Orleans; (2) Abolish all excise tax on sugar, but enforce the collection of taxes on the operation of rum stills; (3) Lower the price of Crown Lands to $1.00 per acre in some areas, and set a $6.00 fee for the survey and title to them; (4) Reduce the tariff on imports; and (5) Establish a thorough system of auditing the public accounts. While these reforms may appear modest, the reaction to them was explosive and their combined effect was considerable.

The mail route change showed creative thought. British Honduras did not have sufficient freight and passenger traffic to make regular steamer calls at Belize economical. This required the government to pay a subsidy for regular mail service. Switching the mail service through New Orleans and giving the subsidy to a company running fruit steamers not only made the proposition economically feasible for the shipping company, but gave Belizean growers a chance to ship bananas to New Orleans. This quick-cash crop, which required little initial capital outlay, proved a bonanza to the colony's agriculture industry and stimulated the nation's trade as well.

Even in the face of the success his program enjoyed from the start, Barlee was not without opposition. In 188?, a group of businessmen petitioned the Colonial Secretary of State, saying that they had been persuaded to change to Crown Colony rule in order to gain more efficiency and economy, but that they now regretted this action and thought it to have been an error. They requested that Barlee's program be disallowed and that the Crown rule be abolished. Barlee was ultimately confirmed and the Colonial Office indicated their support for the terms of his program.

Barlee was a strong-willed man, and his controversial administration left a much healthier economy when he retired in 1882 than that which he had inherited five years earlier.

Unfortunately Barlee's successors, a series of interim executives, took less interest in the colony. Colonel Robert Harley served nominally, first as administrator and then as Lt.-Governor, but most of his term of office was spent in England on "sick leave." General Robert S. Turton took a turn as administrator, followed by the former colonial secretary, Henry Fowler.

Fowler, a long-time resident of the colony and colonial secretary under Barlee (whose policies he disdained), had large personal holdings in the colony. He held mahogany concessions, owned a banana plantation and was a stock raiser. With such power as his office held, it was inevitable that his ability to maintain impartiality in the stewardship of the public welfare, in spite of his own vested interests, would be questioned. Evidence presented in the *Colonial Guardian* in 1884 showed that through some devious manipulations Fowler had blocked the building of any railroad (long sought as a means of opening up the interior of the colony for development) which would not open up his own holdings in the Cayo District. "We had some time ago laboured under the belief that it was impossible for an administration to be worse than that of Sir Robert Harley, but we must confess that Mr. Fowler's has been far more damaging to the interests of the Colony. The sins of the administration of the former were mostly those of omissions, whilst those of the latter have been those of commission."

A major concession by the British Colonial Office in 1884 cleared up a point of contention which had existed since 1841 when the Superintendent of Belize had been directed to deal with London through the Governor of Jamaica. Even upon becoming a British colony in 1862, it was governed by a Lieutenant-Governor under the Governor of Jamaica. This situation had always been resented in British Honduras, as it made it appear that their colony was subordinate to Jamaica. The arrangement had no real advantage to either, as the Governor of Jamaica usually had little knowledge or interest in British Honduras. It often gave rise to problems of conflict of interest, as in the case of the Bay Colony's urgent request for troops to defend their Settlement when troops were needed in Jamaica.

On October 7, 1884, all ties with Jamaica were severed and Lt.-Governor Sir Roger Tuckfield Goldsworthy, the newly-appointed administrator, became the first Governor of British Honduras.

When Goldsworthy first arrived in 1884, the principal matter of business was the implementation of the Baron H. Siccama plan for improving the sanitary conditions of Belize City by filling in lowlands within the city, dredging the two principal sewage-clogged canals of the city, increasing water storage facilities, and the construction of a pier. A local committee had studied the procedures for best accomplishing this work. Their recommendations included working only in the winter months and disposing of the dredgings, twenty-two years of accumulated sewerage, out at sea. The colony had experienced a rise in their yellow fever rate in the past when raw sewage was dredged out and left exposed.

Goldsworthy chose to disregard the committee's report and gave the construction contract, without taking competitive bids, to a Mr. C. T. Hunter whom the *Colonial Guardian* said "had notoriously failed in almost every, if not every, scheme which he has ever undertaken in this colony." Hunter was permitted to deviate in several respects from the contract specifications. He dredged the raw sewage and deposited it along the canal banks. Over the objections of the local physicians, who were very much alarmed by the danger to the health of the colony, the work proceeded through the heat of the summer. To off-set the doctors' condemnation of this practice, Goldsworthy appointed Hunter's brother, Dr. Alexander Hunter, to the post of Colonial Surgeon at a substantial increase in fees allowed for that post. The new Colonial Surgeon had been a member of the committee that had established the health precautions in this work, but to no one's surprise, changed his mind and reported to Goldsworthy that in his medical opinion no health hazard would result from his brother's work.

Soon thereafter, both yellow fever and a disease identified as "canal fever" broke out in epidemic proportion. The regular labor force refused to work near the canals, and the contractor was allowed by the Governor to use prisoners at one-third wages to complete the project, and equipped them with boots at Government expense.

In this and in other ways, Governor Goldsworthy seemed to go out of his way to earn the hatred of the colonists, applying local law with severity against all who opposed him and waiving it completely in favor of his favorites. Doctor Hunter, before serving a year in the office of Colonial Surgeon, retired with a pension such as no other holder of this office had ever received.

By October, 1886, after only two years of the Goldsworthy administration, the treasury had gone from a $90,000 surplus to a deficit exceeding that amount. This proved difficult to explain without admitting to wholesale squander and the lining of the pockets of his cronies. Within two weeks of this news, Goldsworthy's reassignment by the Colonial Office was announced to the great relief of everyone in the colony.

November 2, 1886, was a festive and gala day in Belizean history. All the stores were closed, the schools empty, and large crowds of people paraded in the streets in joyful anticipation of the Governor's 3:00 o'clock departure. The enthusiasm reached the greatest intensity as the departure time arrived. Large crowds, chanting uncomplimentary slogans and carrying large banners, gathered along the breakwater at Fort George to see him off. Goldsworthy embarked from the Government House wharf and received a military salute from the honor guard, but as his barge drew along side the breakwater, he was roundly hissed and booed. When Goldsworthy replied with an obscene gesture, rocks were thrown. A large number of pleasure boats, lighters, and schooners, all decorated with banners and signs carrying derogatory comments concerning the Governor's morality, integrity and parentage, followed the government boat out to the anchorage of the mail steamer which was to take Goldsworthy to England. A large schooner with a full brass band, and a sloop yacht with another musical group, joined the others in circling around the freighter and alternately playing the *Dead March in Saul* and *Rogue's March*. One lighter with a large white banner with red letters reading "Catfish Still Uneaten," referring to the threat that Goldsworthy had made that "he would make the colony eat catfish before he was done with them," passed by and slowly dipped her flag in salute to the despised Governor. (In Belize catfish feed solely on human waste in the Belize River.)

As the freighter sailed, the colony's boats lined the deep channel along which the freighter had to pass, and saw it off with shouts of "good riddance." The band boats kept company with the ship for three miles out at sea with a continuous serenade of the *Rogue's March.* The rest of the day and throughout the night the townspeople in Belize City gave themselves to festivity, with every class and caste joining a celebration rivalling the Christmas revelry of former years.

After Goldsworthy's notable departure, Henry Fowler, the proverbial Colonial Secretary, became acting administrator again. In the climate of good feeling accompanying the Governor's leaving, Fowler enjoyed a popularity he had not before been shown. He was able to enact several important measures. Among these was the cancellation of what was left of C. T. Hunter's dredging contract and attachment of his equipment so that the rest of the work could be completed under more sanitary conditions.

The sequel is not attractive. For reasons best known within the Colonial Office, Goldsworthy was returned to his post in Belize. Whether the Secretary of State for the Colonies was incredibly uninformed, or whether he wished to teach the colonists in Belize "proper respect," it was a devastating blow to the Belizeans. In an emergency meeting held in Belize City on January 10, 1887, the most widely attended public meeting ever held in the colony, two resolutions were passed. The first expressed dismay at Goldsworthy's return, and the second simply stated that the Governor's moral character had been open to censure during his previous term of office. An accompanying memorial listed all of his administrative sins during his two-year term of office.

The resolutions had no effect except to add to the already heady alienation which existed between the Governor and all men of integrity within the colony. Goldsworthy worked in complete isolation, shunned by all but his few less-than-reputable friends. Not long after his return, Mr. Hunter filed a claim for damages against the colony resulting from the seizure of his dredging plant and equipment. This led to the largest scandal of Goldsworthy's colorfully corrupt administration.

The Hunter case consisted of three arbitrations; the first and second were held in Belize City with Goldsworthy himself acting as an agent of the public interest, claiming he was free to do so as he had been out of the colony at the time of the seizure of equipment and was therefore unbiased. Mr. Hunter received an award of $20,000 damages in the first hearing for loss of his plant. The second was inconsequential, but the third arbitration hearing was critical, concerning damages not introduced until after the outcome of the first two had been established. For this hearing, the Colonial Office moved the site to London where colonial witnesses would not be able to testify on behalf of the colony. Two arbitrators were selected, one to represent Hunter and a Mr. John Gentle of Belize to represent the colony's interests. Mr. John Gentle, it was pointed out by the press in Belize, had extensive business dealings with the Hunter Brothers and held a mortgage on property belonging to Dr. Alexander Hunter. Gentle would hardly be an appropriate party to be considered an adversary, nor even one to be properly neutral in regard to the Hunters. In the end this board of arbitrators awarded Hunter another $30,000 in damages.

According to the constitution at the time, only the legislative council could appropriate funds to pay the Hunter arbitral award. Since this had been a suit against the colonial government, Goldsworthy suggested that the legislature vote a tax to raise the money for the Hunter debt. In May, 1890, when the matter came up for vote, the unofficial members of the legislative council resigned rather than vote to appropriate money for the award, and a lengthy deadlock ensued.

The legislature's boycott, while precipitated by the Hunter affair, soon became the colony's stand for representation in government and against open despotism of Crown Colony rule. Governor Goldsworthy was finally recalled in October, 1890, but the colonists did not relent. Their stubborn, shrewd resistance was finally rewarded one year and seven months after the legislative boycott began. On January 1, 1892, a new constitution was given them in which local elected representatives would have a majority in the legislative council. A sense of political unity, never before experienced in British Honduras, was now evident. Behind this common cause, the colony had become united and had won. Congratulations were expressed around the Caribbean for this "people's victory."

Toward the close of the nineteenth century, much emphasis was put on exploration of the Colony. The population had traditionally been centered in a few towns, connected by rivers, which were the highways of the Settlement. Mr. Stephens, in 1841, observed that there were no wheeled vehicles, much less carriages, in the entire settlement. There were very few, even in 1890. The pit-pans and bateaux on the rivers, and sloops on the coastal waters, still provided the only transportation. Even as late as the 1930's there were only approximately thirty-five miles of roads in British Honduras.

A common sight on the Belize River was the government boat, fashioned after the original Maya pit-pan. It was forty feet long, six feet wide, and had been dug out of a single mahogany log. Ten feet from the stern, and running forward, was a light wooden top supported by fancifully-carved stancheons, with side-curtains for protection against sun and rain; it was fitted out with huge cushioned seats for the Governor and his friends, reminding one of a Venetian gondola. The boat was manned by eight black soldiers in red and gold uniforms seated two abreast with two standing behind as steersmen. Their rhythmic chanting, as they paddled up the Belize River, always evoked shouts and cheers from natives on the shore. This sing-song banter became, in time, a polished folk art in which each oarsman would improvise a verse, each verse alternating with a full chorus. The contents of these verses usually were humorous and contained some social comment on the plight of the Blackmen of Belize, or poked fun at some prominent white citizen. Also popular were verses which boasted of the great sex prowess of its author, or the lack of it of one or another of the boat's oarsmen.

Only a small percentage of the interior had been explored and none properly mapped. In 1872 two Americans, Colonel W. T. Mechlin and W. R. Warren, partially explored a section from Belize City to the Guatemalan border. Six years later, Mr. Worth, a miner and Mr. Drake, a sugar planter, undertook an expedition into the Mayan Mountain Range. The following year they attemped a longer expedition, this time accompanied by the Colonial Secretary, Henry Fowler. Concentrating their efforts on the area of the Cockscomb Ridge, they reported on mineral deposits found, and were able to accurately measure the elevations of mountains they encountered.

Other attempts at early exploration were conducted by G. H. Nilson in 1886 and Gordon Allen's party in 1888, both in the Stann Creek District. Four years later, a party of railway surveyors made an expedition up the Sibun River to a point near its source. In 1898 Mr. Monohan opened up a trail from Stann Creek through the mountains to the Cayo District, roughly the route that the Hummingbird Highway now follows.

What mineral wealth the unexplored reaches of the colony's interior might contain was the subject of much speculation at the turn of the century. Gold, both in quartz and in sand, had been discovered and rubies, opals, manganese, graphite and lead were known to exist, although in what quantities was left to conjecture. It was hoped that oil might be discovered and toward that end, the government began informal discussions with private industry to determine the feasibility of obtaining an extensive geological survey; although it was generally felt that agricultural development was the more urgently needed.

Land of Hurricanes and Underdeveloped Resources (1900-1975)

The first decade of the twentieth century was one of modest internal improvement in Belize. Telephone lines were constructed north from Belize City to Consejo near the Mexican border and south as far as Punta Gorda, giving the country its first national communications hook-up. In Belize City electric street lights were installed, and lighthouses and shore lights were constructed to aid shipping. Eighteen miles of narrow-gauge track, called the Stann Creek Railway, was completed and the Bank of British Honduras was founded.

Transportation remained a major problem. Except for two-wheeled horse-drawn carts, commerce was still largely restricted to the murky rivers plied by pit-pan, locally constructed dories, and paddle-wheelers. Two of the latter, the steamers "Africola" and the "Romulus," operated by L. G. Chavanne, made regular scheduled mail runs between Belize City and the northern reaches of the colony with their decks piled high with huge crates, bags of sugar and rice, animals, and furniture. Some small cabins below deck served first-class passengers; however, most were content to travel on deck amid coops of chickens and piles of produce where it was cooler and the air fresher.

The lack of a road system to tie Belize City with the rest of the Colony perpetrated an unfortunate division between city and country, each existing in mutual ignorance of the other. The populations in the outlying districts were deprived of the advantages of what educational, medical, or other social services were being provided the more fortunate city dwellers. The large lumber investors, both local and British, successfully resisted any national capital expenditures for a highway system while their own profits depended solely on the rivers for transportation. Until as late as 1931, not a single road was built to link Belize City with any part of the rest of the country. Ethnic divisions and political apathy, still prevalent to some degree in the interior, are a result of this long separation.

For centuries the urban creole elite acted and behaved as if Belize City *was* British Honduras and the Spanish-speaking Indian-Mestizo peasantry was in the society but not *of* it.

In spite of its fascinating geography and exotic setting, Belize was not a popular post with British Governors. Both Governor Sir Alan Burns and Colonial Secretary Sydney Olivier before him, in 1900, wrote disparaging essays, published in Great Britain, concerning their appointments in Belize. It was found to be so demoralizing that in British diplomatic circles Belize was often referred to as the "slum of the Empire." Most of the Governors, until Sir John Burdon's time, took little interest in furthering the goals of the colony and spent more time, it seems, in scheming to find a way of being reassigned.

Basic to the problem then, and to some degree now, is this territory's geographical and psychological isolation. Not fitting into the British scheme of things as far as colonial advancement, Belize was looked upon by the British only as a source of exploitation of extremely profitable forest products, and little else. Belizeans also have never seen themselves a part of the British West Indian world of plantation economy (large estate-holders employing a strong working class), but instead, as sturdy adventurers and individualists cast in the mold of their free pioneering ancestors who had hacked an existence for themselves out of a hostile jungle.

The twentieth century opened with near-war between the

neighboring independent states of Central America. Hostilities were averted only after an emergency conference was held in Washington, D.C. on November 14, 1907, presided over by William Buchanan, representing President Theodore Roosevelt. Out of this meeting came eight resolutions, signed by all the delegates. One established a Central American Court of Justice, consisting of five judges, which was successful in maintaining peace and sponsoring a spirit of Central American unity. The states realized more fully their dependence upon one another and the importance of presenting a united front to the world.

Guatemala's need for an East Coast outlet, and her realization that Britain was not going to carry out the road project outlined in the 1859 Treaty, led to the building by a private contractor of a railroad connecting her capital with Port Barrios, her only East Coast port. It was completed in 1908.

A proposal before the United States Senate in 1914 to buy British Honduras and trade it, with a sum of money, to Mexico for Lower California and a part of the Sonora Desert, was met with understandable concern in Belize, but was soon forgotten, as in August of that year Britain and Germany became involved in war. Residents of Belize were among those lost on the *Lusitania*, and the first British Honduran volunteer war contingent sailed for Europe.

Governor Sir John Burdon unveiled a red granite obelisk in the small Fort George Park, overlooking the Caribbean, on Armistice Day, 1925, dedicated to the memory of the many men of the colony who gave their lives in the defense of Britain in that war.

BARON BLISS

Near this granite obelisk, on a promontory facing the multi-hued Caribbean, is another monument; the tomb of Baron Bliss, an adventurous eccentric who adopted the colony as his home in his last years, spent on his yacht, the *Sea King, R.Y.S.* anchored in Belize Harbor. Henry Edward Ernest Victor Bliss, J.P., and 4th Baron of the Kingdom of Portugal, was born in

Marlow in Buckingham, England on February 16, 1869. He was educated at Cheltenham, succeeded his father to the Barony in 1890, and married Ethel Wolton the following year. The generous bequest to the colony in his will, found upon his death aboard his yacht on March 9, 1926, was wisely invested and interest from this inheritance has provided for many civic buildings, including: the Baron Bliss Institute, the Town Hall in Corozal, the Health Center in Corozal, the Baron Bliss School of Nursing and the in-transit Lounge Building. It has been used to build public market buildings in Punta Gorda, Stann Creek Town, and San Ignacio and has paid for the road from Burrel Boom to Hattieville and the Baron Bliss Promenade in Belize City. Other civic projects financed by the Bliss fund have included furnishing of the Bliss Institute and Corozal Town Hall, many athletic fields and playgrounds, engineering studies for a water supply for Belize City, and an electrical plant for Orange Walk. It has purchased the Bliss shore light in Belize, an ambulance for the Corozal Health Center and, most recently, the land on which the new capital, Belmopan, is built. His yacht, the *Sea King* is still in use by the Department of Fisheries. March 9th is now an annual national holiday, Baron Bliss Day, in his memory.

Privateering in the seventeenth century, seizing of American ships in the War of 1812, gun-running in the War of the Races in Yucatan, supplying Confederate blockade-runners during the Civil War and rum-running during the United States' prohibition have furnished Belize with its finest financial hours. Fortunes were made during the 1920's by smuggling bootleg Canadian whiskey, purchased for $1.00, into the United States and sold at $6.00. Fast ships kept a regular schedule from Belize City to the Gulf ports of United States, supplying a willing market with their illicit cargoes. This financial boom ended abruptly in 1933, when the U.S. Eighteenth Amendment was repealed.

After years of unchecked mahogany cutting and destructive chicle-bleeding, a Forestry Department was established in 1922 and a Conservator of Forests appointed. The 12,000-acre Silk Grass Forest Reserve near Stann Creek was set aside for a

three-year program of experimentation with sylviculture treatment. The results they achieved gave the government foresters
confidence that, under scientific treatment, valuable timber
could be replaced and restocked. In virgin mahogany logging
forests, where one tree per acre was average, now thirty or more
could be planted. This had a great impact on the colony's
economy, as at that time forest produce represented 83 percent
of the national exports. Mahogany, used for fine furniture in
Britain, and chicle, used by a gum-chewing United States population, were the major products. Experiments with a new technique of tapping the sapodilla tree to obtain chicle without
destroying the tree, as it is now done, also proved encouraging.

The wealth of the colony was still mainly comprised in those
forests that had attracted the first colonists. Logwood, once
used throughout the world in the manufacture of dyes, had
been superseded in importance to Belize by mahogany and the
wood the natives called "cedar" which is really another variety
of mahogany. In the years immediately preceding the World
War, the value of the logwood export was only about 19,000
pounds sterling while that of mahogany and chicle each were
about 145,000. A considerable proportion of the mahogany and
"cedar," however, was being cut beyond the colony's frontiers
and smuggled into Belize City for shipment. The logwood
industry enjoyed a brief revival during World War I when the
supply of German aniline dyes, the chief cause of its earlier
demise, became cut off and foreign countries began to cast
around for substitutes.

Except for the forest species mentioned, little attention was
given to the many other types of valuable timber grown in the
verdant jungles of Belize, although large quantities of various
species of hardwood lumber were sent to Britain during the
World War for use in the construction of airplane components.
After the war, this resource was largely forgotten in favor of the
ever-popular mahogany. Neither the valuable oil-bearing nuts of
the cahune palm, nor the vanilla orchid, had been exploited
commercially.

A Department of Agriculture, established in 1920, concentrated its early efforts on the country's small sugar industry which until that time had not been a major exporter. In fact, in spite of its existence since the mid-nineteenth century as a cash crop, and the exploitation of Belizean Rum derived from the native crop, sugar was still being imported to meet the Colony's need. A cooperative sugar and syrup factory was established, with private planters sharing ownership with the government. Bananas and coconuts were exported, as were plantains, rubber and cocoa on a smaller scale. The natural conditions for the raising of rice, coffee, cotton, tobacco, and all tropical fruits were considered as admirable and their cultivation to be encouraged. Outside of the local breeds of small horses and mules, no livestock was raised and, except for sea food, all of the meat for local consumption had to be imported. The total yearly export trade was about 1,000,000 pound sterling but the imports exceeded this by 200,000 pounds in 1921. During the 1920–1921 fiscal year the total revenue of the colony was placed at 232,500 pound sterling and the expenditure 191,115 while the national debt amounted to 180,000 pound sterling.

Basic to the problem of developing the Colony's agriculture is the inherent aversion of the natives to field labor, which they identify with the plantation life of slavery in Jamaica and other Caribbean islands, or in the case of small farming, considered uniquely disreputable as long as some kind of living could be wrung out of the forest. A deep-rooted preference existed for the intense, but intermittent, work found solely in the log-cutting industry, and there existed a kind of social prestige connected with being a lumberjack.

The other ever-present problem found in the development of small farming lay in the fact that over one-third of the entire Colony was owned freehold by an expatriot capitalist group known as the Belize Estate and Produce Company (the Bookers of Honduras). They were concerned only with exploitation of the Colony's lumber resources and deliberately discouraged cultivation of the soil in order to retain the limited supply of available labor in their lumber camps. Their long-standing reluctance to let out any of their large land tracts for agricultural purposes, which policy had been recommended by the Legislative Council as early as 1879, lasted well into the twentieth century. This meant that the few small farmers could not plan for long-term agricultural development, when their tenure of the land was often by "squatter's rights" alone.

Another possible factor effecting alienation of the Creole logger from agricultural pursuits may lie in the fact that the main participant in the farming sector had always been the Amerindian, so that occupational prejudice may have been compounded by racial disdain; to be a farmer was thus not only socially inferior, but racially degrading. The result of this national disinclination toward agriculture resulted in this Colony, with a potentially productive agricultural economy, importing its basic food stuffs at excessive cost. Even a dietary snobbery of sorts existed, wherein the Creole businessman in Belize City preferred canned meat from Britain and condensed milk from the U.S. and shunned local produce of all kinds at any price.

BORDER DISPUTE REVIVED

In keeping with a current Colonial Office policy in 1925 requiring accurate surveys of all her colonies, the Secretary of State directed the Surveyor General of British Honduras to complete the work of establishing the western boundary line which had been abandoned in 1860. This work was to be done in conjunction with Guatemala, if agreeable with that government, but if not, unilaterally. An attempt to enlist Guatemala's cooperation in 1930 instead resurrected the long-standing, often-acrimonious dispute. Amid heated diplomatic exchanges, the colonial surveyors prepared for the monumental task of establishing a borderline through unhealthy and unexplored jungle. Two parties set out in June, 1932, to demarcate the line; one working south from Garbutt's Falls and one working north from Gracias a Dios Falls ("Thank God" Falls on the Sarstoon). These teams of local residents had been preferred over the originally proposed Royal Engineers because, in the Surveyor

General's opinion, they were as fully qualified and were better equipped to face the adverse conditions of the inhospitable terrain to be traversed.

Although Guatemala carefully avoided official recognition of the line, or of the survey teams, a Guatemalan Boundary Commission was sent over periodically to inspect their work. Toward the latter part of 1933, the two survey parties met midway and erected a stone and concrete monument to clearly mark the boundary. Thus it was hoped that the century-old disagreement could be laid to rest.

Upon completion of the survey, the British Legation in Guatemala asked for official Guatemalan recognition of this frontier line. The Guatemalan Chancellory refused to discuss the matter, "until His Majesty's government was prepared to carry out the bilateral stipulations of Clause VII of the 1859 Convention." Britain responded in 1934 with a demand that Guatemala accept the line delineated by the engineers, while maintaining her integral compliance with the Convention of 1859. An immediate solution was desired to facilitate Guatemalan cooperation required to control smuggling and illegal trade being carried on the Sarstoon River.

Guatemala proposed that the entire controversy be submitted to arbitration by United States President Franklin D. Roosevelt. Britain suggested that a more acceptable means of arbitration would be a judicial decision handed down by the Court of Permanent International Justice at The Hague, Netherlands. Guatemala did not wish to resort to this means of settlement, and has denied this suggestion made several times in later years.

In September, 1936, Guatemala sent Great Britain a multi-optional formula for the settlement of the dispute:

PROPOSAL A

(1) Britain would return Belize to Guatemala, for which the Republic would pay Britain 400,000 pounds and relinquish any claims whatsoever on Britain resulting from the Treaty of 1859.

or

(2) Britain would retain Belize and pay the Republic of Guatemala the same sum, plus furthermore, a strip of land necessary to give El Peten (Department of Guatemala) an outlet to the sea.

PROPOSAL B

The Republic of Guatemala would approve the demarcation of the frontiers as established by the British engineers; would relinquish its claim based on non-compliance by Britain with the provisions of the Treaty of 1859; and, in compensation, Great Britain would pay the Republic the sum of 50,000 pounds plus interest at 4 percent per annum from April 30, 1859, the date of the Treaty. (It is generally understood that the cost to each country would have been 50,000 pounds at that time.) As further compensation, Britain would grant Guatemala a strip of land so that the Department of El Peten would have an outlet to the sea.

Britain did not reply to this set of proposals until March 3, 1938, when a terse reply was sent by the Minister of Great Britain to the Minister of Foreign Affairs of Guatemala which stated: "It would serve no useful purpose to pursue the matter further."

Guatemala now contends that noncompliance with the obligations so incurred has caused the Boundary Convention of 1859 to lapse, and Great Britain now holds illegally the territories of the Anglo-Spanish pacts of 1783 and 1786 and two large areas of which she took control prior to the Convention of 1859. The condition of the controversy was then, as it is today, one of an international dispute unresolved.

In 1939 Guatemala announced "for the sake of unity and peace" that she would set aside her claims until after the Second World War.

Governor Burdon—1925

In 1925 a highly respected and competent Governor, Major Sir John Alder Burdon, K.B.E., C.M.G., M.A., F.R.G.S., a former

Bt. Major of the Cameron Highlanders and most recently Governor of Barbados and Administrator of St. Kitts-Nevis was appointed to Belize. His brief tenure in office, until 1931, left many lasting legacies with the colony. The Burdon Canal linking the Sibun and Belize Rivers was constructed, and the *Archives of British Honduras* were compiled. Since little written record of the colony's fascinating history had been kept, Burdon appointed a committee of local residents, including his Chief Information officer, author Monrad Sigfried Metzgen, who was also chairman of the Belize Literary and Debating Society, to painstakingly reconstruct, from what old records and correspondence did exist, a year-by-year chronicle of the life of the Colony from 1670 to 1884. This book, in three volumes, prepared in the years 1931 through 1935, is now in the Central Library of the Bliss Institute. Burdon, as Chairman of the committee, personally interviewed hundreds of long-standing residents and old-timers to glean all of the information possible to include in this exhaustive history. It was finished by his committee after his death in 1933.

At Burdon's invitation, Charles Lindbergh visited the Colony on his Good Will Tour in December, 1927. One of the largest receptions in the Colony's history was held for him at St. John's College.

The following year, a new road through Pine Ridge and bush country was constructed from Belize City into the Cayo District. M. S. Metzgen led a bicycle survey expedition to initially lay out a ninety-mile route along which fifty miles of dry weather road was eventually constructed with the aid of a Colonial Development Fund Grant from the British Government.

Hurricane of 1931

Not since a hurricane desolated the Bay Settlement on September 2, 1787 had Belize City been visited by a treacherous Caribbean cyclone, so the thousands of people gathered there on September 10, 1931 to celebrate St. George's Cay Day paid little heed to the storm warnings broadcast that morning and proceeded to organize the traditional children's parade. As Belizeans thought their country to be outside the hurricane belt, even the peculiar yellow-toned sky with densely piled alto-cumulus clouds blocking out the usually intense mid-day sun was not sufficient forewarning to stop the festivities.

A fury of hard, blinding rain hit the city late in the afternoon with a force of steel buckshot driven by 150-mile-an-hour winds, tearing houses apart and uprooting trees. The storm lasted an hour before subsiding. Curious Belizeans emerged from their shelters to view St. John's Cathedral, with its roof missing and windows gone, and the streets blocked by the debris of splintered houses and fallen trees. Hundreds gathered along Bliss Promenade to stare in bewilderment at the riled sea from where the storm had come. Suddenly the wind freshened and the storm again raged over the city, this time from the opposite direction, dragging a ten- to fifteen-foot tidal wave behind it. 2500 people were killed that day, nearly twenty percent of the population, and virtually all the survivors were left homeless, their little pole houses scattered like straws by the giant wind. St. John's College, near the sea front, had been totally destroyed with many of the students and priests lost. Whole families were killed; one family alone had 45 relatives listed among the casualties. Governor Burdon was able to save the *Archives* but many current Colonial documents were destroyed. Food and medical supplies were rushed in by the American Red Cross and many countries sent aid, but it was several years before the city was restored and it took another murderous hurricane, thirty years later, to blot out the memories of this national disaster.

Great Britain granted Belize a loan for reconstruction following the hurricane, but in so doing took over absolute control of the Colony and its finances, in 1932. The old Legislative Council was replaced by a new one, with the Governor as president. The Council of five official members and seven unofficial members, of which two were nominated by the Governor, met for the first time on the 12th of March, 1936.

Although business was conducted by democratic vote and a portion of the legislature was popularly elected, the Governor had the reserve power under the new constitution, should the Council fail to pass a bill he thought necessary, to declare the bill, resolution, motion, or vote to be in effect as if it had been passed by the Council. A Board of Agriculture for food inspection was established and ordinances against dangerous drugs and counterfeit money were among those bills passed in the 1936 session of legislature.

During the Thirties, roads were built to link Orange Walk and Corozal Town with Belize. Unfortunately these all-weather roads were constructed mainly of stone taken from hundreds of Maya Indian mounds found along the route. Today one can still find bits of Maya pottery and artifacts along the roadways. Travel was further improved with the building of a bridge over Haulover Creek in 1936 with funds obtained from a British grant. Education got a boost from the new legislature, with more money being allocated to improve the system of education by appointing a full-time Superintendent of Schools and providing scholarships for secondary school study.

But for the few reforms, the Belizean society in the Thirties had many ills. Most of the population was employed in the forest industries; a migratory labor force working seasonally and precariously for a corporate employer who enjoyed monopolistic advantages while paying unrealistically low taxes. The Creole-loggers were subjected to the widespread fraudulent practices of timber contractors and had no recourse to a labor relations board or trade union. They were kept in a constant state of semi-serfdom by their indebtedness to a labor contractor, stemming from the popular practice of pre-payment and forced employee trade with the company stores. Employees were subject to a private penal legislative system which levied severe fines and prison sentences on defaulting payees.

The plight of the Maya Indian in the chicle industry was even worse; so much so, that a board of commissioners recommended in the Moyne Commission Report that a post of Special Commissioner for the Mayas be set up to oversee their interests.

This industry became very hard hit, in the years following the Second World War, by competition from U.S.-discovered synthetics and trade competition from the Orient.

WORLD WAR II

In 1941 a Belizean merchant ship became wrecked near Panama and its passengers and crew took refuge in the U.S. Canal Zone. They found an acute labor shortage there and remained. Letters sent to relatives and friends in Belize touched off a "Panama Fever" at home. This availability of well-paying jobs was a panacea for Belize, which suffered from a chronic problem of unemployment. In the next few months, over 1000 able-bodied men went to the Canal Zone to work on the building of the Third Locks Project. Some arrived in illegal ships, which hastily unloaded their passengers at night and sailed back to Belize. Others traveled on the "La Plata," the first chartered boat on a Panama run, operated by Captains Gough and Hill. For over a year, ships of all sizes transported British Honduran laborers to the Canal Zone.

Eight hundred forty-three forest workers answered Britain's plea for manpower in 1942, and were shipped to Scotland to relieve men needed in the war effort. Many young men joined the Armed Forces of the United States, as well as Great Britain, and a battalion of volunteers from Belize served with the British forces in Europe.

During the confusion of the early days of the war a number of prominent residents of Belize were seized and held as suspected spies in Jamaica. Among those imprisoned was Captain George Gough. After suffering from smeared reputations and loss of property taken from them by their government, all were released for lack of evidence. They were later publicly exonerated of any charge. Gough returned to his shipping business and spent the duration of the war running through the submarine zones, carrying men to work in the United States and Panama, and returning with food for the Colony cut off from normal shipping trade.

Toward the end of the war, the United States War Manpower Commission arranged for the employment of all remaining eligible men in the Colony. Over 1000 more went to work in the United States for the war effort.

The period following the war was marked by an extreme unemployment problem resulting from the laborers and soldiers returning from Panama, the United States and Europe to the already-depressed economy in Belize. The expenditures in the Colony in 1945 out-weighed its revenues, requiring a grant-in-aid of $666,474 from the British government to balance the budget. Strict import control on certain expendable items led to an attempt to encourage home industries, but skilled labor was scarce and no procedure existed for the training of technicians. Wages were low; laborers working for the Public Works Department earned $2.00 a day and store clerks from $7.00 to $15.00 a week. Price controls, begun during the war, remained in effect and many products were rationed.

There was little political activity in the Colony. Owing to the severe restrictions of the property and income qualification for voting, there were only 822 registered voters in the entire Colony in 1945. The only open opposition to colonial policy was from the Knights of Labor, led by Gabriel E. J. Adderley, but his pamphlets and speeches were taken seriously by only a small minority of the population. Carlos Meighan, another opposition leader, left the Colony for the United States to join the Honduranian Society in New York, a group of former Belizeans and their descendants working for the advancement of their homeland from the United States. Adderley himself went to Guatemala when it became obvious he did not have his people's support.

The Evans Commission Settlement Report—1948

From time to time, the British government appointed a commission to study the situation extant in the Colony and report on its findings. The Evans Settlement Report of 1948 was a startling departure from previous reports. In contrast to the most recent Moyne Commission Report, which recommended mixed peasant farming, the Evans Report made a revolutionary proposal for planned plantation economy, operated by large multi-industrial corporations, and the replacement of the small owner-farmer with a wage-earner employed by the mechanized agricultural corporation. This report, however stillborn, recognized a need, for the first time, for national planning to meet the economic dilemma. It also stressed the need to realize that the heretofore remorseless exploitation of the nation's natural resources, without this planning, would someday result in their total depletion.

The Evans Report called attention again, as all reports had done since 1914, to a depressing list of social evils: the low standard of community hygiene and preventive medicine, widespread illiteracy, and the remaining prevalence of malarial diseases (the principal cause of death in the colony), unchecked in some of the more remote areas of the country.

The Evans Report only touched on a very basic problem, a source of local irritation and political frustration—that of Treasury control. Since the tragedy of the hurricane in 1931, when Britain extracted gubernatorial reserve powers from a reluctant Assembly as the price demanded for grant-in-aid status, the Governor had enjoyed complete control of the colonial finances for as long as colonial indebtedness to the Crown existed. In a vicious cycle, Britain denied the Colonial Assembly power to either reform the outdated taxation system or to exact more equitable tax returns from the British-controlled foreign business empires, and then cited the low revenue level caused by this denial as the excuse for continuing Treasury control. These big interests, principally the timber combine, so controlled the government that politicians could do little to stop such unethical practices as the consistent under-valuing of timber exports on customs declarations which consequently meant lost revenue to the Colony. Treasury control meant the sacrifice of any chance of large-scale, long-range planning and kept the Colony a perpetual and resentful prisoner of British exchecquer domination.

A subject of the Evans Report, as well as a matter discussed at the 1947 Montego Bay Conference, on possible federation of all of the remaining British Caribbean colonies into a West Indian Federation, was that of immigration. For many obvious geographical, economic and cultural reasons, British Hondurans had little proclivity toward West Indian affiliation and, for differing reasons, were nearly unanimous in their opposition to uncontrolled immigration from the overcrowded West Indian islands. The Creole workers feared an influx of unskilled labor which would provide only more competition for their already underemployed work force. The Mestizo population was apprehensive about the type of people, predominantly Creole, which would be attracted, and would tend to reinforce the strong existing Creole culture.

The main criticism of the Evans Settlement Report has not been of its content, but that the same problems that had been minutely delineated in official reports before 1914 were still being delineated in the same detail in official reports in the 1940's, with no apparent progress having been made for alleviating them.

Devaluation of the Dollar—1949

However well-meaning British intentions were for the advancement of British Honduras, their confidence was destroyed in 1949. In 1936, and again in 1949, sterling had been devalued in Britain. In each case, the British Honduran dollar had remained at parity with the United States dollar, as it had been since 1894. Although it was the only British possession to do this, there was a very good reason for so doing. Half of the Colony's imports, including most of its food, came from the United States, while only 12 percent came from the United Kingdom. Farm machinery and manufactured goods, badly needed in Belize, were nearly impossible to obtain from Britain at this time.

Great Britain, however, considered that the anomaly of one small colony's maintaining parity in its rate of exchange with the U.S. could not be tolerated. To support its stand, the Colonial Office pointed out that the export trade of British

Honduras was changing, and with the rapid rise of its citrus industry closely linked with Britain, the devaluation was likely to make the Colony's exports to Britain more competitive. This was a hollow excuse since Great Britain was already committed to purchasing a substantial part of Belize's citrus production.

News of an impending devaluation brought near-panic in Belize, and unanimous opposition from the elected constituency of the Legislative Assembly. Lord Listowel, Minister of State for Colonial Affairs, came to Belize on October 13, 1949, to assure the Assembly that the British Honduras dollar would not be devalued. This was met with relief and short-lived optimism by Belizeans. But controversy continued for the next two months in the Assembly, with the Governor favoring alignment with the policy of other British Colonies. On December 31, 1949, Governor Sir Ronald Herbert Garvey used his reserve powers to override the opposition of the legislature, and devalued the British Honduran dollar in conformity with the sterling devaluation in Britain. This made the B.H. dollar worth $2.08 to the pound sterling instead of $4.03, and in terms of U.S. dollars, the British Honduran dollar was now worth about seventy cents.

THE BIRTH OF POLITICS IN BELIZE

With the dramatic rise in their cost of living, public opinion became aroused to the point of riot. It was obvious that the interests of the Colony had been overridden for the convenience of the Colonial Office and British big business interests. To make matters even worse, the whole affair had been seriously mishandled by the British Ministry of State.

The plan being promoted by Britain at the time for combining all the Caribbean Colonies into a single West Indian Federation, including Belize, which was looked upon by some as the ultimate solution to Belize's Guatemalan problem, lost what support it might have had in the Colony. This incipient devaluation incident gave polarity to an already popular anti-colonial movement. Bitter anti-British feeling throughout the country was general. Political ferment in the General Workers Union and allied groups even gave rise to talk of immediate secession from the British Empire and association, in some way, with the United States.

In order to use a Belize City Council election campaign as a sounding board for their new reform platform, a group of inexperienced but enthusiastic young men, closely allied with the General Workers Union, organized a People's Committee which became the political party now called the People's United Party (PUP). George Cadle Price, Belize's present Premier, was a leader and moving spirit from the inception of this party which, forwarding a policy favoring termination of colonial rule and opposition to entry into the proposed West Indian Federation, won control of the Belize City Council in 1950.

The colonial administration, openly hostile from the first to the new City Council, used legislative subterfuge to intimidate the new Council members. At one time, the Council was legally dissolved because of its refusal to hang a picture of the Queen in the City Hall. Leigh Richardson, the PUP party chairman, and Philip Goldson, its assistant secretary, were imprisoned for "seditious writing" in the *Belize Billboard*, a newspaper jointly owned by the two PUP leaders. The seditious article, written by attorney Goldson, had been an account of a visit he made in September, 1951 to Guatemala as a guest of the Newspaper Association. In it he gave a favorable account of life in Guatemala and a corresponding denunciation of current conditions in British Honduras. These, as in the case of similar incidents in British colonies, only served to enhance the popularity of the party.

The PUP consisted of young middle-class Creole radicals, imbued with the ideals of Catholic Socialism, evident in the elaborate system of consumer and producer cooperatives of their proposed programs. They possessed, as best exemplified by leader George Price himself, qualities of rigid Catholic morality, social zeal, and private asceticism not unlike Catholic missionaries operating a foreign mission. The PUP leaders were all products of St. John's College, the most important educational foundation in British Honduras today. The dozen or so American Jesuit priests from St. Louis, Missouri, who maintain St. John's, are highly suspect by the British who point out this pro-American group, many with Irish names and backgrounds, have been influential in fostering and encouraging anti-British feeling within the Colony, and have "stirred up the people to clamour for unqualified universal sufferage in the name of Democracy."

PUP leaders maintained that their members were anti-British only in the sense that they were expressing a natural indignation at Britain's failure to deal seriously with any of the very serious problems of the Colony. The agitation between the British colonial government and the colonists became especially high-pitched during frequent open-air political rallies, which invariably concluded with the crowd marching to the United States Consulate House on Hutson Street to serenade the Consul General with "God Bless America," substituting the American lyrics for the British "God Save the Queen." This practice was finally stopped by the American consul, who pointed out that it was embarrassing to his country's relation with Great Britain. This singular act of "disloyalty" so unnerved the British Administration that before the proposed visit of Princess Alice of Athlone to Belize, the Governor proposed to the citizens of Belize that if they would refrain from singing their "God Bless America," the Government would see to it that "God Save the Queen" was not played during her stay in Belize. More than simple harrassment tactics, these acts were the result of a basic realignment of Belizean thinking. For the first time, Belizeans were considering that their country's natural destiny, as the United States had long claimed, was Central American.

However dedicated the young PUP radicals were to their cause, their organization was not without internal strife. A bitter quarrel between George Price and John Smith, the party's first party leader, concerning, among other things, the settlement of the "seditious writing" charge out of court, thus avoiding imprisonment of two of the party's leaders, favored by Smith, led to Smith's resignation in November, 1951 and his subsequent removal to the United States in 1955. Smith was gravely concerned that Goldson's writings were only encouraging Guatemala's territorial ambitions, more unacceptable to him than all the evils of British colonialism.

1954 Election

Not until 1954, after four years of mass meetings and demonstrations pressing for change, did Britain finally concede a new, more liberal, constitution. This constitution conferred the right to vote on all literate adults, and established a Legislative Assembly of which nine of the members were to be popularly elected and six nominated by the Colonial Government with a nominated Speaker. In the Executive Council, the control of the Governor was still absolute and his reserve powers were retained. A general election was scheduled for May of that year.

Working relentlessly for representation in the new Legislative Assembly, Price and his fellow PUP leaders thought nothing of starting at dawn, traveling over miles of pelvic-pounding roads, for a day's campaigning in remote villages with such improbable names as Never Delay, Gallon Jug, Double Head Cabbage, or Guinea Grass. They would present their case for complete self-government and the end of British colonialism, teach as many natives as possible to write their names (a prerequisite for voting), and be back in Belize City by night. George Price, the mild-mannered Party Secretary, seemed to be everywhere at once, characteristically dressed in an open-necked white shirt and faded khaki trousers, waving at passers-by from his mud-splattered Land Rover and greeting them equally enthusiastically in English, Creole or Spanish.

Just one month before the general election, in a desperate last-minute attempt by the colonial administration to discredit the PUP leaders with their followers, a Commission of Inquiry was staged. British attorney Sir Reginald Sharpe was rushed to the Colony and commissioned to investigate allegations that PUP leaders had been in contact with the Guatemalan government and, furthermore, had received financing from that government. In a double-barbed indictment of the party, it was determined by the Commissioner, after hearing evidence of the PUP's embittered ex-party leader John Smith, among others, that the PUP indeed *had* been receiving aid from the "Communist-influenced Government of Guatemala."

This revelation, coming when it did and under the circumstances that it occurred, was given little or no credibility by the colonists for, on the one hand, strong ties with the Catholic church precluded any serious thought of Communist infiltration into the PUP, and on the other hand, cooperation with a neighboring government which openly covets sovereignty of Belize would make little sense for a party whose minimum demands were complete self-government and independence.

In an official party statement the People's United Party replied to the Communism innuendos of the Commissioner's charges, saying: "There are no Communists in PUP and PUP shall continue to oppose Communism as a world conspiracy against freedom, democracy, and religion, and no solution to economic problems." They resolutely denied any Guatemalan influence, or other foreign control over PUP policies.

To the day of the election, the colonial government in Belize City stoutheartedly maintained that the mass of the Baymen were loyal to the Crown and, at least publicly, remained resolutely confident that the pro-British National Party (NP), which clung tenaciously to colonial attachments, would have little trouble in polling a majority in the election in spite of its apathetic and disorganized leadership. When the votes were counted, the People's United Party possessed eight of the nine elective seats in the Assembly. One very large step had been taken in the direction of independence of Belize.

1957 Election

Within a few months of their victory at the polls, the PUP's ranks became deeply split. No sooner had Leigh Richardson and Philip Goldson assumed their portfolios as Ministers of the new government than they both voiced favor in Belize's joining a

West Indian Federation—a reversal of the very policy which had helped put them in office. By mid–1956 Nicholas Pollard, who had been expelled from the secretaryship of the General Workers Union (still controlled by Richardson), over allegations of peculation from union funds, joined George Price in the PUP. Leigh Richardson and Goldson left the party to form their own Honduran Independence Party (HIP).

The principle issue of the 1957 election campaign was the one of the country's entry into a federation of former British colonies, now actively supported by HIP, and a cornerstone of British Policy in the Caribbean. Price concentrated his argument on the importance of keeping clear of such an arrangement for fear of possible domination by Jamaica or Barbados. He stressed the danger of Belize losing its identity in a great amalgamation of West Indian states, where its small population would be over-shadowed by the greater states.

As an alternative, Price suggested the possibility of some association with the other Central American Republics. The exact association was left undefined, however. Richardson and Goldson feared any closer association with Latin America, for racial and social reasons, and counted on support from their fellow Creole rank-and-file Belizeans. George Price's charismatic appeal, and his ability to represent his Central American sentiments in a nationalistic context, was attractive to Creole and Spanish-speaking Belizeans alike. At this time, it was enough to sweep the 1957 election for PUP, which won all nine of the elective seats in the Legislative Assembly. The outcome was a blow to British Colonial policy in the Caribbean and a tribute to the electioneering ability of George Price. Leigh Richardson, bereft of support and his council seat, faded from politics and left the country to go to work in Trinidad.

The association to which George Price alluded in his campaign speeches obviously was with the Organization of Central American States (now the Central American Common Market). Price had been in contact with the member states of that organization. Until shortly before election day in 1957, presidents of all the Central American republics, except Guatemala, had stated their intentions of supporting an independent Belize. In 1957 this organization, under pressure from Guatemala, declared its solidarity with its member nation in her territorial dispute with Belize, and pronounced the re-incorporation of "Belice" (the name by which British Honduras is known in Spanish-speaking countries) to be a Central American affair and pledged their support in "incorporating Belice into the movement of economic integration of Central America." If Belize was to take its place among the Central American republics, it was going to have to first deal with Guatemala.

In November, 1957 George Price, as the Assembly's Member for Natural Resources, led a delegation to London to confer with the British Colonial Office on matters of constitutional reform and the pressing financial problems of his country. While in London Price committed the indiscretion of accepting, for his colleagues, the invitation of the Guatemalan Minister in London to discuss their countries' differences. At this meeting, the proceedings of which unfortunately were soon made public, the Guatemalan ambassador was reported to have told the Belizean delegation that Britain was bound to leave their colony to fend for itself soon, and that they should anticipate this by forming an association with Guatemala now. He proposed that Guatemala handle foreign affairs and finance Belizean development. He also intimated that, should Belize not choose to accept this offer, Guatemala would break off trade relations. In response, George Price is reported to have said something to the effect that this offer would be a good lever to use in case the current financial talks with Britain showed signs of failing.

Alan Lennox-Boyd, the Secretary of State for the Colonies, was shocked by reports of this meeting, a serious breach of protocol, and of the statements allegedly made by Price at the meeting. He immediately broke off any further discussions with the Belizean delegates. Upon his return to Belize, Price was dismissed from the Executive Council by Governor Sir Colin Thornley, who explained in a broadcast over Radio Belize that he could only conclude that "Mr. Price was prepared, in certain eventualities, to see you, the people of British Honduras, handed over to the Guatemalan Republic lock, stock and barrel."

George Price survived even this blow. Although Pollard left the party over the incident, Price still retained the confidence of most of the elected members of the Assembly, though now reduced to a minority leader as a result of the defection of several of his parliamentary constituents. In order to bridge the gap with the colonial administration and preserve his political life, he was obligated to collaborate with political leaders more acceptable to the administration. Thus he closed ranks with the National Independence Party, NIP (the result of a merger of the ill-fated HIP and the old conservative NP), to present a united front in opposing a constitutional report prepared in 1959 by Sir Hilary Blood, which called for only slight constitutional advance and roundly condemned past PUP proposals for self-government within the geographical framework of Central America. Sir Hilary's discouraging report cited the "danger signal" of the Guatemalan pressure now being intensified by the new Guatemalan President, Ydigoras Fuentes, for his objections to self-government at this time, and failed to discern the difference between the PUP policy of incorporation in the Organization of Central American States as an independent state and a complete take-over by Guatemala.

Another London constitutional conference was held in 1960 to air the differences resulting from the Blood Report. At this conference, Price joined with the NIP in concluding a declaration, inserted as a preamble to a constitutional agreement, stating that they agreed not to introduce into the Assembly any measure for integration with any other country without a clear mandate from the electorate arising from a general election.

The PUP–NIP coalition, having been formed out of expedience, of course was not maintained beyond the London conference. Out of that conference did come a new spirit of cooperation shared by the two rival political parties of the colony and Britain as well. This allowed for more long-range planning and joint efforts toward common goals of the colony in the 1960's, with a degree of freedom from the strain of mistrust, the conspiratorial politics, and intense conflict of the past decade. Partly contributing to this change of attitude was the softening of British policy toward Belizean independence. Having failed in the attempt to incorporate all her former colonies into one manageable entity, Britain now began to think in terms of liquidating the residue of her empire in the Caribbean. Criticism at home, best seen in a contempory *London Times* editorial which read, "all the dilemmas, contradictions, and frustrations of the colonial situation in the second half of the twentieth century are present (in British Honduras) as a political laboratory. This territory is no longer of any conceivable economic or strategic use. On the contrary, it absorbs large sums of development money which are spent either on non-remunerative social services or on projects which are very difficult to justify economically," forced the Colonial Office to gradually accept, and even encourage, PUP's Central American aspirations.

1961 Election

The 1960 London constitutional convention led to a reformed and more democratic legislative structure. This new Legislative Assembly was to consist of eighteen elected members, five nominated ones, and two ex-officio members. The new Executive Council was comprised of a First Minister (to be the leader of the winning party), five Ministers (chosen by the Assembly from their membership), and two ex-officio Ministers. The Governor was to be Chairman of the Assembly.

George Price's campaign speeches in 1961 were modified only slightly from those of 1957. While the agreement to remain in the Commonwealth, to which he had been a party, precluded any immediate possibility of political association with Central America, it did not stand in the way of economic association. Membership in the Central American Common Market was now his party's primary goal. By honoring his 1960 London commitment, Price made less credulous Philip Goldson's charges of his being "a traitor intent on Guatemalan annexation of Belize." The NIP's only other plank, federation with other British Caribbean colonies, was now abandoned as a possibility even by Britain. When the results of the election of February, 1961 were known, the PUP had taken all eighteen of the eighteen elective seats in the Assembly and George Price was his country's First Minister.

New Constitution

With the clean sweep of the 1961 elections behind him and, his party having held all elected seats in the legislature since 1957, First Minister Price attended a constitutional conference in London held in July, 1963 with a hand full of aces. At this conference, a new constitution was drafted allowing the Price Government full internal self-government, to come into being on January 1, 1964.

This new constitution, which is in effect today, provides for a bi-cameral legislature, called the National Assembly, comprised of a House of Representatives and a Senate. The eighteen members of the House of Representatives are elected under the system of universal adult suffrage. The Senate consists of eight members appointed by the British Governor, of whom five are appointed on the advice of the Premier, two on the advice of the Leader of the Opposition Party (if such a party is represented in the House of Representatives), and one after consultation with such persons as the Governor considers appropriate.

The President of the Senate is similarly chosen—either from among the Senators who are not also Ministers, or from outside the Senate. The Speaker of the House is elected either from among the members of the House of Representatives who are not Ministers, or from outside the House.

A Cabinet, with the Premier (Leader of the Majority Party) as Chairman has, by this constitution, replaced the former Executive Council as the chief instrument of policy.

The British Government, represented by a Governor, retains responsibility for foreign affairs, national defense, internal security, and civil service employment. There is an independent judiciary whose members are appointed by the Crown. The highest court in Belize is the Supreme Court headed by a Chief

Justice. The legal system is based on the common law of England.

Gatemala's reaction to this move toward an independent Belize was swift in coming. Colonel Enrique Peralta Azurdia, the head of Guatemala's governing junta, called Britain's promise of self-rule "a flagrant violation of the sovereign rights of Guatemala." He broke off diplomatic relations with Britain, and an editorial in Guatemala City's daily, *La Hora*, grandly threatened war: "We haven't fought a war for a half a century. The English always have been good soldiers, but that doesn't mean they are any more masculine than we are."

Britain remained as unrattled by these newest threats as did the then British Foreign Secretary Ernest Bevin in the 1950's when Guatemala's Ambassador to the Court of St. Jame's barged in on him demanding that British Honduras must be turned over to Guatemala instantly. Bevin is reported to have heard the fellow out, then leaned over, tapping him on knee, and cut him down to size with a single question: "What did you say you called your country?" Bevin's one-upmanship won that round, but the Guatemalans have never given up in their claim to this territory which they have never occupied nor ever governed.

Returning to Belize from the London conference as his nation's first Premier, George Price launched into the business of nation-building with a fervor. He gave his country a new flag, officially renamed it Belize, gave it an anthem and a national prayer. He has even written a pageant to be performed on Independence Day, whenever that may come. No effort was spared in instilling a new sense of nationality in his diverse and easy-going countrymen.

In keeping with the provisions of the new constitution, a national general election was held March 1, 1965 to fill the newly-created seats in the Assembly for a five-year term of office. Price's PUP party succeeded to sixteen of the eighteen seats in the House of Representatives and five of the eight in the Senate. Price voiced his determination to bring his country, as a totally independent nation, into the United Nations to replace

Iceland as the smallest member before the end of his five-year term of office.

Of course, the first order of business for the new nation of Belize, toward whose very political and economic idealogy is geared, was in the settlement, once and for all time, of the Guatemala Question. Since Britain, by the new constitution, retained responsibility for external affairs and defense, the resolution of this international dispute is legally out of the hands of the people of Belize. It is especially frustrating for the government of Belize to know that the final outcome, and in fact their very future as a nation, depends largely on factors beyond their control.

The solution is not an easy one. Belize is named as a district of Guatemala in their constituion, and is shown as "Guatemalan territory illegally held by Great Britain" on their official maps. The dispute is brought very much to the forefront during election time in each country. There exists in Belize a very real fear of a military take-over by Guatemala after independence. Premier Price has warned his countrymen repeatedly that if circumstances suited Guatemala, that country would not hesitate to invade Belize.

In May and June, 1965, talks were held in Miami and in London between representatives of Britain and Guatemala in an attempt to reach a settlement. Throughout the negotiations, Guatemala insisted on turning the problem over to the United States for mediation. Britain eventually conceded to this means of resolving the question, and in September, 1965 a joint request for mediation by the President of the United States in the Belize Question was forwarded to Washingtin.

News of the choice of United States as mediator caused a great deal of consternation in Belize City, as only a few years before General Miguel Ydigoras Fuentes, then President of Guatemala and a puppet of the C.I.A. and of President John Kennedy, had allowed his country to be used as a staging grounds by U.S.-equipped and trained Cuban refugees for their ill-fated Bay of Pigs fiasco. It is widely believed throughout Central America that one of the concessions made at that time by the C.I.A., as a price for Guatemalan cooperation in the Cuban attack, was that the U.S. would make no effort to interfere in a future Guatemalan take-over of British Honduras. The exact concession made by the U.S., if any, is not known, however, President Fuentes, in a public address made on January 1, 1962 stated unequivocally that the United States had agreed to "lend its good offices to mediate Guatemala's claim against Great Britain for the territory of Belize." The Guatemalan press has repeatedly stated that the United States' C.I.A. base was not built at Retalhuleu, Guatemala, until the C.I.A. was able to relay President Kennedy's solemn promise of a well-defined stand against Britain by the United States on this issue.

After a long delay, President Johnson indicated to the two countries that the United States, while willing to suggest a list of nongovernment American citizens as mediators, was unwilling to be dragged into the dispute as official referee. Guatemalan diplomats at first objected, saying that they must insist on an official U.S. role if only because this would give any solution so reached a greater chance of success, since U.S. prestige would be involved. Later, both parties agreed to the President's appointment of the distinguished New York attorney Bethuel M. Webster, noted U.S. authority on international law, as mediator.

During the two and a half years in which the future of the country was being considered by the New York attorney, political life in Belize did not remain in limbo. George Cadle Price was hard at work with his party's plans for creating a viable economy, through a seven-year plan, which could eventually support itself without annual handouts from Britain, and in lobbying for future membership in the Organization of American States and the Central American Common Market.

Not without antagonists, Price came even more under attacks from a rival party leader, attorney and publisher Philip Goldson, whose accusations of collaboration with Guatemala led to a confrontation in July, 1966 when Goldson publicly called Price a traitor. George Price, not one for ignoring an insult, matter-of-factly and unemotionally explained that Goldson's accusations were "a product of a fearful and confused mind." Price clarified his position on Guatemalan cooperation somewhat by stating that he was willing to make only one concession to Guatemala; a road from the Belize Coast to the Peten area of Guatemala, as included in the 1859 Treaty. He also stated that he believed economic cooperation between the two countries was a possibility. Goldson contended Price was "ready to sell out to Guatemala at the first opportunity." Political feelings continued to run high and apprehension was strong.

On April 2, 1968 U.S. Secretary of State Dean Rusk relayed the long-awaited report of Bethuel Webster, the result of nearly three years work by the attorney and his staff, to the heads of state of the two governments. When made public, the "draft" treaty he proposed drew sharp criticism and feelings of dismay from all sides.

The Webster Plan, characterized by its unusual naivete and impracticability, proposed an "association" of Belize and Guatemala and provided that Belize would "consult" with Guatemala on all foreign affairs, after which Guatemala would act in Belize's behalf. Guatemala, in a sort of "big brother" role, would cooperate with Belize in the areas of defense, communications, and economic development, leading to a limited Belizean independence by 1971 but with close ties to Guatemala.

The Webster Plan assumed that the predominantly Negro, English-speaking, and now fiercely nationalistic Belizeans would be willing to accept annexation to their Spanish-speaking Indian neighbor Republic who had been openly hostile to them from the very founding of the Guatemalan State. It also assumed that Guatemala, once it has annexed Belize, would be willing to work in cooperation with the leaders of Belize in strengthening that country's economy toward the day when Belize would become a sovereign nation. The workability of this plan was inconceivable.

The only favorable comment on the arbitration report came

from the British Foreign Secretary, Michael Stewart, on April 30, 1968 when he termed it "reasonable," but after consultation with colleagues in his government and the government of Belize—Premier Price flatly rejected the Webster Plan on May ninth, saying it would "limit independence of Belize"—he announced London's abandonment of the plan, stating it had been "dropped because of opposition by the Belizeans" on May 20, 1968. In September, 1968 the United States formally notified all parties that "the U.S. had concluded its role as mediator of the Belize-Guatemalan dispute."

The one logical solution to the problem, proposed by Premier Price, that of a defense agreement with Britain after independence, has been given little serious consideration by Great Britain and, in fact, comments made in the House of Commons on June 25, 1969 by Under-Secretary of State for Foreign and Commonwealth Affairs, Mr. Maurice Foley, indicate that it is doubtful that any commitment of this sort will ever be forthcoming. Not satisfied with the *status-quo* which Britain seems to prefer, the Belizean government continues to press for a resolution of the question. Diplomatic consultations on a local level between Guatemalan representatives and the Governor of British Honduras, Sir John Paul, led to nothing, and Sir John reported in 1969 that the two countries were still far from reaching an agreement.

Frustrations, caused by the seemingly insurmountable deadlock of the Anglo-Guatemalan dispute, contributed to the violence of the 1969 National election campaign. With little difference between the platforms of the pro-independence PUP party of George Price and the opposition NIP party led by Philip Goldson, the campaign degenerated into one of personal slander and name-calling. Riots and violence erupted following a PUP political rally in Belize City on September 21, 1969, and led to the burning of the *Billboard*, the newspaper plant owned by Philip Goldson, minority party leader. Rumors of the theft of a case of dynamite from the government warehouse added to the tension of the riot, which lasted for 72 hours despite efforts by the government leaders and the police to put down the rampage.

In the National Election held on December 5, 1969, Premier Price was returned to office for another five-year term by an extreme majority. The PUP won 17 of the seats in the House of Representatives. The one remaining seat was taken by a combined effort of the NIP and the People's Democratic Movement (PDM), made up of former NIP leaders who had broken away and formed their own party. The NIP had been severely shaken by dissent within its ranks since 1965. There were three parties and one independent contesting the 1969 election. Philip Goldson filled the lone seat won by the NIP–PDM coalition. Voter turnout was 22,377, or 75% of all eligible voters.

Belmopan

Much of the nation's time and attention following the election were taken up by the grandiose national project—the construction of the new national capital. Plans that were made immediately following the destruction of Belize City by the tropical storm Hattie, in 1961, were being realized in concrete and masonry at a site some 50 miles inland from Belize City. The purpose of the new capital was twofold; first it would be relatively safe from future hurricanes, and secondly, the population and economic pressures on Belize City, caused by a rapid population growth rate and heavy migration from rural areas, would be alleviated.

The new capital is about the geographic center of the country and conveniently located near the Belize River, its source of water supply. The project is designed to be built in five stages; the first, now complete, is planned to accommodate 5,000 residents in 740 small modern homes of 11 different designs, on lots of varying sizes to add visual interest to the community. The houses sold for from U.S. $3900 to $10,200 when completed in 1970. The city is planned for an ultimate population of 25,000 to 30,000 people. The capital has its own diesel-generating plant, a water purification plant, 600,000 gallon reservoir, and a radio-telephone link via Belize City to international service.

The House of Representatives finally concurred on a name for the new capital on March 22, 1970, when they officially named it Belmopan after a Maya Indian tribe native to Belize. Some governmental offices moved to the new capital in May, but the majority did not relocate until August, 1970.

Near the National Government complex, a Civil Plaza will soon be built to accommodate a Magistrate's Court, future City Council Chambers, and bank buildings. A Commercial Center for private developers has been provided, where hopefully a supermarket, cinema, restaurant, bowling alley, and all the other amenities necessary to serve the transplanted residents, mostly Government employees and their families, will be built. The far-ranged master plan has allocated space in the surrounding area for industrial sites, residential expansion, and farms for providing fresh produce for the local market. An area has even been designated for a future University of Belize.

The cost of the project: U.S. $13.75 million, of which $11.25 million is being financed under the aid program of the British Ministry of Overseas Development through its Caribbean division. Administration on behalf of both governments is being carried out by the Crown Agents for Overseas Governments and Administrations in London in collaboration with the Reconstruction and Development Corporation, under the chairmanship of the Hon. George C. Price, Premier of Belize. It has been designed by British architects and engineers and built by British contractors.

The economic impact on the nation's economy of the investment in this project has been enormous. In the 1968 national budget, almost 75% of the capital expenditure went into the building of Belmopan. In 1969, expenditure for Belmopan amounted to $7.5 million out of the total capital expenditure of $8.75 million.

Of the work force at the new capital, only about 2½ percent were foreigners, giving the Belizeans not only the advantage of increased employment, but allowing local workers an opportunity of learning new trades. Until recently all building in the country was of wood construction but, since Hurricane Hattie, most new structures have been of concrete or concrete masonry. At Belmopan, all public buildings were designed to withstand winds of 140 m.p.h. and residences 110 m.p.h. This offered a training ground for local craftsmen, teaching them to work with concrete and masonry. Foreign superintendents gave initial on-the-job training as long as needed, but the construction was completed by local workers.

On January 22, 1971 G.T.E. International, a subsidiary of General Telephone and Electric Corp., received a $3 million contract for construction of a nationwide modern telecommunications system which doubled the number of telephones in the country.

Gunboat Diplomacy

Since the failure of the U.S. arbitration attempt, Guatemalan newspaper editorials, directed at Belize, grew increasingly more antagonistic and inflammatory, with threats of "driving the Niggers of Belize into the sea." In January, 1972 the situation reached a crisis stage when Guatemala was reported concentrating troops near the Belize border. Premier Price flew to London to confer on the tense situation in his country.

The *Ark Royal*, Britain's largest ship and its only remaining aircraft carrier, at the time was enroute to New York for a good-will tour of the United States and sea maneuvers off the Virginia coast. It was diverted in mid-Atlantic when news of "threatening gestures" made by Guatemala toward British Honduras reached the war office. Steaming southward, when the big ship reached the vicinity of Key West, Florida, her Commander, Captain John Oliver Roberts, launched two Buccaneer low-level bombers on a record 2500-mile round-trip sortie to "show the flag" over Belize. After its "fly-over" the planes returned to the carrier and it made its planned call at the Port of New York, the first by a British ship since 1959. It was greeted by water-streaming fireboats and a 21-gun salute.

Explaining the incident in New York the ship's flag officer,

Rear Admiral John Devereaux Treacher said, "it is a small storm in a tea-cup. There is a thing the military deal with occasionally called 'presence'; as soon as this was realized in Belize, the operation was called off."

The operation was not called off, however, and on February 11 the *Ark Royal*, its hanger decks filled with F4K Phanton interceptors, Buccaneer bombers, Gannet early-warning planes, and Sea-King helicopters sailed from New York, bound, not for the Virginia coast, but for the Caribbean and more "gun-boat diplomacy." The *Ark* was joined by two frigates and a guided-missile destroyer as her escort.

Spurred by reports from sources in Guatemala that Guatemalan warplanes were waiting in readiness and "pointed toward Belize," a contingent of Grenadier Guards were flown in to reinforce the 2nd Battalion already in the country. The Defense Minister announced that 3000 more British servicemen would be in the area in the next month and would be carrying out amphibious exercises which he said "had been planned months ago."

In exchanges, primarily through the news media—Britain and Guatemala have had no diplomatic relations since 1963—Guatemalan Foreign Minister Roberto Herrera Ibarguen, on January 27, 1972 protested the entry of troops from Great Britain. He said that Guatemala had no invasion plans and termed the British show of force an "unfriendly action" and indicated that his government considered this "tantamount to the presence of foreign troops on Guatemala soil."

The following day in Parliament the Minister of State in the Defense Ministry, Lord Bainiel, rebutted the speculation that the airlift of troops to Belize and the sea maneuvers of the aircraft carrier task force in the Caribbean was intended to deter any pressure on British Honduras by Guatemala. Nevertheless, Colonel Felix Roman Beteta warned Britain that Guatemala's American-equipped Air Force, Navy, and Army had been alerted. "The armed forces will remain on alert because we must defend our territory, according to circumstances," he said. Guatemalan newspapers claimed that the troop movements which started the incident had been aimed not at neighbors but at internal rebels operating in the border area.

The situation remained tense. Guatemala made it clear on March 10th that any further negotiations between that country and Great Britain concerning Belize were indefinitely suspended, and reaffirmed her claim to sovereign rights over the entire territory of "Belice."

In answer to the new assertions of territorial claim by the Guatemalan government and a continuation of Guatemalan guerilla activities near the Belizean border, the British Government announced on March 21 that it had doubled its garrison of "regulars" in Belize. Also, the series of air, land and sea maneuvers, begun in February, would be continued at least through April.

At the same time the Foreign Office told Premier Price, who was attending another meeting in London, that in spite of Guatemala's recent renewal of her claim to sovereignty in Belize, Great Britain still intended to negotiate a lasting settlement with Guatemala.

At the second General Assembly of the Organization of American States (OAS) held on April 11, 1972 in Washington, D.C., Guatemala protested the presence of British troops in Belize, charging that these forces "posed a threat to peace and security in the hemisphere." Delegates from the 23 member nations unanimously adopted a resolution condemning military, political, and economic intervention.

After a heated debate, a majority of the delegations agreed on April 21 that the OAS had the authority and should send an observer into Belize—which is not a member of the organization—to assess Britain's military strength there and to determine if it constituted a threat to Guatemala.

After a short tour, Major General Alvaro Valencia Tovar, the OAS official observer, reported that he considered that "the British Forces are fundamentally of a defensive nature." Premier Price notified the OAS that "unless the government of Guatemala unequivocally declared that its country would not invade Belizean territory, the people of Belize have no alternative but to welcome British forces in her defense."

Impatient at Britain's seeming inability to reach a satisfactory agreement with Guatemala, Premier Price began a series of discussions in late 1972 with Salvador's President, Colonel Arturo Armando Molina, which led to a tentative agreement for Salvador to act as intermediary with Guatemala in an attempt to permit Belize independence in 1973.

Interest in Salvadoran emigration to Belize also resulted from the discussions, and Belize offered to auction off an 18,000-acre estate along the Guatemalan frontier to Salvadoran immigrant interests. This land in the Cayo District shares an eleven-mile boundary with El Peten, and extends all the way to the Orange Walk District. The Belmopan government said the land was offered for auction to recover arrears in taxes.

Land of Promise
(1975–)

Any projection of the future of Belize must be contingent upon a satisfactory resolution of Guatemala's claim to sovereignty in Belize. Failing this, Belize must either follow patiently in the course she is taking: moderate internal advancement while depending, as a colony, on the protection of Britain; or by obtaining an alternate defense agreement, as an independent nation, with another power to insure Belize's territorial integrity.

Premier Price's government has investigated this latter alternative through continuing informal discussions with Mexico, the United States, and Canada but has found little encouragement. It is clear that a defense agreement with Great Britain after Belizean independence is not a possibility. Meanwhile, Britain is building permanent facilities for her military forces in Belize and is making use of their extended stay by training her troops, on a rotating basis, in jungle warfare. This is one of the few remaining territories in her shrinking empire affording this advantage.

Belize has neither the manpower nor the capital to support an army of its own, especially one capable of defending the country against the well-equipped Guatemalan army with a standing force in excess of 8,000 men, plus a trained reserve.

Under the shadow of the yet-unresolved "Guatemala Question," Belize continues to move forward both economically and politically; confident of its eventual independence from the nominal colonial bonds, and freedom from the threat of a Guatemalan take-over. Belize's parliamentary type of democratic government can only be described as politically stable— even conservative by world standards.

The only ripple in the otherwise calm waters of internal politics in recent years has been caused by a small but vituperous Black Power Movement (UBAD). Fortunately, this party has chosen to work within the framework of existing institutions. UBAD, led by Evan Hydr, an American-educated black power advocate, joined in coalition with the minority party (NIP) in the 1972 Belize City Council elections. Its objectives, largely misinterpreted by foreign newsmen, are not so much race-oriented, as North Americans are prone to see them, but are in sympathy with the lower classes who, in this case, happen to be predominated by Blacks.

1974 NATIONAL ELECTION

The country's long-established two-party system was strengthened by the results of the 1974 general election which placed members of the United Democratic Party (UDP) in six of the eighteen seats in the National Assembly. This represented a gain of five for the UDP minority party, the successor of the NIP of the 1970 elections, and will give the nation's conservatives more voice in government for the next five years. Philip Goldson retained his Assembly seat and his job as party whip. Dean Lindo was named Leader of the Opposition in the Assembly.

Three seats went to independent candidates, although two of these have close PUP connections and will probably vote with the majority party on most issues.

The election campaigns of the two major parties in the 1974 election were conducted without any serious incidents of violence as has marred previous elections. The issues were trivial, with both parties generally in agreement on two basic national goals—the securing of a fail-safe total independence, free of fear of a Guatemalan take-over, and the stabilization of the national economy, although neither party advanced any clear-cut method for achieving either goal.

UDP candidates charged the powerful PUP leaders with abuse of power and with fostering run-away socialism. PUP party chiefs made full use of government-controlled Radio Belize to extoll the progress and good works achieved by the country under PUP leadership during the past five years and to beat the drum for their proposed progressive action programs for the next term.

Socially, Belize has few of the problems experienced by other developing nations. According to Premier Price, "We have an inter-racial cosmopolitan people; therefore, we can be something to all men." A factor influencing the stability of the social, as well as the political, clime of the country is the relatively even distribution of wealth. Although a poor country economically, there is no great disparity between the "haves" and the "have nots" so common throughout Latin America. Opportunities for advancement and education, such as now exist, are equally available for all.

The proverbial national problem of under-employment (of special concern to residents of Belize City) has recently been determined to be not so much one of job shortage (Mexican laborers have to be imported during the season of citrus and sugar cane harvest) but one of immobility of labor. The government is working on this problem and with improved transportation and realignment of industrial labor priorities, the situation is improving.

By 1966, the country became free of treasury control by the United Kingdom, which they had inherited along with rehabilitation loans acquired after a disastrous hurricane of 1931. During the worldwide depression of the Thirties, continual assistance in the form of annual grants and loans from Britain were required to balance the national budget. In order to obtain this assistance, the finances of the country were made subject to rules and regulations dictated by London.

Today, through long-range planning and local control of her finances, though still far from a wealthy country, Belize is taking its first steps down the road toward economic stability. The gross national product (GNP) averages something around U.S. $46 million, or about $400 per capita—higher than most of its Central American neighbors. Belize's biggest economic problem is its huge deficit in the area of foreign trade. Its imports, mainly foodstuffs, machinery, transportation equipment, and manufactured goods, amount to nearly twice its exports. The deficit must be financed through tourism, foreign investment, and foreign aid. The three principal areas for development which are open for immediate expansion are agriculture, light industry, and tourism.

Although microscopic in global terms, the economy of Belize can offer a prospective investor some interesting opportunities. Clouds of social unrest or political instability are admirably lacking. Various positive developments in recent years—CARIFTA membership, a higher U.S. sugar quota, increased agricultural production—indicate a definite impetus for continued and increasing growth.

NEW OPPORTUNITIES IN AGRICULTURE

Highest on the list of national priorities is the increase in production of agricultural commodities, both for export to help offset the required import of capital goods, and for local consumption to reduce the unnecessarily high level of foreign foodstuffs imported yearly to satisfy the local market. In 1967 food imports accounted for 27 percent of the total value of all imports, and what is more significant, the value of foodstuffs imported was 70 percent as much as that produced locally and retained for domestic use. Clearly the problem facing the country is that of developing the vast unused land areas. With its abundance of natural resources—principally a fertile fallow land—Belize is potentially one of the richest countries in Central America and the Caribbean; yet only approximately 5 percent, or one acre per capita, is now under cultivation.

According to the latest report of the Survey Department (1966), at that time, of the 5.6 million acres of land in Belize 1 million was held by the Belize Estate and Produce Company, the forest syndicate which is gradually relinquishing its land holdings; 1.3 million additional were privately owned and 3.3 million were government owned (Crown lands). With the exception of certain reserved areas, small lots of these government lands, ranging from 20 to 50 acres, may be purchased from the government under a plan initiated in the 1950's designed to stimulate cultivation of undeveloped land. Called the Location Ticket System, this plan allows for purchase and repayment over a five-year period. Provided the purchaser has developed the land in accordance with the terms of his contract, at the end of this period the land becomes his property on unconditional freehold. Larger parcels of government land (in excess of 50 acres) can be obtained on a lease arrangement with the possibility of eventual acquisition.

Land purchased from private individuals is usually sold in blocks of 1000 acres and ranges from U.S. $10 to $20 per acre for undeveloped, uncleared land. Land clearing costs in 1974 averaged about $40 to $80 per acre, depending upon the density of the jungle growth.

The relatively small domestic market of 120,000 people has been a severe limitation to agricultural production of products aimed solely at the local market, making large-scale production methods economically impossible. Therefore, there has been a shift of emphasis to those crops which not only find a local demand but have a potential for export. Considerable interest has been shown by foreign investors in this field. To encourage them, as well as help local growers, the government offers attractive tax incentives. Under the Development Incentives Ordinance of 1960, a tax holiday of ten years plus one to five years development period is granted. Therefore, it is possible to operate tax-free for as long as fifteen years. In addition building materials, plants, vehicles, machinery, tools, appliances, etc., can be imported duty-free. This represents a savings of 3 percent entry tax and customs duty averaging about 27½ percent on the general tariff or 15 percent on the preferential tariff. Dividends and profits are free of income tax during this period up to the point where the amount paid out in dividends or profits equals the amount invested in the company or plantation.

For investors with the necessary skills at their disposal, agriculture presents a most inviting prospect at this time. Land prices are still comparatively low, even considering the additional expenditure required to prepare the virgin jungle-covered land into farmland, but the prospective entrepreneur must be prepared to find financing for any venture from outside sources. The largest stumbling block to rapid expansion of Belizean agriculture is its lack of ready sources of development capital. The country's four banks are generally restricted to only short-term commercial loans.

U. S. investors in Belize are fully insured by the U.S. Investment Guarantee Program (AID) which guarantees against currency inconvertibility, confiscation, expropriation, and damage to assets attributable to war, revolution, insurrection, and certain other extended risks.

An Agricultural Credits Fund and a Small Farmers Loan Fund are in existence. Some B.H. $100,000 was available for loans by mid-1970 with prospects for increased repayments making further funds available after that time. The general policy of the Ministry of Agriculture is to grant loans up to B.H. $500 at 4 percent, loans between B.H. $500 and $3,000 at six percent, and those over B.H. $3,000 at eight percent. The smaller loans are subject to approval of a loan committee, but those over $3,000 are subject to Ministerial approval. Loans have been granted under these provisions for the purchase of livestock and to cooperatives for mechanized rice farming.

A Government Marketing Board has continued since 1948 to buy up, at guaranteed minimum prices, any locally produced rice, corn or red kidney beans offered, thereby assuring the farmer an outlet for surpluses. To stimulate production, more buying posts are being established with drying, rice milling, and storage facilities throughout the country. To meet a growing demand, the Marketing Board is also venturing into the field of providing agricultural supplies, especially feedstuffs, fertilizers, and agricultural chemicals.

TRADITIONAL EXPORT CROPS

As a colony, British Honduras exported only a few primary products, namely chicle, lumber, citrus fruit, and sugar. The level of economic activity depended almost exclusively on unpredictable demand and price levels of foreign markets. In 1968, agricultural exports amounted to 15.3 percent of the gross national product.

Today, both the public and private sectors realize that the country cannot prosper if traditional export levels are maintained. The timber business, once the nation's chief industry, has shown a dramatic decline due to changing market demands and local exploitation of the nation's forests without proper concern for its reserves. The amount of lumber exported, and consequently the number of persons employed in this industry, today is only approximately one-third of what it was in the 1950's. The possibilities, however, for expanded markets for sugar, which is rigidly controlled by quotas in the U.S. and the United Kingdom, and of citrus fruits appear equally good.

Sugar

The most highly developed agricultural export operation now is the expanding industry which produces, processes, and exports Belizean sugar. Sugar's importance to the national economy is a fairly recent development, even though it has been a local commercial enterprise since the mid-nineteenth century.

Mestizo refugees, fleeing the horrors of the Caste War in Yucatan, brought sugar cane cuttings with them; by 1860 over 800 acres were planted in cane. Export of this product began with the first shipment of sugar and rum sent to Britain in 1857. Planting increased so that by 1883 nearly 3000 acres of cane was supplying some sixty small independent mills. This was the high point of the nation's sugar production for many years as, after that year, it gradually declined, until by 1935 it had reached an all-time low with only six inefficient mills remaining in operation.

A new company, the Corozal Sugar Factory, Ltd., breathed new life into the industry by acquiring used, though modern, equipment from Cuba belonging to Messrs. Bacardi, the rum producers, and establishing a new factory at Libertad in the Corozal District. When new capital became available in 1954 for expansion, they scrapped the Cuban equipment and replaced it with totally new machinery capable of processing ten tons of cane per hour.

A big boost was given the sugar industry in more recent times when Belize Sugar Industries, Ltd., a wholly-owned subsidiary of Tate and Lyle, Ltd. of London, one of the world's largest growers and processors of sugar cane, took over the Corozal Sugar Factory in 1963. This company again overhauled the Libertad factory at Pembroke Hall (locally pronounced Pimbrokell), thereby increasing the capacity of sugar production to approximately 40,000 tons per year.

Meanwhile, Tate and Lyle constructed a new fully-automated sugar factory at Tower Hill, near Orange Walk, at a cost of nearly U.S. $3 million which, when completed in 1967, was capable of producing some 100,000 tons per annum. Along with the improvement in facilities, improved planting techniques—using the Louisiana mound system—were introduced. This procedure not only improves yield per acre, but allows for convenient machine harvesting of the cane.

Because of the unique soil and climatic conditions in the Corozal District, cane grown there has one of the highest sucrose content in the world, comparable to the best grown in Cuba and superior to that of any of the other Caribbean islands. With favorable growing conditions, the 1973 season produced a record crop of 70,170 tons (long tons) and 1974 production approached that figure.

The sugar industry does, however, suffer from some limiting

factors. The International Sugar Agreement, while stabilizing prices, restricts outlets. Belize joined the International Sugar Association as a full member in May 1969. Her sugar exports are subject to quota limitations established by her three major markets: the United States, Great Britain, and the International Sugar Association.

Considering this, Tate and Lyle have been investigating a more diversified approach. Sale of molasses, a by-product of sugar manufacture, has been increased and will probably continue upward. Production in 1970 was 26,400 tons. The company also has sufficient undeveloped land to support a major cattle industry, and many U.S.-based firms and individuals have been looking into the possibility of a joint venture with the sugar company in this project.

In order to gain added empathy in Washington for their requests for an increased U.S. sugar quota, Belizean sugar lobbyists convinced the Belize Government and the Tate and Lyle group to give independent farmers more share in that growth pattern of the sugar industry. U.S. policy is favorable to developing nations, but encourages small-farmer participation. Under an agreement with the Belizean Government, Tate and Lyle has been selling off its cane lands and concentrating more and more of its activities solely on the milling and refining of cane purchased from small cane growers, most of whom operate through a cooperative. By 1969, fully two-thirds of the entire acreage under sugar cane in Belize was tilled by independent farmers and by December, 1972 the company estimated this figure to be 96 percent.

U.S.-controlled prices are higher than world prices, and competition for the U.S. sugar market, since the U.S. turned away from Cuba, has been keen in the Caribbean. It was a boon to the entire country when the United States, in 1971, finally agreed to more than double the existing Belizean sugar quota. A long-fought campaign by the efficient sugar industry to expand its market paid handsome dividends. Although much of the increased earnings resulting from this most recent U.S. sugar legislation will have to be used toward repaying some of the industry's past loans, a fair share can be expected to enter the local economy and provide further impetus for growth. Belize's 1973 U.S. sugar quota was 36,689 tons.

One of the major drawbacks to this philosophy has been in maintaining a steady labor force, especially at harvest time. There are now approximately 1000 independent cane farmers, of which only about fifty are sufficiently large enough to warrant a year-round work crew. Considerable difficulty is encountered by the others during harvest season. This is due in part to a great many of the cutters being also small sugar cane farmers, with quotas ranging from 5 to 200 tons, who look after their own interests before making themselves available to the larger producers. Also, many of the field workers of Corozal are *Milperos*, who own a small plot of land called a *milpa*, miles away from their place of work, and frequently leave their jobs at irregular intervals to plant their own crops of corn and beans or otherwise tend to their holdings.

Today sugar exports account for 67% of all agricultural exports and 53 percent of total exports. Some 2500 farmers gain their livelihood from this crop and over 3000 workers make up the industry's supporting labor force. Improved yields from existing acreage are nearly certain as the froghopper (Spittle-bug) menace has been brought under control (although infestation did occur in the Orange Walk region in 1970), and there is optimism for an increased International Sugar Association quota. Sugar will, for many years to come, retain its importance as a mainstay of the nation's economy.

The sugar industry is regulated by a Sugar Board established in May, 1960 to control the industry and the production of sugar cane. A Cane Farmers Association has been formed by the growers to represent their interests and to give member farmers technical and financial assistance.

Belize Sugar Industries, Ltd. initiated a million dollar expansion of their Tower Hill factory in 1973 and a program of continued modernization of the old Libertad factory. These programs provide Orange Walk farmers with quotas amounting to 70,000 additional tons of cane. "These substantial new investments," a BSI spokesman said at that time, "demonstrate the company's continued faith in the country's sugar industry, and in the ability of the cane farmers to continue to supply an adequate quantity of cane now that over 96 percent of cane production is exclusively in their hands."

In 1972, the Belize Sugar Industries increased their hauling fleet by adding four new sugar barges and a $200,000 Belizean-built tug. Expansion plans call for increased expenditures through 1975.

The 1973 sugar and molasses crop earned a little more than $20 million, with $19.5 of that exported. Belize Sugar Industries purchased about 760,000 tons, with approximately 80,000 tons left for the local market. In 1974, the government approved an increase in the ceiling price for local white sugar sold in the country from ten cents to twelve cents, the first such price increase in twenty years.

The 1974 season yield was slightly less than 1973; but the world price of sugar hit a new high late in 1973 and prices remained good through the 1974 season.

Table 5
SUGAR PRODUCTION

	1968	1969	1970	1971	1972	197
Tons Cane Ground (1000 long Tons)	642.51	528.72	675.17	N/A	667.65	760.
Tons Sugar	63.59	52.14	66.80	64.90	69.75	71.
Tons Cane per Ton Sugar	10.10	10.10	10.12	N/A	9.55	10.
Export Value B. H. $ Million	9.94	9.58	N/A	14.41	N/A	19.

Table 6

CITRUS PRODUCTION

Crop Year	Production (Boxes Million)	Calendar Year	Export Value (B. H. $ Million)
1967-68	0.96	1968	3.2
1968-69	1.13	1969	4.4
1969-70	0.81	1970	N/A
1970-71	1.30	1971	4.4
1971-72	1.36	1972	4.4

Citrus

Citrus, another traditionally important export commodity, has also enjoyed a dramatic up-turn. The 1971 production was fully 50 percent over that of the previous year and 1972 exceeded 1971. 1972 production was approximately 1.4 million 90 lb. boxes; 2/3 of the crop was oranges and approximately 1/3 grapefruit. Some 9000 acres are currently under citrus, of which about a quarter are growing grapefruit and the remainder oranges.

The Citrus Industry in Belize relies to a large extent on the U.S. market and, at times, overproduction in the U.S., with resulting low prices, has been citrus growing hazardous. Belize enjoys many natural advantages which help to make this industry attractive and at times highly profitable. The climate is ideal, rainfall is sufficient, no irrigation is required, and the soil is fertile. High temperatures assure rapid growth and the incidence of disease is low. There are several factors which give Belize an edge over competition from foreign producers (chief among her competitors are Spain, Israel, South Africa, and Morocco), and from U.S. Growers. The richness of the soil requires little expenditure on fertilizer, the cost of labor is far lower than in the U.S., and the quality of the produce is extremely high. Large quantities of orange concentrate from Belize at times are sold in Florida to improve the quality of their local product.

Overall, the market is an expanding one. The U.S. and Canadian markets are still the most important, although Sunglo Groves, a London firm, operates in Belize and there is no reason why, given tough and efficient marketing, Belize could not compete on the European markets to a greater extent than she now does.

Hurricane damage and Mexican Fruit Fly infestation are the only natural crop hazards. Scientists are studying the control of the fruit fly and hopefully it will be eradicated soon. In contrast to the sugar operation, nearly all of the large groves that produce citrus—mostly Valencia oranges and Marsh and Duncan grapefruit—are owned by the processors. The two major plants, both located in the Stann Creek Valley directly south of Belize City, are owned by the British Honduras Fruit Company, Ltd. (owned by Salada Foods, a U.S.-Canadian combine), and the Citrus Company of British Honduras, Ltd. (a Jamaican group controlled by Sharpe interests). While most of the citrus activity is confined to the Stann Creek area, some citrus is also grown in the Cayo District.

The two large Stann Creek plants are working to near capacity and a third is planned to handle the increased production anticipated. Sunglo Groves reported 2,800 acres in production with option on an additional 8000 acres, with a quarter million trees in its nurseries ready for planting as land is cleared or for replacement. By 1970, yields of oranges in Belize had already essentially equaled that of the state of Florida. Citrus amounted to 25 percent of the total national exports and is the country's second most important agricultural export.

One of the best organized of Belize's agricultural industries, the citrus growers have an association which was incorporated in 1966. The Citrus Growers Association limits its membership to the larger producers and has as its main object the representation of the nation's citrus growers with a view toward encouraging development of the industry and the maintenance of orderly marketing. A Citrus Control Board, a statutory body also founded in 1966, is financed through a tax levied on each box of fruit delivered to the processor. Its responsibilities include the determination of the basic quota for each producer, arbitration of disputes within the industry, advising the Minister of Trade and Industry on the granting of export and import licenses, and on the control of sale and pricing of citrus within the country. This board also fixes the annual price of citrus after discussion with the producers and processors.

Bananas

A banana industry of some magnitude was in existence in the Stann
Creek Valley in the 1920's, but Panama Disease virtually wiped out the entire cultivation, and citrus fruit groves were planted in

A banana industry of some magnitude was in existence in the Stann Creek Valley in the 1920's, but Panama Disease virtually wiped out the entire cultivation, and citrus fruit groves were planted in their place. Until 1970, there was increasing optimism among Belize's banana growers that someday this product would again reach the magnitude that it was before the epidemic. Today a new variety is planted in the Southern Stann Creek and Belize River Valley regions that is resistant to the Panama Disease, and in 1969, 35.2 million pounds were exported.

In 1970, winds accompanying Hurricane Francelia caused very severe damage, with some of the major plantations reporting losses as high as 85 to 95 percent of their crop. Only one of the four major producers was able to replant immediately.

Although the banana industry in Belize remains in poor condition, plagued by poor access roads, low world market prices, and irregularly scheduled shipping, talks between the Government, the United Fruit Company, and local growers have led to a renewed interest in production and subsequent export to the United Kingdom.

Projections are for over 6000 acres to be ultimately planted in bananas, but this would be a considerable increase over the 2600 acres which were in bananas before the storm of 1970, and would have to be in the distant future.

"Golden Beauty," a dwarf variety, is mainly planted now, and some plantains are grown for the local market. Commercial plantations still in operation are those of Green and Atkins at Waha Leaf, and the Caribbean Empire Co., Ltd., at South Stann Creek River, which has received government development concessions.

In March, 1973, a newly-organized Banana Association of Belize, consisting of 60 small growers, was able to put together an ambitious ten-year contract with the Fyfes Shipping Lines for exporting local bananas to Great Britain. The Fyfes Group agreed to buy all the produce of the Association members, up to 70,000 tons a year, at a guaranteed price. This represents approximately half the bananas consumed in England, the rest coming from Jamaica.

To fill the order, the Association obtained a service agreement for technical assistance from the Riversdale Service, Ltd., who will take care of packaging and forwarding of the fruit as well as maintaining quality control over the export product.

Plans call for the immediate cultivation of 4000 acres, of which 100 have been planted, in the vicinity of Cowpen and Riverdale. Growers are expecting help from the Caribbean Development Bank to finance the initial planting. The government of Belize has constructed a road and a pier at Riverdale and is guaranteeing a loan from the Caribbean Development Bank for one million dollars B.H.

Mr. Mike Williams, manager for Riverdale Service, says "The whole idea is to concentrate on high production and quality. We are starting from scratch using the latest techniques. The plantations will be the most modern, complete with cableways, draining systems, and a modern packing plant. In fact, it is reasonable to assume that in five years a small community will have sprung up in the banana-producing belt. This industry can someday surpass the citrus industry, and go on to rival the sugar industry in the north. With the signing of this contract, Fyfes will make money, the growers will make money, and more important than these two, the country will make money."

Chicle

Another of the traditional export products, chicle, has undergone a drastic decline in national importance through the years. This latexian ingredient of chewing gum is obtained from tapping the sapodilla tree. When carefully tapped, a sapodilla yields about 1½ pounds of gum and can only be tapped again after five years. In the southern part of the country, where rainfall is the highest, an inferior type of chicle is obtained known as "crown gum." Skilled chicle workers, called *chicleros*, collect the latex during wet weather when it flows freely. It is then cooked in special pots to remove excess moisture and poured into molds and left to harden.

Chicle is exported in blocks of 20–30 pounds. It is referred to as "dry" chicle, meaning that it has less than 33.3 percent water content. The largest exporter of chicle is the Belize Estate and Produce Company, Ltd., the London timber monopoly, but exports had fallen to only 61,000 pounds (all to the United Kingdom) in 1969, when the last figures were available, and it is assumed that today production is even less.

Cocoa

Caribbean Investments, Ltd., which owns some 64,000 acres of land near Belmopan and enjoys concessions under the Development Incentives Ordinance, now has over 1100 acres of it in cocoa. An ambitious rehabilitation plan was carried out in 1970 with the growth thinned out to reduce the number of bearing trees per acre. The 1970 crop amounted to about 37 tons, while that of the following year realized 60 tons. There is speculation of additional dramatic increases in production in the coming years due to more scientific farming.

Coconuts

Prior to the 1966 Hurricane, coconuts were grown in "cocals," as the groves are called, on the sandy soils of the mainland and on the Cays in respectable numbers and a major export industry for them was envisaged at that time. Unfortunately, the groves suffered so greatly from Hurrican Hattie that the government has made no plans to re-activate the plantings. Coconuts for local use were imported from neighboring countries until 1968.

Before the hurricane nearly all of the Turneffe Islands and certain other cays were thickly covered with coconut palms, but now only small odd-shaped areas of them remain with little, if any, attention paid to them.

Some private growers introduced dwarf varieties of coconuts in 1962 and 1963, which are now coming into bearing. Annual production of coconuts is only about 700,000 nuts, a small proportion of which is actually exported, and in recent years exports have shown a declining trend.

Plantations on Ambergris Cay, which were replanted after Hurricane Janet in 1955, are now producing and a small quantity of these nuts are exported annually to the U.S. and Mexico by truck. Copra production has not been resumed, since all the copra drying facilities were lost in the hurricane of 1951.

In 1968 a coconut survey was undertaken to determine the feasibility of a factory to produce margarine and coconut fat from coconut oil, though the supply is still insufficient to warrant such a plant.

Cohune Nuts

Every report or treatise ever written concerning the natural resources of British Honduras has included the plentiful Cohune Palm. Yet to date, no attempt has been made to exploit it. The nuts of this palm are about the size of a turkey egg and contain a kernel which yields a high-grade oil used for cooking purposes. The extremely hard shell can be converted into charcoal, carbon, or wood flour. As carbon it is highly absorbent, and cohune nut charcoal burns cleanly and gives off an intense heat.

The wood flour is an excellent molding material and can also be used as a base for face powders. Currently, primarily due to the relatively high cost of its extraction, there is no commercial application being made of the cohune.

CARIFTA MEMBERSHIP

Its entry in the Caribbean Free Trade Area (CARIFTA) on April 26, 1971 marked a very important turning point in the future of Belizean agriculture. This trade association of 12 former commonwealth countries in the Caribbean includes membership of Antigua, Barbados, Guyana, Trinidad and Tobago, Dominica, Grenada, St. Christopher (St. Kitts) Nevis-Anguilla, St. Lucia, St. Vincent, Jamaica, and Montserrat.

CARIFTA was an outgrowth of the ill-fated West Indies Federation and is broadly based on the agreement made in 1965 between Antigua, Barbados, and Guyana aimed at furthering regional cooperation in the Caribbean.

Like its predecessor, CARIFTA's main objective is to facilitate the economic development of its member countries through the expansion and diversification of trade within its area. Toward this aim, and to assure that the benefits of free trade would be distributed equally therein, all barriers to the movement of commodities between member nations have been removed. Although not specifically stated in the agreement, there are implications that the intention is for the free trade to develop into a common market.

Late in 1972, prime ministers of the Caribbean Commonwealth nations met in Trinidad to discuss the formation of a common market. It was agreed at that meeting to establish a regional common market and to seek some form of association with the European economic community as a single unit rather than as separate countries. At the same meeting in October, 1972 it was agreed that action should be taken to remove the Organization of American States (O.A.S.) ruling which bars entry to countries (Guyana and Belize) who have territorial disputes with member nations.

Membership in some regional market group was recognized as essential by the government of Belize at an early date. Membership in the Central American Common Market was investigated. Also, after independence, Belize has hopes of following Jamaica's lead by joining the Organization of American States (O.A.S.), but Guatemala has effectively blocked either of these avenues, at least until some form of agreement between the two countries can be reached.

Membership in CARIFTA has the advantages of widening its agricultural market several-fold, thereby making large-scale production of certain products now economically feasible where it was not with only the domestic market to supply. With growing deficits in food products among the CARIFTA member nations, as well as the protected markets which the Association offers, Belize agriculture appears to have a bright future. The most promising prospects for export to the Association (primarily Jamaica) in the immediate future are beef, rice, and red kidney beans, with exports of corn and peanuts to follow shortly. The government's development program is designed to boost production in these crops in order to fully enjoy the opportunities afforded by CARIFTA membership.

The terms of membership in which the Minister of Natural Resources and Trade, Hon. Alexander Hunter, and his committee were able to negotiate with the CARIFTA Council were very favorable to Belize; the country was classified "Less Developed," a status which allows her tariffs to be lowered more slowly than "More Developed" member nations; certain tariffs will be eliminated over a period of ten years, others over a period of five years—privileges which Belize could only have expected had she joined at the Association's inception; and the Council agreed, in principle, that commodities consistently produced by any member could be added to the agricultural protocol. Since prospects for export to member nations are now good, there is optimism in Belize for dramatic reduction of their trade imbalance.

Rice

The most remarkable agricultural success in recent years has been in rice, the country's food staple. Traditionally, the rice-growing area had been considered to be in the south, around the Punta Gorda area, and it was considered impossible for Belize to become a major rice producer. All polished rice sold in Belize had to be imported.

Starting in the early 1960's rice was planted, on an experimental basis, by Tennessee Farms, Ltd. on the Belize River west of the International Airport at Burrel Boom. The results were satisfactory, though less than impressive.

In 1964 Al Bevis, a seasoned rancher from Patterson, California established Big Falls Ranch, Ltd. further upstream on the Belize River, and by using modern methods proved that it was possible to grow rice in that area in substantial quantities with high yields per acre. Bevis introduced a new planting method recommended by Louisiana State University—flooding of the rice plants only to a certain height, not completely submerging them as had been the practice. This, together with planting by aircraft, experimentation with rice varieties, irrigation control, and mechanical harvesting has brought outstanding results. From an initial crop of 400,000 pounds of paddy rice sold to the Government Marketing Board in 1967 from 800 acres under cultivation, in 1972 Bevis harvested close to 10.6 million pounds of rice—enough to make Belize self-sufficient for the first time in rice production—and since 1973 has been bringing in export revenues.

Bevis cautions prospective investors to be prepared to furnish all their own infrastructure. In order to operate economically he had to build his own roads, his own $750,000 milling plant, and to obtain operating capital for expansion of his multi-million dollar operation had to go as far away as Peru to obtain favorable financing. Even before he could economically ship surplus export rice to Jamaica, Bevis found it necessary to buy part-ownership in a shipping company.

Long-range projections for Big Falls Ranch call for having 32,000 acres under cultivation within ten years, and production to increase at the outstanding rate of 10 million pounds annually.

Other small growers in Toledo and Orange Walk Districts contribute to the national rice production, which is purchased and milled through the Government Marketing Board. The Board has a number of threshers which it operates for the small planters, chiefly in the Toledo District. Total rice production for 1972 exceeded domestic consumption by approximately 6 million pounds.

Livestock

Belize has a very high potential for cattle and beef production, yet very little of its ideally suited rangeland is being utilized. A United Nations' study concluded that Belize could support a cattle population of 1.5 million. Cattle numbers today are estimated at only about 40,000 head.

As early as 1950 Ford Young, an American real estate broker in Belize City, became convinced that cattle could ultimately become an important bulwark of the nation's economy, and proved the feasibility of this theory. Obtaining some open grazing land in the Mountain Pine Ridge area from the government for experimental use, Young introduced a herd of cattle which he allowed to forage and graze freely on the native grasses available throughout that region. The results of his experiment proved conclusively that cattle can be raised quite successfully that way.

Frank Norris, another American from Illinois who came to Belize in the early 1950's, established the country's first ranch in the Cayo District between Roaring Creek and El Cayo. Norris stands out as an example of what one can accomplish in Belize through modern techniques, careful planning, and hard work. Starting in a dense jungle-covered area in the Belize River Valley he has, bit by bit, hacked out and bull-dozed away a sizeable ranch planted in citrus, cashews, dwarf coconut palms and cocao trees, but it is the cattle industry, of which he is the strongest promoter, that he feels will be the largest national foreign exchange earner in the future.

For many years after the introduction of cattle, little use was made of them for local consumption; they were fattened for export in the form of live animals to Mexico. Of those slaughtered locally, the yield was extremely low—about 250 pounds of beef per animal—and domestic slaughtering facilities were limited.

A long-awaited government slaughterhouse was commissioned late in 1970 and is now producing beef and pork for the local market. The United States Department of Agriculture certification for the plant has been granted, and the government believes that the U.S. and the CARIFTA countries will become future markets for Belizean beef which will stimulate foreign and domestic investment in this industry.

Retail price controls on beef have had some inhibiting effect; nevertheless, over the past four years prices of good steers of the over-1000-lb. liveweight class have gone from 19 to 34 cents per pound. The national herd has increased 25 percent in the past two years. Government control of the slaughter of female cattle and those animals less than 500 pounds, together with its ban on the export of live cattle since 1968, has resulted in the yield per animal slaughtered rising to 330 pounds by 1970. A surplus of the domestic requirements was reached in 1971 exclusive of any live cattle imported for breeding. 1972 production was 1.69 million pounds of beef. Both the government and the private sector are now engaged in scientific breeding experiments with importation of grade cattle to improve the stock which, until recently, had been nearly entirely composed of feeder stock imported from Guatemala. Pedigree Jamaica Black, Brahman, Charalais, and Red Poll stock has been introduced.

A National Livestock Association is forming and some discussion has been given to the possibility of allowing this organization to receive a tax revenue from slaughtering to give the Association more viability. Cattle auctions, though popular with traders, suffer from restrictions of price controls.

Hog slaughter and pork production has fluctuated with the corn crop. 1969 was a poor corn year leading to high corn prices and consequent reduction of hog production, further aggravated by an outbreak of hog cholera in the Corozal District. 1970 was a bumper crop year for corn and saw a marked increase in activity in the pork industry. 1972 production was 892,000 pounds of pork. Indications are, with the increase in importations of quality breeding stock by the government and with the outlet afforded by the modern Meat Packing Plant, the pork industry will continue to expand. As more feedstuffs become available it will become less susceptible to seasonal fluctuations.

Mutton production is hardly started, averaging only four to six thousand pounds annually, but there is keen interest in development of sheep raising in Belize and experimental breeding is already taking place.

Poultry production is expanding, both of broilers and layers, with the goal of meeting domestic requirements in the near future. Production is now at about 1,280,000 pounds per annum and 900,000 dozen eggs.

Red Kidney Beans and Corn

Corn has always been a major food crop in Belize, and its production has been expanding at a rapid rate. In 1964, 9.1 million pounds were produced from 11,383 acres. By 1969, 23 million pounds were harvested from 17,544 acres, and the 1971 harvest produced approximately 35 million pounds from 25,000 acres. 1972 figures were substantially unchanged from 1971, although foreign and domestic interest in commercial poultry production will undoubtedly induce more farmers to plan corn. 2.05 million pounds of poultry had to be imported from the U.S. in 1970.

The rice and bean diet of the Caribbean produces a constant demand for Red Kidney Beans among the CARIFTA member nations. Due to the low prices received in 1970 on the local market, many farmers had switched to other crops which resulted in a 31 percent decrease in the 1971 harvest. Now with CARIFTA export opportunities—Jamaica has given a firm commitment for 10,000 one hundred pound bags—together with constant local demand, future years should show a healthy increase in production of this commodity. 1972 production was 2.6 million pounds.

Cucumbers and Tomatoes

One of the real sleepers in the food export industry has been in cucumber raising. Intended strictly for export to the U.S., cucumber production before 1966 was virtually non-existent in Belize. On June 18, 1966, after some experimental growing the previous year, the Belize Offshore Growers, Ltd. (predominantly an American combine) acquired 5000 acres and prepared to export in time to reach the United States in the winter off-season to take advantage of that ready market.

The first cucumber crop, from some 900 initially planted acres, produced 13.4 million pounds when harvested between December and March 1967 but, because of transportation problems and excess handling, nearly half the crop was too damaged to market and resulted in only 7.8 million pounds of cucumbers reaching their Florida destination.

The shipping problem was solved the following year with the building of a small deep-water pier at about mile five on the Western Highway. The location of this docking facility, far from the coast, required the company to dredge a 100-foot-wide by 12- to 14-foot-deep channel to connect it with deeper water. This allows the use of "landing craft" type of vessels to haul the produce from their own pier without the expensive process of lightering by barge to waiting freighters. The company has since chartered two refrigerated cargo ships, each with a 350-ton capacity.

Offshore Growers have added tomatoes to their exports, but the success of their venture has been mixed. Cucumber acreage in 1968 was reduced to only 475, but has steadily increased to

1700 in 1970. 1970 was a poor crop year and resulted in only 7.1 million pounds of cucumbers being exported and 1.3 million pounds of tomatoes. The same acreage was planted in cucumbers in 1971 season but tomatoes were not grown, as the projected profit therefrom was thought to be too slim. The 1972 season production and acreage was up substantially, with cucumber exports approaching 22.4 million pounds.

Offshore Growers claim, however, that cucumber production has not been a profitable enterprise. Farm production costs are estimated at $2.50 per bushel (50 pounds), but the ever-present high loss rate inherent with cucumbers—only the straight, unbruised cucumbers are acceptable for export—and high transportation costs make the break-even point for a duty-paid price of $6.50 per bushel.

The company concedes that it has found it impossible to successfully compete with Mexico, the major supplier of cucumbers for the U.S. market. They can produce cucumbers at a competitive price (on the farm) but cannot deliver them at a competitive price in the U.S.

A wholly-American-owned company, Savannah Products, Ltd., has been experimenting with producing vegetables in the Mango Creek area near Placentia in the south, and became operational for the 1972 growing season.

Mangoes

In 1969, Tropical Produce, Ltd. was approved for development incentives to establish a plantation of 1000 acres of mangoes for the export market on the company's leased government lands in the Monkey River area of the Toledo District. The first of the trees came into bearing for 1973 export to the U.S. market. The first shipment was sent air freight and sold in the Los Angeles area. Belize mangoes were reportedly rated "top quality," and superior to Florida mangoes. The shipment was 100,000 pounds. Tropical Produce Company plans to increase this to 300,000 pounds during the 1974 season, according to Dr. C. J. McCleary, owner of the mango plantation.

Sea Crops

The same vibrant blue waters, endless Barrier Reef, and myriad of sequin-like cays on a satin sea that hold such promise for an outstanding tourist industry seem destined to become a vital element in the future economic and financial structure of the country for another reason. They provide an extensive feeding grounds and, as a result, provide the best fishing found anywhere in the Caribbean. Already ample supplies of fish are caught for the domestic needs and provide an important potential for expanding export trade.

Among the first legislation passed by the Belizean Government, upon gaining control of its internal affairs, was in the field of protection of this natural resource by establishing strict rules and regulations concerning commercial fishing in its waters. Commercial netting of bonefish, prized by sports fishermen, was outlawed to save them for the sportsman. Seasons and quotas were established for many fish, especially the lobster, which heretofore had been indiscriminately trapped, resulting in many egg-laden females being taken. Today these laws are dutifully enforced and respected.

The most important item to this industry is the export of "crayfish" (rock or Spiny Lobster) shipped to the United States and the Central American Republics. Financed by U.S. private capital, three seafood freezing plants began operation in Belize in the post World War II era. The plants first began exporting only lobster tails to the U.S., but now also ship a variety of edible fish fillets, including Belize's delicious red snapper.In 1961, shipping was temporarily halted due to the destruction of the processing plants by Hurricane Hattie, but has now resumed and the industry is again on an upward trend. Approximately two-thirds of the lobster crop is exported to the U.S.

Belizean spiny lobsters (Panulirus argus), known locally as "crawfish," are found in relatively shallow water inside the Barrier Reef. This crustacean bears a strong resemblance to the common lobster, but lacks the heavy crushing claws. As the name implies, the spiny lobster has a number of short spikes projecting from the carapace, leg joints, and antennae. The shell is normally a mottled brownish-red color but may even be deep magenta or olive green, depending on the type of bottom the animal inhabits.

Having a great number of natural enemies, the lobster must remain near cover and consequently avoids areas where there are soft, shifting bottom sediments or unusually strong currents. The central lagoons associated with the atoll-like Turneffe Islands, Glover's Reef, Lighthouse Reef, and the Banco Chinchorro in Yucatan, all provide ideal environments to support large populations of lobsters.

After a long career as a sailing captain, Captain Frank Foote, an energetic Canadian of impressive physical appearance, came to British Honduras in 1921 for reasons of health and engaged in the coconut trade. He soon became familiar with his new surroundings and became interested in the commercial possibilities of the spiny lobster. Foote found that the tropical lobster could be successfully trapped in the traditional "pot" used in his native Nova Scotia.

Encouraged by his early results, Foote imported equipment to outfit a small barge-mounted canning plant. The barge was initially located near the south end of Water Cay where there were shallow wells capable of furnishing enough potable water to be used in the primitive canning process. Steam heat for boiling the lobster tails was provided by a crude boiler fired with mangrove wood.

For the first few years of operation, the packing plant employed no more than a dozen women to process the catch, delivered to the barge by fishermen trained by Foote to build and set the new traps.

In 1925 an apparent scarcity of lobster in the surrounding area caused the plant to be moved further north to the windward entrance to Baldwin's Bogue. As production slowly increased in volume, organizational difficulties began to occur. Foote had been working with a small group of Creole fishermen based in Belize City who were paid one cent per pound for lobster tails. There was, more or less, continual agitation for a higher price, and the quantities delivered to the barge became erratic. Rumors of greatly exaggerated profits allegedly being made by Foote at their expense kept the fishermen in constant unrest. When the price was later raised to five cents per pound, the retail market apparently was not yet developed sufficiently to yield a profit at this rate. The resulting dilemma was solved by the disastrous hurricane of 1931, which demolished the barge and caused a temporary halt in all fishing activity.

In 1932 another barge and packing plant was acquired, and the operation moved still further northward to a protected location in a shallow bay on the leeward side of Cay Caulker. The labor problem was resolved by training an entirely new group of fishermen from Ambergris Cay and Cay Caulker. Production was relatively high in the following years, as it was virgin fishing ground. At the peak of operations at Cay Caulker, some twenty-five women were employed and perhaps a dozen lobster boats were kept busy during most of the year. After an initial surge in production, the operation began to falter due to uncertain market conditions in the U.S. By 1935, the enterprise was abandoned and Foote concentrated his efforts once again to establishing coconut plantations.

In spite of commercial failure, the lobster fishing techniques that Foote introduced were firmly instilled in fishermen from Belize City to Cay Caulker, and lobster fishermen on that cay continued to harvest spiny lobster, on a reduced scale, for their own consumption.

Today, lobsters are processed in several fishermen's cooperative plants where they are weighed, sorted, frozen, and packed in boxes to await air freight shipment to wholesalers in Miami, Florida. Air freight has proven to be altogether more reliable and economical for the cooperatives in Belize City than ocean transportation, since ships with refrigeration seldom call at Belize. Even if there was enough cold storage space available at the plants to await their arrival, delays in transporting the lobster from the plants by barge to be reloaded onto ships would result in excessive spoilage because of the perishable nature of the cargo. So, it is apparent that the expansion of the lobster export industry depends on an efficient air freight system capable of delivering the product at an economical rate.

There are six fishing cooperatives now operating in Belize. The Sarteneja is the smallest. It does not have its own freezer plant but sells its produce through the shrimp plant. The Caribena Co-op in San Pedro on Ambergris Cay freezes and exports its own lobster tails which are picked up by vessels enroute to the U.S. A similar lobster pick-up station is operated on Cay Caulker by the Northern Fishermen's Cooperative who transport their produce by boat from the station to their freezing plant in Belize City, where it is processed, and awaits air freight to U.S. markets. Many local Belize City fishermen share the facilities of this cooperative as well as those of the National Fishermen Producers Cooperative also located in that city. The two plants in Belize City also pack red snapper, grouper, saltwater catfish, and conch meat for export.

In 1967 Booth Fisheries financed and built a modern freezing plant in Placentia which is operated by the Placentia Cooperative in the southern area. This company owns freezer ships which serve its shrimping operations in Nicaragua as well as the lobster industry in Belize. These ships call at Placentia to pick up lobster for delivery to its distribution center in Brownsville, Texas.

Commercial fishing is now confined to five cooperatives. An annual quota for lobster is allotted to the cooperatives by the Fisheries Department; the quota for 1971 was 510,000 pounds (tails). Conch (both meat and shell) is also being exported, and its price has remained consistently high.

Shrimping as a commercial venture was virtually unknown in Belize before 1965, but increased rapidly from 23,000 pounds exported in 1966 to a high of 149,000 pounds in 1969. In recent years this production has dropped off drastically due, not to depleted stocks, but to decreased fishing efforts, with local fishermen preferring the more lucrative conch and lobster.

A temporary shrimp processing plant was built in Belize City in 1966, and plans are for construction of a permanent packing plant at Big Creek on the southern coast nearer the fishing grounds. The A and S Corporation, a subsidiary of Alberti

Foods, Inc., of Hinsdale, Illinois has extensive interests in frozen shrimp and has been granted a permit to exploit the shrimp potential.

The projected development in scale fisheries has not yet begun due to the same reason as the shrimp decline: the high prices maintained by the lobster and conch markets.

A breakdown of the various fish products marketed in 1970, a typical year, is as follows:

Lobster (Crayfish) .... 400,000 lbs. (tails)
Conch .... 800,000 lbs. (all-time high)
Scale and corned fish .... 240,000 lbs.
Shrimp .... 4,000 lbs.

Relative to its land area and population, Belize has one of the largest areas of sheltered fishing water in the tropics, or indeed anywhere in the world, yet its entire Caribbean coastline is remarkable in its lack of well-developed scale fishing industry. In spite of the ready accessibility of the fishing grounds, Belizean fishermen continue to provide the local market with daily subsistence catches, but show little inclination to increase their efforts on a more commercial basis with an eye toward a healthy export trade that their efforts could produce. Governmental attempts to encourage this industry have met with no appreciable degree of success; the scale-fishing industry remains today much as it was fifty years ago.

Estimates vary as to the total number of full or part-time fishermen working in Belize today. The majority are found north of Stann Creek, in the Belize City area, and in the two fishing villages located on Cay Caulker and on Ambergris Cay. This northern group of fishermen may contain as many as 500 full-time fishermen. South of Stann Creek, there are perhaps another 100 distributed along the coast, particularly in the Placentia area. Many of the coastal Black Caribs are considered fishermen, although they devote considerable time to agricultural pursuits as well. If this group is included in the total, the figure would approach 1000 with concentrations in Stann Creek, Seine Bight, Monkey River, Punta Gorda, and Barranco.

Of the total population of Belize this is a very small percentage, and of this number, even fewer are equipped to engage in commercial fishing.

The fishing fleet based in Belize City has traditionally provided the town with most of its daily supply of fresh fish with some contributions coming from the fishermen of San Pedro and Cay Caulker. More and more of these fishermen have turned to the trapping of spiny lobster, since the government has established relatively low maximum domestic market prices for fish and exporters continue to pay top dollar for lobster tails.

There are some rather complex cultural factors involved, which surely have a bearing on the situation. Fishermen are keenly aware of the disparity of price and of the social benefits gained by an individual who advances himself in the hierarchy from conch gatherer, to scale fisherman, to lobster specialist (called *Chambista* locally). The lobster fisherman has considerable prestige and obtains easy credit from local merchants, while the common fisherman must not only clean his catch but peddle it himself at the local market, a task less than appealing to the Belizean. Most recently, with the unusually high prices on conch, even conch gathering has been more popular than fishing.

Privately financed studies have indicated that there are enough fish present to provide a sustained yield for a major fish cannery and it would appear that foreign investment in this industry would be of great benefit to the aspirations of the government of Belize, although any attempt to improve the static state of the fishing industry in order to increase export earnings could result in the reduction of its more valuable spiny lobster exporting business. Since it is the same limited group of fishermen which would be required to perform both duties, one industry could decline at the expense of the other. Thus it will be necessary to introduce modern commercial fishing techniques, as yet unknown locally, and provide large and efficient fishing boats requiring less manpower per fish-pound of produce.

The Belizean fishermen are not entirely complacent. Many are looking to the future, and believe that their future might lie in deep sea fishing. Presently the United Nations research vessel, *Alcyon*, is working in the Belizean waters. On board are representatives of the fishermen's cooperatives being trained in modern deep sea fishing.

Meanwhile in another area of the fishing industry, the Caribena Fishing Co-op has acquired a large shrimping trawler, at a cost of $50,000, and began exporting shrimp in early 1973.

The fishing industry of Belize is under strict control of the Fisheries Section of the Department of Forestry who employ whatever restrictions are considered necessary in the interest of enlightened conservation of this natural resource. A license from the Minister of Trade and Industry is required for commercial fishing and a tax is levied on all fisheries exports. There is a Fisheries Advisory Board comprised of eight members appointed by the Minister of Trade and Industry.

LIGHT INDUSTRY

Any entrepreneur adept at utilizing techniques of mass production slanted toward a small market can find a bonanza in Belize. This underdeveloped country needs manufactured goods and skilled services of almost every type. Imports of manufactured items far exceed exports. The small population is increasing at about 3 percent per year, and the rise in living standards accompanying the steadily expanding economy will engender demands for increased services and for more material goods.

Not only is the opportunity seemingly unlimited, but the actively responsive government invites and cooperates fully with any developer proposing a serious project. This governmental attitude, with its liberal tax exemptions for up to fifteen years for projects in the public interest, its liberal duty-free concessions, and the security provided by the U.S. Investment Guarantee Program, are more than justifiable reasons for considering investing in Belizean industry.

Excluding the area of industry concerned with the processing of forest and agricultural products, the greater part of the nation's industry, and with fishing, some very diverse and imaginative manufacturing industries have recently gone into production in Belize. A brewery, established by Bowen and Bowen, Ltd., commenced production in 1972, bottling the first Belizean beer, called "Belikin" after a Maya Indian word which many claim to be the origin of the name of Belize. Signs throughout the country now proudly tell its citizens: *"Be Belizean–Drink Belikin."* In order to add incentive to try the new brew the government imposed a 300 percent import duty on its competitors, the largest being the Dutch Heinekin brand. The plant has the capacity to produce 100,000 32-gallon barrels per year, considerably more than the current domestic market of 15,000 barrels.

A cigarette manufacturing plant has been in production for several years, producing two local brands from imported Virginia and Turkish tobaccos. The name of their best seller, Independence, reflects the nationalistic attitude Belizeans have for their locally produced goods. As in the brewing industry, the government encourages increased production for home consumption by raising the import duty on foreign cigarette brands.

A paint mixing plant with an annual production of 48,000 gallons has been recently established and a development concession has been granted for a fertilizer plant which opened in 1972. A newly formed steel company, Belize Steel Products, Ltd., rolled 360 tons of billets in 1970, the raw material coming from Germany, and nearly doubled that production in 1971. Belize Industrial Gases produced a record one million cubic feet of oxygen in 1970, all of which was sold locally, and a quarter of a million cubic feet of acetylene gas.

The government is especially interested in broadening the economic base by encouraging the establishment of many small- to medium-sized industries rather than fewer large ones. Among the small plants now in operation are those producing furniture, aluminum windows, batteries, soap, edible oils, footwear, power and sailboats, as well as rum, alligator skin items, honey and candles. In late 1972 a plant began producing toilet paper, which alleviated the necessity of importing this item for the first time.

There has been a revival in the traditional boat building industry, mainly supplying small craft for the U.S. market. In addition, many boats are still constructed for use in the waters around Belize, some of the luxury class but most of the sloop or fishing trawler size. An infusion of U.S. capital has given new impetus to this industry. A ship repair and shipbuilding yard is located at Robinson Point, an island about nine miles southeast of Belize City. Currently it is one of the largest such operations along the entire Caribbean coast from Mexico to Panama. The new operating company, Robinson Point Shipyard, Ltd., not only offers modern dry-docking facilities and general ship repair but builds boats and coastal vessels, many of which are purchased by neighboring countries as well as the U.S.

A typical example of the type of small industry that can best be supported by the 120,000 population of this country is the garment factory opened in the early 1960's by Williamson-Dickie Corporation of Ft. Worth, Texas. One of the considerations that this firm gave before locating in Belize was the problem of finding skilled labor. There was no question about finding experienced help—there was none—but there was a question as to whether natives could be trained in this work. Operational results have proved significantly successful. Not only is the plant supplying the local market (this was not their initial intent), but it is exporting larger quantities to the U.S. than originally planned.

Oil & Minerals

Legislators in Belize have for many years speculated on the discovery of oil as being the very panacea needed to bolster the little country's lagging economy. Oil exploration has been conducted for many years—both off-shore and inland—but so far no oil-bearing formations of consequence have been located. Traces of their efforts in the Caribbean are seen in the seemingly bottomless holes, evidenced by eerie yellow-colored fifty-foot circles appearing a few miles off the coast near Belize City, where oil-exploration companies have blasted shafts in the coral bottom in an attempt to locate oil-bearing strata. In the interior, like elephants traveling head to tail, huge rubber-tired vehicles churn through the murky ooze of the jungle, their heavy oscillating metal plates bearing down on the earth to create seismic waves whose echoes reveal sub-surface topography. Hopefully, through information so gathered, their owners will be able to pinpoint probable oil-bearing areas.

The entire northern half of the country, formerly under concession to Belize Chevron Oil Company, is now under oil exploration license to the Anschutz Corporation. With the exception of the Maya Mountain range, the entire southern region is under oil exploration license to Harding Brothers Oil and Gas Company. In addition, Belize Chevron is exploring along the northern coastline for off-shore sources, and the southern off-shore area is being prospected by Ajax and Ariel Petroleum Companies.

On September 8, 1961 the Esso Standard Oil Terminal in Belize City was completed at a cost of $500,000. It is supplied by ocean-going tankers and has a capacity of 30,000 barrels of petroleum products including aviation fuel, diesel oil, paraffin, and gasoline.

In October, 1971 Belize Refining and Terminal, Ltd. began discussions with the Ministry of Trade and Industry concerning plans for a multi-million dollar oil refinery to be located in the Monkey River area. The company started construction of the facility in mid-1973. This company reportedly already has under contract a sufficient quantity of crude oil to keep the plant in operation for over a three-year period after the commencement of refining operations. Foremost of the problems being worked out by Belize Refining is the anchorage for their super tankers.

There are also two small mineral-prospecting licenses in force, both operating in the south of the country and one in the north. To stimulate activity in this field, the government retained the Institute of Geological Sciences (London) to conduct a geological survey of the entire country. This study was completed in mid-1970 and became available in 1971. Until this time, the only reliable geological data that had been available was the Dixon Report, but it had only covered the southern half of the country.

There is no Department of Mines in Belize. The inspection of mines is under the aegis of the Forestry Department with the Chief Forest Officer acting as Inspector of Mines.

TOURISM

Unquestionably the largest, or at least the most obvious, El Dorado for investors in this country would seem to be in its undeveloped tourist industry. Belize possesses the natural ingredients for a multi-million dollar tourism business. All the basic elements sought by vacationing North Americans are here—sun, sand and sea, plus several natural endowments found nowhere but in Belize, and it is only 800 airmiles from the U.S., the largest generator of tourist travel in this hemisphere.

Today, Belize is an unspoiled little-known Caribbean Paradise for the visitor wishing to escape the crowds of the tourist circuit or looking for the unusual advantages offered by this off-beat country: jungle expeditions to nearly-lost Mayan Indian cities, jaguar hunting safaris, or cruises among palm-fringed cays whose surrounding waters teem with record blue marlin, sail and kingfish. Skin diving and underwater photography are unexcelled anywhere in the tropics. It will not escape "discovery" for long.

As in other developing countries, the government is already looking toward tourism as a means of aiding economic development. Experience in other countries, principally in Mexico and the Caribbean islands, has shown that tourism can indeed make a significant contribution to foreign exchange earnings and employment. This industry was given momentum by the government in 1968, when the runway at Belize International Airport was lengthened to accommodate medium-sized jets at a cost of 925,000 pound sterling. The country is now connected by direct flights from Miami, New Orleans, Mexico City, Guatemala City, Kingston, San Salvador, San Pedro Sula, and Tegucigalpa. In December, 1972 SAHSA Airlines, Central America's largest carrier, began service to Belize from New Orleans and became the third major airline serving Belize City. TACA and TAN have had regular service to Belize for some time.

The lack of proper facilities has long been a major handicap to the development of even a reasonably large tourist trade. Belize's only first-class hotels, the Fort George and the Bellevue, run high occupancy rates and lack of available hotel rooms limit the country's capacity for increased tourist traffic. The Fort George is the larger of the two and it has but 35 rooms. Both are located on the waterfront.

With the exception of the two hotel dining rooms and one or two private clubs, like the Pickwick, Belize does not have restaurant or night club facilities that in any way compare with those of other Caribbean resort areas. The reason is understandable; of the 42,000 residents of Belize City, perhaps only 6000 could afford the luxury of a first-class restaurant and the 40,000 or so tourists which visit the country annually are not sufficient to warrant them.

Thus, until the tourist influx increases, tourist enterprises cannot survive and, conversely, until tourist amenities are provided, Belize cannot expect to draw the tourists. The local people have been slow in realizing the tourist potential of their country, and therefore little attention and local money has been invested in tourist attractions. For example, it is difficult to find any suitable souvenirs in the country, and even picture postcards are scarce.

Perhaps the largest drawback to development has been the lack of infrastructure. The building of roads and the provision of adequate water and electricity supply, among other things, require a heavy capital outlay which the government cannot afford. The country's roads still remain a deterrent to all but the most hardy motorist. Although a few tourists still cross the

Table 7
TOURISTS VISITING BELIZE*

	1970	1971	1972**	1973***
Cruise Ship Visitors	68	851		
Air Passengers	9,003	17,860		
Overland Visitors (principally from Mexico)	22,075	27,226		
Others		521		
TOTALS	31,146	46,458	50,651	58,000

*Based on figures released by the Tourist Board, Belize, December, 1972.

**No breakdown available

***Provisional figures

Table 8
COUNTRY OF ORIGIN – TOURISTS VISITING BELIZE
1971

Great Britain	2,000
Europe	1,500
United States	12,000
Canada	1,700
Guatemala	8,685
Honduras	1,803
Mexico	15,605
Other	3,165

borders from Mexico and Guatemala by automobile, each year thousands who normally would visit Belize do not because of the poor road system. The government is improving the situation, but progress has been slow.

The country lacks a strong tourist board. A shortage of funds and its "unofficial" capacity limit the activity of the one it does have. There are no tourist pamphlets available for travel agents to hand prospective visitors, nor paid advertising in foreign newspapers. Tourism has to rely on word of mouth and limited promotion by TACA airlines and other private companies. The tourist board is extremely cautious in promoting tourism until the country is able to absorb a large influx of tourists, and favors a slow, well-controlled growth in the industry.

These deficiencies, however, can in no way negate the tourist potential of Belize, and private interests as well as the government recognize this. Private capital from the U.S., Canada, and Jamaica, already invested in Belize tourism, indicates a strong optimism for its future. Currently the government does not have enough money to make the necessary investment, nor does it have the necessary revenue to carry out a full-scale promotion and advertising campaign. Tourism remains a poor third on the list of national priorities, behind expansion of the agriculture and manufacturing industries. The government would prefer that the entire business of tourism—construction of facilities, development, and promotion—be handled by private entities. As a means of attracting this capital, the government offers tax holidays. In principle, hotels are granted a tax holiday during a three-year period of establishment, plus another ten years of operation if they have one or more of the following facilities: swimming pool, yachting and watersport facilities, and ample grounds developed for golfing, horse-back riding or other outdoor sports. If they provide none of these facilities, the tax holiday for the establishment period is reduced to two years.

In addition to the tax exemptions offered, there are exemptions from the entry tax and import duties on most imported goods. If a hotel is financed by outside capital, the enterprise can be granted "approved status" under the exchange control regulations, and convertibility is guaranteed for the remittance of profits, capital, and gains.

To date, there are resort developments in San Pedro (Ambergris Cay), Maya Beach near Placentia, Stann Creek Town, and on the Augustine Pine Ridge; but in retrospect, progress has been disappointing.

In the 1960's a Philadelphia firm purchased Cay Chapel, a palm-covered island 16 miles from Belize and, amid high expectations and encouragement from the government, began construction of a 36-room hotel, an airstrip, and supporting facilities. A nine-hole golf course, a shopping complex and single family residential units were planned for the future. The project gained much attention and publicity but, due to lack of long-range planning and poor management, the developers went bankrupt before the project could be completed. This has had an adverse effect on the attraction of new large-scale resort developers.

Another ambitious development scheme for resort facilities to be located on 35,000 acres 22 miles north of Belize City by the Olla Hotels, Inc. of New Jersey, which was to have included a 200-room hotel to be operated by the Holiday Inns, a golf course, residential community and hunting and fishing facilities was announced in the mid-1960's but was cancelled in 1972.

Such large-scale tourist developments, while representing a much-needed stimulant for their economic doldrums, are viewed locally with a mixture of zeal and apprehension. Some feel that a wholesale influx of tourists could upset the ecological balance of their communities. Many fear the fate of other of the Caribbean countries who complain that massive tourism and outside investors have turned their youth into a "nation of waiters and busboys."

Closely related is the question of casino gambling. Several major tourist developers have reported interest in investing in Belizean resorts only if government licenses are granted for gambling. Opinion in Belize is divided on this question. Many believe that due to the lack of facilities, the only way to attract large investments in tourism is by legalizing gambling. The other, and so far dominant faction, fears that casino gambling would bring in undesirable people which the country could not control. There has already been an incident of attempted Mafia infiltration through resort development in Belize and, thus far, the government has not sanctioned any casino gambling operations.

Land speculation, especially on the off-shore cays, has increased in recent years, with many North American investors buying up prime ocean-front parcels for subdivision and resale in the U.S. for retirement homes and summer cottages. In Ambergris Cay, for example, land that sold for nearly nothing in the early 1960's now sells for $2000 per acre or more for small parcels. Lots with street frontage in Belize City now sell for $1600. The fastest growing center for retirement homes is in the Maya Beach area near Placentia which is being developed by Canadians.

To date, the most successful tourist-oriented operations have been small-scale enterprises which capitalize on some of Belize's unique attractions—"outdoor" sports and pleasures—especially for explorers who wish to penetrate into little-known regions of the interior searching for Maya ruins, big-game hunters, sports fishermen, skin divers or beach lovers. Fishing and hunting resorts for small parties are now operating successfully on the Belize River, Salt Creek, Big Creek, and on several of the cays.

One of the first to recognize the potential of Belize for this type of business was Vic Barothy. He had operated a flourishing sports fishing lodge in pre-Castro Cuba's Isle of Pines. After studying the entire Caribbean, he chose Belize to locate his new resort—the Barothy Caribbean Lodge—some nine miles up river from Belize City. From this base, Barothy can guide his parties on trips on the Belize and the Sibun Rivers and their tributaries to fish for tarpon and snook; to the coastal flats for the highly prized bonefish; and he is also equipped with larger boats for venturing beyond the Barrier Reef for king mackerel, marlin and sailfish.

Today Barothy has several competitors with similar facilities. The Foreman brothers were among the first local Belizeans to get into the sports fishing business, and provide charter fishing accommodations for Ft. George Hotel guests from their pier adjacent to the hotel.

Jaguar hunting safaris (the natives call them tigers) with government-licensed big game guides, are provided by two companies. The average safari takes four days and in addition to the 250-pound spotted cat, included on the bag list are the mountain lion, deer, ocelot, giant tapir, and peccary.

Belize is rich in archaeological treasures and the most extensively excavated of all its Mayan cities, Altun Ha, is just 30½ miles from Belize City. This archaeological site, the remains of a mysterious prehistoric culture which flourished there in 200 B.C., offers a unique and unforgettable tourist experience. The hour-and-a-half trip by Land Rover from Belize City takes one through dense jungle, alive with extraordinary plantlife (240 varieties of wild orchid alone), and such exotic birdlife as the brilliantly-colored parrot and macaw.

While only ten percent of the site of this former trade and ceremonial center has been unearthed, the results are impressive. Its major pyramid, the Temple of the Masonry Altars, rises like a mirage from the jungle floor with the dignity of Chartres Cathedral, hand-hewn in the middle of this trackless bushland.

Tourists are met at the site by a government guide who, being part Mayan and having spent his lifetime in this remote area, is able to impart a vast amount of knowledge of its history while walking among the jungle-covered mounds which had been homes, temples, tombs, and palaces of this once-great city state. Visitors are allowed to climb the pole and rope ladder used by the excavators to the top of the great limestone pyramid which affords a breathtaking view of the dense jungle through which he has traveled, and from this vantage point is able to make out profiles of hundreds of lesser mounds concealing yet-unexcavated buildings which housed the 10,000 or so inhabitants of this once-thriving city.

As the guide describes the area, a visitor has the uneasy feeling of being an uninvited witness of forbidden rites. A masonry table atop the great temple was used by priests to contain their ceremonial fires. By "magic" (a piece of jade thrown into the fire to change its color, or a piece of flint to explode in a shower of sparks) these priest-rulers were able to hold their subjects in superstitious awe. One can well imagine the priest, his robes flying in the warm breeze, partially engulfed in incense (small niches still exist on the platform that once concealed the incense burners), chanting for the benefit of his subjects standing in the kilometer-square paved courtyard below.

Vestiges of the ancient Maya civilization dot Belize. Pottery and other relics have been found throughout the country, even deep in some of its limestone caves. Another of its major archaeological sites, Xunantunich, near the Guatemala border in the Cayo District, is accessible to tourists, through further from Belize City than Altun Ha. The government has provided minimal facilities: simple open, thatched-roof huts for resting in the shade, but there are no restaurant provisions at either site for even purchasing soft drinks. There are no hotel facilities for overnighting at Xunantunich, requiring visitors to return over the spine-punishing roads to Belize City after dark.

Limestone caves offer some unexpected adventure for a courageous explorer. The caves, largely inaccessible and unexplored, are scattered throughout the country and often yield ancient Maya artifacts and bones. None is commercially exploited and, in fact, except for a few avant spelunkers, mostly ignored by the local people. The largest known single room is in the Rio Frio caves and is approximately 525 feet long, 135 feet across, and about sixty feet from floor to ceiling. The longest, yet explored, runs about 3000 feet long. Most of these caves are "wet" caves and still in the forming stage. Many have wierd and beautiful formations; one is noted for its "frozen" waterfall.

Though not all of the several hundred caves in Belize are accessible, a few of those generally known may be visited without too much difficulty. Ben Lomond and the Manatee caves, both in the same general area south of Belize City, may be reached by boat from Belize City and a short hike. One of the most publicized is the Blue Hole (not to be confused with the undersea cavern in Lighthouse Reef Lagoon) on the Hummingbird Highway south of Belmopan. It is highly advisable to arrange for a guide before exploring caves in Belize, as none have been surveyed, and natural dangers such as "bad" air and bottomless shafts present hazards to the uninitiated.

For private excursions into the country's wild interior Land Rovers may be hired, with or without driver, although the demand is great and arrangements must be made well in advance. Small power cruisers and sailing dories are available for charter for fishing or exploring the Barrier Reef. Scuba gear is easily obtained from several sources.

Sightseeing trips to the cays by light plane provide a memorable treat. There are landing strips on Amergris Cay and on Cay Caulker. Both of these Tahitian-like atolls have overnight facilities for visitors.

For those more passive visitors seeking only to escape the anxieties of a more complex lifestyle, Belize offers an unhurried tranquility rare in a world characterized by tension and frustration of everyday life. Each of the rooms at the Fort George Hotel has a private terrace for sitting and contemplating the unique beauty of the multi-hued Caribbean a few feet below.

This British-built hotel is run with the seemingly incongruous pomp and circumstance of a good British resort but moderated with the warmth and friendliness of its local staff. The rooms are air-conditioned, but most guests prefer the natural ventilation of the balmy trade-winds which blow off the Caribbean throughout most of the year. The rooms have a fully-louvered exterior wall facing the sea which provides a delightful means of tempering the humidity. Lazy days under the soft West Indian sun can be spent beside a salt-water swimming pool, sipping local rum, or just gazing out at the white-sailed coastal schooners slipping out to sea for a day or spear fishing, or returning late in the afternoon laden with many varieties of fish, conch or lobster to sell at the native market in Belize City.

In most countries the tourist potential must be fully developed to be enjoyed, but in Belize her most valuable assets need no developing.

BELIZE 1980: An Epilogue

Ir the five years which have passed since the first edition of this book was published much has changed in Belize—and little. The Belizean dollar is now based on US dollar parity instead of the pound sterling, the fixed rate of exchange is US $1.00 to $2.00 Belize, and the economy has undergone steady expansion. Gross national (domestic) product is now about US $96 million and per capita annual income has increased to about $700. The population is now 156,000.

A hurricane—this one named Greta—followed by two weeks of constant rainfall in early 1980 caused very serious flooding and crop loss. Hurricane damage reduced the output of some industries but was more than offset by increases in other areas of the economy. Fortunately no lives were lost.

Archaeologists, still intent on solving the mystery of the Maya civilization, announced in May 1980 some significant finds in Belize that lead them to believe the Maya civilization to be much older than previously reckoned. While being very cautious in their public statements until the results of their field work can be properly evaluated, it appears that the Mayas of Belize were important seafarers and fishermen at a very early date.

University level education has been introduced in Belize with the formation of the Belize College of Arts, Science and Technology.

George C. Price's PUP party is still firmly in control of the government and the Guatemalan question is as surely unresolved as it was five years ago. Premier Price met in December 1980 with the British Minister of State in London to once more discuss prospects of solving the conflict in a peaceful way. For the first time in the nation's history, on January 1, 1978, a standing national army was established. The army, called the Belize Defense Force, is under command of Lt. Col. Graham M. Longdon, M.B.E., and consists of both a regular army and civilian volunteer element. Volunteers are being trained at home in jungle warfare and attend courses overseas.

Among the industries which have expanded in the past five years are those of the garment industry, steel fabrication, auto battery assembly, tire re-capping, furniture manufacturing and food processing. Diversification in light manufacturing and further mechanization in agriculture has been responsible for more than modest gains and a wider economic base.

Tourism has increased in Belize and existing tourist facilities have been expanded. The marine industry has increased production in both scale fish and in deep-sea fishing catches.

Infrastructure facilities have made significant gains. The first section of the Northern Highway is complete and work is underway on the second section which includes a new alignment. The Hummingbird Highway has been greatly improved and the old Western Highway between Belmopan and Benque Viejo del Carmen is being rebuilt. The Southern Highway has also been improved with the addition of new bridges in several locations. Work is still underway in improving agricultural feeder road systems for sugar and grain-producing areas. Expansion of rural electrification, improvement of the performance of Radio Belize, and providing potable water supply to farm areas continue in 1980.

A modern deep water pier, officially dedicated in 1979, now makes off-loading of freighters less difficult and has improved the volume of Belize's trade with other countries.

Agricultural Outlook

Even with the damage brought by hurricane Greta, the agricultural sector showed overall gains in 1979. Fall in the expected output of sugar and citrus was counterbalanced by significant increases in banana, livestock, and grain crop production.

Sugar production decline, from 114 thousand tons in 1978 to 99 thousand tons in 1979, was due to problems with pests, "smut" disease, and machinery failure. A government survey has been conducted to determine the extent of acreages in danger of smut infestation and a program of informing farmers on smut-resisting varieties has been undertaken. It is felt that 1980 production will again be over 110 thousand tons.

Output in citrus fruit production declined from 987 thousand boxes to 755 thousand in 1979 due mainly to the flood damage done to the grapefruit orchards following the 1978 hurricane. Rehabilitation funds, to replace damaged orchards, have been made available to growers. Citrus, too, is expected to be back to normal in 1980, and further expanded in future years when the trees planted with rehabilitation monies mature. Many growers took this opportunity to enlarge their plantations.

Production in both of the two major grain crops—rice and corn—has shown steady yearly increase in production due to better farming techniques and increased mechanization of the small farmers. Red kidney beans and other bean crops were especially damaged by flooding in 1979, and fields are being rehabilitated through loans made available from the United Kingdom.

Exports of bananas in 1979 amounted to 700 thousand boxes, and that figure is expected to exceed one million boxes in 1980. This industry has received loan commitments of $11.8 million from the Commonwealth Development Corporation and the Caribbean Development Bank for expansion programs and irrigation.

Honey, one of the newer export crops in Belize, suffered a set-back in 1979 when 150 bee colonies in the Yo Creek area of the Orange Walk District were destroyed by insecticide. Losses to the bee-keeper in that area amounted to $90 thousand. An investigation is underway to determine the source of the poison. It will take at least a year for the six bee-keepers affected to recover their lost colonies.

Fruit and vegetable crops for local consumption continue to be in adequate supply. Livestock production also continues to meet local demand. The emphasis in that industry is on improving the breed of cattle and pigs raised in Belize. Several new livestock enterprises started in 1980, and ranch locations are now more widely distributed in the country.

The Construction Industry

Early in 1980 construction was finally completed on the housing projects in Belmopan and Ladyville. Reclamation of land near Belize City is underway for more low cost housing units. Loans for residential construction are available through the Reconstruction and Development Corporation and the Development Finance Corporation. Three bedroom homes on 75' × 100' lots in Belmopan may be purchased from the Government of Belize in conjunction with the Development Finance Corporation for about $33,000. Two bedroom homes sell for $21,000. Private lots in sub-divisions near Belize City can be purchased for about $2,500 with utilities.

Recent expansion by hotels and some manufacturing enterprises have given considerable impetus to the construction industry. Although nails, roofing materials, and lumber are available locally, steel and cement must still be imported.

At the end of the third quarter, 1979, the commercial banks had loans outstanding to the construction industry of over $8.2 million while the Development Finance Corporation made forty two housing loans amounting to $848 thousand.

Manufacturing

The Belize Flour Mill, Ltd. produces several types of flour and satisfies local needs. The company's mills have adequate capacity to meet the projected needs of the immediate future.

Cigarette manufacturing interests do not expect an increase in production due to continued competition from imported brands and the increased cost of local production.

Beer and stout output from the two Belizean breweries was 800 thousand gallons in 1978, but slightly less in 1979 due to a series of mechanical breakdowns in one of the plants. One of the companies plans major expansion in 1980.

Domestic production of paper products now supplies 75% of local market demand. The paper producers have expanded their activities to include plastic bags, facial tissue, and paper napkins. A new factory building has been acquired.

Garments produced in Belize for export amounted to a value of $18.9 million. This industry has substantially expanded, although we have been told that a crew of fifty only produce about fifteen garments a day. On the local market they are, however, competitively priced with imported goods and therefore provide a saving in foreign exchange for imports.

Tourism

Data available on aircraft and passenger movements indicate a decided increase in tourism in Belize, although the government does little to encourage this industry. Scheduled aircraft movements increased from 5,296 in 1977 to 6,104 in 1978. Private aircraft entering Belize doubled in 1978 from what it had been in 1977. Two thousand seven hundred and fifty-eight private planes visited Belize in 1978. Total passenger visitors in 1977 were 57,584 compared with 59,494 in 1978. By all indications, 1979 figures will show an increase over those of 1978.

Hotel expansion has been modest but hotel rates have risen sharply in recent years.

Trade and Finance

Total exports in 1978 reached $160 million and total imports were

$210 million. This shows a reduction of $6 million in the trade deficit compared with the previous year. Most of the imports represent capital goods—machinery, equipment, and fuel, which help to increase the productive capacity of the economy.

Partial data indicate that the trade deficit continued to drop in 1979 as export items increase at a greater rate than imports.

At the end of November, 1979, loans outstanding at the commercial banks amounted to $89.9 million compared with $67.1 million at the same time the year before. Nearly 25% of this amount went as loans for agricultural purposes.

Demand deposits stood at $21.2 million, while time and savings deposits were $62.4 million.

Currency issued was $19.1 million. The net foreign position of all commercial banks and the Monetary Authority was $9.8 million. The other major leading institution, the Development Finance Corporation, approved loans totaling almost $3.7 million between January and September, 1979. More than 50% of these loans were made for expansion in the areas of sugar, livestock, and mixed farming production.

The Caribbean Development Bank has been a major source of capital for Belize. So far, this bank has provided funds totaling over $70 million for facilities in the sectors of tourism, manufacturing, and agriculture.

The Belize Monetary Authority continues to play a crucial role in the country's development and foreign exchange activities. The Authority reported the country's money supply at the end of November, 1979 to be $37.3 million cash and $99.7 million including fixed deposits and savings. Foreign assets stood at $15.2 million.

Preliminary figures as of 31 December 1979 show the central government's recurrent revenue to be $64 million against recurrent expenditures of $54 million. This surplus of $10 million, when added to local capital revenue of $1.8 million, gives fully financed local capital expenditure total of $11.8 million. Capital expenditures on grants and loans totaled some $40 million. Expenditures on U.K. aid schemes and C.D.B. have not been reported.

The Next Decade

In his New Year's address to the people of Belize, Premier Price quoted the prophet Isiah: "The people who walked in darkness have seen a great light, and you have brought them abundant joy and great rejoicing." This is yet another variation on the familiar PUP theme, "we can see the light at the end of the tunnel." Since January, 1964 when Belize became fully self-governing, their premier has promised to lead his people out of the darkness of foreign rule into the sunshine of independence. Although great studies have been made and independence appears eminent, the people of Belize are growing increasingly impatient.

The key to independence remains to be in finding a satisfactory solution to the Guatemalan question. In the face of continuing territorial claims by Guatemala, Belize cannot envisage independence without some form of defense agreement with a major power. Negotiations in 1978 between Great Britain and Guatemala, on behalf of Belizean independence, are reported to have involved discussions of the cession of the southern portion of Belize (which is thought to contain oil), but this concession is totally unacceptable to the Belizean government.

Perhaps the eventual solution to the problem will come about more as a result of changing conditions inside Guatemala than due to British-Belizean diplomacy. Today the military government in Guatemala maintains order only by employing death squads who systematically hunt down and murder opponents to their right wing regime. Marxist insurgents are gaining strength daily and there are indications that they will soon be able to overthrow the ruling Junta. Once done, any "hands off" promise that the United States may have made to Guatemala will be invalid. This, together with similar conditions in Honduras, a Marxist state in Nicaragua, threat of Marxist takeover in El Salvador, and uncertain government in Panama, makes a friendly independent and democratic state of Belize of great strategic value to the West.

While one cannot be sure of what the next decade may hold for Belize, it can be stated with some surety that the spotlight of world attention will be on events in Central America and perhaps, too, on the tiny enclave of democratic individuality known as Belize.

Annotated Bibliography

BASIC COMPREHENSIVE SOURCES—History and Politics

BANCROFT, Hubert Howe. *History of Central America*, vol. II. San Francisco: A. L. Bancroft and Company, 1883.

BRISTOWE, Lindsay W. and Phillip B. Wright. *The Handbook of British Honduras: Comprising Historical, Statistical, and General Information Concerning the Colony, compiled from official and other reliable records.* Edinburgh and London, 1888, 1890, and 1892. A very valuable contemporary work. These three volumes are all that remain in the Jubilee Library in Belize City of the biannual series. The 1892 issue is on microfilm at the Bancroft Library, University of California, Berkeley.

"British Honduras." *The Statesman's Yearbook*. London: St. Martin's Press, 1971.

"British Honduras (Belize)." *Europa Yearbook*. London: Europa Publications, 1972.

"British Honduras." *The Honduras Almanack for 1826*. Belize. Also available in the Jubilee Library, Belize City are the Almanacks for the years 1827, 1830, and 1839 as well as some later years. Contains interesting contemporary accounts of conditions as they existed in Belize at the time of their printing.

BUCHAN, JOHN, ed. *British America*. Boston: Houghton Mifflin Co., 1923.

BURDON, Sir John Alder. *Archives of British Honduras*, 3 vols. London: Sifton Praed and Co., 1931-1935. A basic tool for the colony's history through 1884. Prepared by a local committee under Burdon's editorship.

CAIGER, Stephen L. *British Honduras: Past and Present.* London: George Allen and Unwin, Ltd., 1951.

CAIN, Ernest E., ed. *The British Honduras-Guatemala Boundary.* Bristol: Bristol Typesetting Co., Ltd., 1967. A copy of an address delivered by Henry Clifton Fairweather. MBE, at Belize City on July 13, 1967; edited and arranged by Cain. A summary of the boundary survey work.

CLEGERN, Wayne M. *British Honduras: Colonial Dead End, 1859-1900.* Baton Rouge: Louisiana State University Press, 1967. A thoroughly documented study of the history and political development of British Honduras in the late nineteenth century. Important bibliography with reference to availability of microfilmed records in the U.S.

DAMPIER, William. *Dampier's Voyages (1697-1701).* John Masefield, ed., 2 vols. New York: E. P. Dutton and Co. A reproduction of a volume prepared by a participant in Caribbean piracy in the seventeenth century.

DONOHOE, William Arlington. *A History of British Honduras.* Montreal (Canada): Provincial Publishing Company, 1946. A chronicle of Belizean history; especially interesting are the author's first-hand observations of the colony in the post-World War II years.

ERNEST, Morris L. *The Comparative International Almanac.* New York: The Macmillan Co., 1967.

ESQUEMELING, John. *The Buccaneers of America.* New York: Dover Publications, Inc., 1967. An unabridged reproduction of a work first published by Swan Sonnenschein and Company, 1893. A personal account of piracy in the Caribbean in the seventeenth century.

EVANS, Sir G. *Report of the British Guiana and British Honduras Settlement Commission, 1948.*

GIBBS, Archibald R. *British Honduras: An Historical and Descriptive Account of the Colony from its Settlement.* London: Sampson Low, Marston Searle, and Riverton, 1883. The definitive work on the subject in its day.

GRENFELL, *Capt. Russell, R.N. Nelson the Sailor.* New York: Macmillan Co., 1950. Includes a brief account of Horatio Nelson in Belize City.

HENDERSON, G. *An Account of the British Settlement of Honduras.* London: C. and R. Baldwin, 1809.

HOLMES, Vera Brown. *A History of the Americas: from Discovery to Nationhood.* New York: The Ronald Press Co., 1950.

HUMPHREYS, R. A. *The Diplomatic History of British Honduras, 1638–1901.* London: Oxford University Press, 1961. A standard work which material found in the British Foreign Office archives.

METZGEN, Monrad Sigfried and Henry Edney Cain. *A Handbook of British Honduras.* London: Waterlow and Sons, Ltd., 1925.

MITCHELL, Sir Harold. *Europe in the Caribbean.* Stanford, Calif.: University of Stanford Press, 1963.

PARRY, J. H. *The Spanish Seaborne Empire.* New York: Alfred A. Knopf, 1970.

PARRY, J. H. and Philip M. Sherlock. *A Short History of the West Indies.* London: Macmillan and Co., Ltd., 1956.

RODRIGUEZ, Mario. *Central America.* Englewood Cliffs, N.J.: Prentice-Hall, 1965.

SANGER, Clyde. "British Honduras." *Latin America and the Caribbean: a Handbook.* Claudio Veliz, ed., New York: Praeger Publishers, 1968.

SHERLOCK, Philip. *Belize: a Junior History.* London: Collins, 1969. Prepared for classroom use in the Belizean schools.

SIMPSON, Lesley Byrd. *The Encomienda in New Spain.* Berkeley, Calif.: University of California Press, 1966.

WADDELL, D.A.G. *British Honduras: a Historical and Contemporary Survey.* London: Oxford University Press, 1961. Though out-dated, a useful general interest survey of Belize — thorough and well-documented.

____. *The West Indies and the Guianas.* Englewood Cliffs, N.J.: Prentice-Hall, Inc., 1967. Waddell explores and compares the influence the past has had over the development of 23 Caribbean territories.

____. "Developments in the Belize Question (1946-60)." *American Journal of International Law*, April 1961.

SOCIO-CULTURAL TOPICS

HOROWITZ, Michael M., ed. *Peoples and Cultures of the Caribbean.* Garden City, N.Y.: The Natural History Press, 1971. A compilation of articles dealing with anthropological topics common with the Caribbean peoples. It includes an interesting article on the Black Caribs of Belize.

LEWIS, Gordon K. *The Growth of the Modern West Indies.* New York: Modern Review Press, 1969. An in-depth analysis of the forces shaping West Indian society since World War I. It offers a good panorama of the Caribbean.

TAYLOR, Douglas M. *The Black Carib of British Honduras.* Viking Fund Publications in Anthropology, No. 17, New York: Wenner-Gren Foundation for Anthropological Research, Inc., 1951.

GEOGRAPHY, FLORA AND FAUNA

CRAIG, Alan K. *Geography of Fishing in British Honduras and Adjacent Coastal Waters.* Baton Rouge: Louisiana State University Press, 1966. This study goes far beyond its subject and introduces some interesting historical data not previously published.

CROSS, Cliff. *Yucatan Peninsula.* North Palm Springs, Calif.: Cliff Cross Publications, 1971. A good current travel guide.

FOWLER, Henry. *Narrative of a journey across the Unexplored Portion of British Honduras.* Belize: Government Press, 1879.

SANDERSON, Ivan T. *Living Treasures.* New York: Pyramid Books, 1965. Reprint of a book printed by Viking, 1941. Report of this naturalist-author's expeditions in the jungles of Belize and descriptive accounts of wildlife encountered there.

____. *Book of Great Jungles.* New York: Simon and Schuster, 1965.

STEPHENS, John L. *Incidents of Travel in Central America, Chiapas, and Yucatan,* 2 vols., New York: Dover Publications, Inc., 1969. An unabridged reproduction of first edition as published by Harper and Brothers, 1841. Vol. 1 contains Stephen's description of the Settlement of Belize as he found it in 1839.

ECONOMICS

BARCLAY'S Bank, DCO. *British Honduras (Belize).* London: April, 1971. An economic survey with emphasis on the state of the nation's agriculture.

BRADLEY, John. *Financial Times Survey: Belize (British Honduras).* London: The Financial Times, July 29, 1969.

DOWNIE, Jack. *An Economic Policy for British Honduras.* Belize, 1959.

LURIE, Richard G. *Passports and Profits.* Garden City, N.Y.: Doubleday and Co., 1964. A tourist handbook with advice for businessmen doing business in Belize.

MARSHALL, Ione. *The National Accounts of British Honduras, Social and Economical Studies.* Jamaica: The University of the West Indies, 1962.

U.S. Department of Agriculture Economic Research Service. *Agriculture and Trade of the Caribbean Region.* (ERS-Foreign 309). Washington: U.S. Dept. of Agriculture, May, 1971.

THE MAYA

COE, Michael D. *The Maya.* New York: Praeger Publishers, 1966. An excellent accounting of the civilization of the ancient Maya, concentrating mainly on the achievements of the Classic Period.

MORLEY, Sylvanus G. *The Ancient Maya.* Stanford, Calif.: Stanford University Press, third edition, 1956 as revised by G. W. Brainerd. The classic work on the subject, written for non-professional archaeologists.

PENDERGAST, David M. *Altun Ha: A Guidebook to the Ancient Maya Ruins.* Belize: the Government Press, 1969. An accounting of the author's work at Altun Ha and the recent important discoveries there.

____. *Palenque: The Walker-Caddy Expedition to the Ancient Maya City, 1839-1840.* Norman, Okla.: University of Oklahoma Press, 1967. The first printing of a very interesting diary kept by one of the explorers and residents of the Belize Settlement.

REED, Nelson. *The Caste War in Yucatan.* Stanford, Calif.: Stanford University Press, 1964.

THOMPSON, J. Eric S. *The Rise and Fall of Maya Civilization.* Norman, Okla.: The University of Oklahoma Press, 1954.

PERIODICALS

"The Atlantic Report: British Honduras." *Atlantic Monthly*, 1966.

"British Honduras: Ballot for the Baymen." *Newsweek*, April 26, 1954.

"British Honduras — Delightful." *Sunset Magazine*, December, 1963.

"British Honduras: Let George Do It." *Newsweek*, March 15, 1965.

"British Honduras: Promise of self-government." *Time Magazine*, August 9, 1963.

DE LA HABA, Louis. "Belize, the Awakening Land." *National Geographic*, January, 1972.

GRANT, Cedric. "British Honduras and Guatemala." *Venture*, June 6, 1970.

HAINES, Ralph E. "Ambergris: Caribbean Haven." *Travel Magazine*, September, 1958.

HAMMOND, Norman. "The Planning of a Maya Ceremonial Center." *Scientific American*, May, 1972.

OLSEN, Jack. "Land of Wild Men and Tame Devils." *Sports Afield*, April 1972.

"Report of British Honduras," William A. Gaudet, ed. *Latin American Report*, August, 1962.

RUSSELL, Jack. "Belize." *Travel Magazine*, October, 1967.

SETZEKORN, William D. "Belize for Blue Skies, Blue Marlin." *San Francisco Sunday Examiner and Chronicle*, August 20, 1972.

TEAGUE, Dorwin. "The Offbeat Caribbean: British Honduras." *Yachting Magazine*, March, 1970.

NEWSPAPERS — CURRENT

The Belize Times, Belize City.

The Reporter, Belize City.

Belize Billboard, Belize City.

The Beacon, Belize City.

The New Belize, Belmopan. Published quarterly by the Government Information Service.

NEWSPAPERS

Belize Advertiser. Belize. 1839–1840 and 1881–1889 are on microfilm at the Bancroft Library, University of California, Berkeley. Also, the *British Honduras Colonist and Belize Advertiser*, 1864–1868.

Central American Telegraph. Belize, 1873. Microfilm in Bancroft Library.

Colonial Guardian, Belize, 1882–1913. Microfilm in Bancroft Library.

Honduras Gazette and Commercial Advertiser, Belize, 1826–1827. Microfilm in Bancroft Library.

Honduras Observer, Belize, 1844–1845, in Jubilee Library, Bliss Institute, Belize City.

New Era and British Honduras Chronicle, Belize 1871–1872. Microfilm in Bancroft Library.

Observer. Belize, 1885–1886. Microfilm in Bancroft Library.

The Times of Central America. Belize, 1894–1896. Microfilm in Bancroft Library.

INDEX